FLEXIBLE LEARNING STRATEGIES IN HIGHER AND FURTHER EDUCATION

Flexible Learning Strategies in Higher and Further Education

Edited by
Diana Thomas

CASSELL

Cassell
Wellington House
125 Strand
London WC2R 0BB

215 Park Avenue South
New York
NY 10003

British Library Cataloguing-in-Publication Data
A catalogue record for this book is available from the British Library.

ISBN 0-304-33068-X (hardback)
      0-304-32986-X (paperback)

Typeset by York House Typographic Ltd, London
Printed and bound in Great Britain by Redwood Books, Trowbridge, Wiltshire

Contents

Acknowledgements

I have had the pleasure and privilege of working with most of the contributors to this book over a number of years and am indebted to them for their support, generosity and endlessly fertile exchange of ideas. A number of us would like to thank John Fairhurst of the Open Learning Foundation for the lucid and far-sighted contribution he has made to many discussions, and Bob Sang of the King's Fund College for both his staunch support and his ability not only to see analogies between higher education and almost everything else but endlessly to suggest new ways of designing learning which is humane and purposeful. I should like to add thanks to John Davies for his insight and wisdom in this and earlier projects and above all, though he would not recognize it, for never being cynical about the purposes of learning.

We are all indebted to numerous colleagues, friends and students in our own institutions who have taken the time to talk through the ideas developed in this book and who have left us in no doubt about what works and what does not and why. Jacki Proctor and Ruth Wright would particularly like to thank Peter Chambers for his contribution; David Baume to thank Stephen Cox and Carole Baume; and Bruce Gillham to thank Peter Eagle and Derek Wallace. John Bothams is indebted to his co-facilitators on the Medical Directors' Management Development programme, Christine Huxford and George Wright.

We should like to acknowledge the support of the University of Plymouth in allowing us to use their diagram of the learning transmission system; the University of Strathclyde for permission to use a screen from *COPE* cognitive mapping program; and Anglia Polytechnic University for permission to use sample screens from *Motion: A Visual Database*.

My thanks also go to Thelma Murray and Pam Barnfather for their practical help and support.

This book and the work which it documents could not have been accomplished without the patience, support and, for several of us, the direct involvement of our partners and families, to whom many thanks. I should particularly like to thank Graham, my resident IT manager and very constant help and companion, without whose expertise, hard work, loyalty and optimism the book would not have been completed.

Preface

This book is an attempt to encapsulate some of the innovative work being done in higher education and at the interface of further and higher education. It is written by contributors from all over Britain, several of whom are working with universities in Europe and the United States, so it covers a pretty wide spread both geographically and in terms of level of programmes and disciplines to which the programmes relate.

The contributors are all practitioners in some aspects of the design, development and delivery of flexible approaches to learning, and are all working with adults in the universities or in partnership with colleges or client organizations. Between them I estimate that they have a somewhat daunting two hundred years or so of experience in the field. There is sufficient body of knowledge and experience, therefore, for some of the contributors to risk looking back and to summarize and appraise developments (progress is something else) over the past twenty years, in order to offer guidelines for future development.

Any description of current projects is necessarily a snapshot in time and risks being overtaken by events, but the messages that these chapters contain will, I think, hold up, because they are concerned primarily with the quality of the learning experience and the extent to which particular configurations of expertise, learning resource and learning interest meet an identified learning need. That equation is what teaching and learning are all about, and is at least one reason why a number of the chapters allude to follow-on projects, parallel developments or alternative applications for what they have done. Analogies between fundamental problems of learning addressed here and similar challenges in any college or university are not hard to find.

The contributors have aimed to be essentially practical and, in a variety of contexts, to explore what has worked, what has not and why. We hope, therefore, that this will be of interest to teachers in any discipline who are looking for new ways of meeting learner needs with resources which probably increase in technical capability and decrease in terms of available expenditure per head; to managers working towards an institutional strategy; and to students of education looking for an insight into not only the range of some of the approaches to learning being adopted but also the current perception of learning and learning needs which underlies them.

None of us would claim that this is a comprehensive treatment of innovative approaches nor, as it stands, a turn-key solution to problems of resourcing learning. One problem with a book is that it is linear. This book was neither conceived nor developed as a linear product. Any linear organization of chapters implies a sequence, even a priority, which with this book is not the case. These chapters, like the elements in the model of flexible learning in Chapter 1, refuse to stay neatly compartmentalized and are forever metamorphosing into treatments of new issues. The matrix of themes and topics on p. x identifies the themes addressed and the chapters which relate to them.

The chapters have been written in parallel and reflect much shared thinking and discussion. All of them are concerned with the dynamics of the relationship between learners, sources of expertise, learning resources and opportunities, and with the determinants of the purpose of learning in the contexts examined. All of them reflect an undaunted creativity, a financial realism and a concern to provide the best learning opportunity possible with the available resources.

A Matrix of Themes and Topics

Chapter	1	2	3	4	5	6	7	8	9	10	11	12	13	14	15
Reflection on earlier developments	#	#	#			#	#	#	#			#	#		#
Projection of likely change	#	#	#				#	#			#	#	#	#	#
Adapting to a changed environment	#	#	#		#	#	#	#	#	#	#	#	#	#	#
Adapting to local/regional needs		#	#		#	#	#	#		#	#	#	#		#
Adapting to business needs								#							
Partnerships and collaboration:															
with employees and public bodies	#	#					#	#	#	#	#	#		#	#
between FE and HE	#				#		#		#	#		#			#
with learners	#	#	#					#	#	#		#	#	#	#
Using the workplace as a learning resource	#	#	#	#	#		#	#		#		#	#	#	#
Staff development needs and opportunities	#		#	#	#	#		#				#		#	#
Staff perceptions of flexible learning	#		#	#					#			#			
Learner perceptions and responses			#	#	#				#	#	#	#		#	#
Developing materials					#	#			#	#	#	#			#
Using different media					#				#	#	#	#			
Institutional learning strategy	#	#	#	#	#	#	#	#	#	#	#	#	#		#
Course design, delivery and assessment			#	#	#		#		#		#	#	#	#	
Practical techniques			#	#	#				#					#	

The Contributors

Alison Baker is management development manager at the Institute of Health Services Management. She began her career as a research assistant with the Schools Council and then took a post in higher education as a lecturer in sociology. She moved in to the business school at what was then Ealing College of Higher Education and completed a doctorate which looked at the founding and running of small businesses. After a short secondment to the Open Tech she was appointed to the Development Services Unit of the Council for National Academic Awards, from where she moved to her present post. She is currently involved in initiatives in open learning, quality assurance, ethics and management for professionals.

David Baume is head of Educational Development and Support Services at London Guildhall University, and chair of the Staff and Educational Development Association (SEDA). He was previously staff development manager for the Open Learning Foundation. Before that he worked for Calibre Training, producers of open and distance learning materials, and for many years at the then Polytechnic of East London. After initially teaching Underwater Technology, he later worked at East London's legendary School for Independent Study, where he formed his view of education as being primarily about empowering and skilling students to plan and undertake their own learning.

George Boak is a senior consultant at the Northern Regional Management Centre (NRMC). In addition to working on the development of management learning contracts, he has worked extensively on the design and use of competence models for managers. In 1993 he led the NRMC team that developed the personal competence model for senior managers for the Management Charter Initiative.

John Bothams is academic admissions manager at Strathclyde Graduate Business School (SGBS) and lecturer in Human Resource and Operations Management. Until May 1992 he had been course leader for the MBA in association with SGBS for over four years, and principal lecturer in Management at Newcastle Business School. He was course leader for the Certificate in Management Studies, which won a prize in 1986 for being the best of the 100-plus BTEC programmes running at that time. His lecturing followed a career which included research chemistry for BP Chemicals and production and factory management in food and pharmaceutical companies including MSD and Winthrop Laboratories. He has worked extensively with Health Service personnel from many different categories and has been a consultant to Middlesbrough Public Protection Department on total quality for three years.

Elisabeth Clark is distance learning co-ordinator at the Institute of Advanced Nursing Education of the Royal College of Nursing, with responsibility for developing award-bearing distance learning programmes for nurses throughout the UK. In 1992–93, Elisabeth was seconded to the Open Learning Foundation to work as the academic co-ordinator for Health Services. In this role, she was responsible for creating a coherent framework within the 23 member institutions for the development and delivery of flexible learning materials for pre- and post-registration nurses, midwives and health visitors. She also ran a series of workshops to prepare teaching staff to use and evaluate open learning within new and existing programmes. From 1988 to 1991, she was director of the Distance Learning Centre for Health Care Studies, South Bank University – a specialist producer of open learning materials for nurses, midwives and health visitors. She has authored numerous open learning modules that were developed for the first validated Diploma in Nursing by distance learning, and was project manager for a highly successful Research Awareness series that has been widely used by educational institutions throughout the UK and abroad. She has acted as open learning consultant for a range of projects including some by the National Extension College, Cambridge and the English and Welsh National Boards for Nursing, Midwifery and Health Visiting.

Bruce Gillham is managing director of a company producing and designing training materials and providing associated workshops. Recent work includes, among other things, a project for the United Nations on policies related to the environmental management of hazardous waste; the development of educational resources associated with palliative cancer care for medical personnel in hospices; and, with a team of local headteachers and senior staff, the production of a series of materials on developmental planning and quality management for schools. Recently retired from the University of Northumbria, Bruce retains an interest in the development of reading. A past president of the United Kingdom Reading Association, he has also been chair of the Teacher Education and Research Committees and a member of the adjudication panel for the Association's Research Awards. He has been an open learning specialist since the mid-1980s, working on projects commissioned by the Nuffield Foundation, the National Confederation of Parent–Teacher Associations, the then Training Agency, the National Council for Educational Technology and the Open Learning Foundation. He was for several years a senior consultant for the Open Tech Training and Support Unit.

Gil Graham is senior lecturer in Physics at Anglia Polytechnic University in Cambridge. He has taught physics over the full academic range from pre-O-level to final honours degree work, specializing in optics and geophysics at the upper level. He has also taught undergraduate courses at Marshall University, West Virginia, USA, and is currently director of a UK/USA undergraduate exchange programme including Marshall and other American universities. He is actively involved in the use of interactive video for undergraduate students of physics. With David Glover and Rod Macdonald he produced the interactive videodisc *Motion: A Visual Database* in 1987. In 1993 *Motion* won the Partnership Awards BT Prize for Technology for Learning in Science.

Euan Henderson is professor of Educational Technology at the Open University. He has been involved with the NHS Training Division's Management Education Scheme by Open Learning (MESOL) project since 1987, first as a member of the MESOL Project Group which planned the project, then as co-director for the development of the Managing Health Services materials, and latterly as co-director for the development of the Health and Social Services Management programme.

Virtue Jones is a freelance radio and audio producer. She teaches radio and tape production at Gateshead College and is involved in the training of contributors to community radio. She was seconded for several years from Durham Further Education Department to produce education programmes for the BBC, and was a member of the authority's curriculum development groups for Broadcasting and Low Level English. In 1979 she was appointed education producer at BBC Radio Newcastle, where she was responsible for a substantial daily schedule of mainly adult and continuing education programmes and led a team of teachers seconded from schools, and both further and higher education. From 1991 to 1992 she was employed by Sunderland Polytechnic to explore the use of community radio both as a medium for distance learning and for the dissemination of course information, and to produce audio and written open learning packages.

Geoff Layer is head of Access and Guidance at Sheffield Hallam University. He has been responsible for the development of the University Access strategy and oversees all links with colleges. He was involved in the creation of the South Yorkshire Open College Federation and is still actively involved in that organization. He is a regular contributor to conferences and seminars on Access and continuing education.

Timothy Lehmann is director of the National Center on Adult Learning and a Professor in the Graduate Studies Program at Empire State College (SUNY). For the past twenty-five years he has conducted studies and written extensively about adult learning, adult education, programme evaluation and the sociology of higher education. He received his PhD from the University of California at Berkeley in 1971 and has taught at the Ohio State University, Chabot Community College, Colorado State University and Empire State College (SUNY). As director of the National Center, Dr Lehmann is responsible for administering the practitioner research fellowship programme and for planning national conferences on topics of major interest to adult education.

Rod Macdonald is head of Media Production in the Faculty of Educational Services at Anglia Polytechnic University in Cambridge. A classics graduate of Sydney University, he taught Greek drama and philosophy before moving into more contemporary media. As well as numerous educational programmes his linear video productions include *Hamlet*, with Cambridge Experimental Theatre. With Gil Graham and David Glover he produced the award-winning interactive videodisc *Motion: A Visual Database* in 1987.

Jacki Proctor worked in further and higher education in Bradford for twenty-seven years. She moved from teaching English as a foreign language to work with art students and then into teacher education. She was PGCE course tutor for three years before moving into open learning development. Since taking early retirement she has worked mainly with the National Health Service and the Health Policy Advisory Unit, a national charity. She has a particular interest in the experience of women managers.

Mac Stephenson is director of the Northern Regional Management Centre. Its remit is to explore new approaches to management development. After a career in industry, local government and higher education, he has concentrated on competence-focused, work-based learning for managers. He is currently piloting a learning community, as a way of attaining world-class performance and supporting lifetime learning.

Andrena Telford is head of the Open Learning Unit at Newcastle Business School, University of Northumbria. She was previously a senior training adviser at Newcastle Polytechnic, and has had a long and varied career in the UK and Canada in adult education and training and in counselling adults seeking a change in career direction.

Diana Thomas is associate principal lecturer at the University of Northumbria and a consultant in learning methods and materials development. She was previously project manager for the Open Learning Foundation on the Health and Social Services Development programme, and as such led the design and development of learning materials being written in eleven different universities. She is currently contributing to development work on learning resources for several UK universities and for the National Examining Board in Supervisory Management.

Pauline Thorne is associate head of Curriculum Development at Sheffield Hallam University, based in the Learning and Teaching Institute. Her background is as a market research practitioner and lecturer. As a teacher, she increasingly recognized the value in 'live' projects in teaching research methods to students, and from this developed a broader interest in work-based learning. For the past four years, she has been actively involved in setting up an Accreditation of Prior Experiential Learning (APEL) centre and systems at Sheffield Hallam University as well as being involved in work-based learning projects across several disciplines.

Ray Winders is Satellite Projects co-ordinator at the University of Plymouth. He taught in school, further education and teacher training before moving to Plymouth as course tutor to the Post Graduate Diploma in Education Technology. Throughout, his interest has been in the use of media in both face-to-face and distance education and training. Following a successful project in the use of telephone conferencing, for the last four years he has been directing STEP-UP, the University of Plymouth satellite delivery system. His current research is in the convergence of television, satellite and computer technologies.

Ruth Wright taught briefly in secondary modern schools before moving into further education. She became interested in providing for the development of language skills while teaching sociology to Access course students. For the past ten years she has been manager of the Communication Workshops at Bradford and Ilkley Community College.

Chapter 1

Learning to be Flexible

Diana Thomas

INTRODUCTION

The pleasure in editing this book has been to be on the receiving end of such diversity of evidence that, sometimes despite the odds, there still operate an undaunted creativity and an ability continually to adapt while staying firmly focused on the needs of the particular learners targeted. It is that which is of lasting interest and is worth celebrating.

The drive to implement more flexible learning strategies is often presented as an economic and political expedient. Implicit in that is that the change is a short-term response, reactive rather than proactive, at best only secondarily determined by educational considerations and judged by externally determined criteria which neither learners nor teachers would necessarily endorse. That is not what this book is about.

The projects and initiatives discussed demonstrate as much as anything an attitude of mind. Whether capital-intensive or not, whether high- or low-technology, what characterizes the thinking behind them is the following:

- an ability to see the learning process in context, whether within the confines of an undergraduate class, in a company, in a region or industrial sector, or in the economic and social needs of an institution's international market
- within that context, an ability to identify the learner's need
- an ability and willingness to respond to the learner's capabilities, expectations and uncertainties
- skill in taking into account a number of learning variables such as available technology, sources of expertise, and, yes, available funding, in the design of a learning solution which meets the purpose
- the ability to keep on doing it.

By that last I mean endlessly to learn from their own and others' current practice, to adapt and reconfigure resources to meet emerging needs.

None of the projects or developments referred to here is standing still. Almost invariably the next potential development or different application is in mind: an interactive video (IV) intended for physics undergraduates is taken up by Sports Science students (Chapter 9, '*Motion: A Visual Database* – Learning with Interactive Video'); a community radio programme for GCSE chemistry revision can be adapted as open learning material for basic chemistry across a range of university courses (Chapter 10, 'Using Audio and Community Radio'); a Certificate-level programme for Health Service managers can be extended to Diploma level and to managers in social services too (Chapter 8, 'Open Learning for Health Service Managers'). Although a number of authors refer to problems in obtaining continuation funding for new work and the difficulty in obtaining cross-faculty, let alone cross- or trans-institutional, strategic commitment, there is much evidence of the cross-fertilization of ideas. At the end of the day perhaps little is lost, though the wait for results can be long. As Jacki Proctor and Ruth Wright point out (Chapter 6, 'The Development of Open Work-shops: How to Make it Happen'), considering the focus of government funding on, successively, investment in physical resources, especially information technology (IT), centralized control and funding targeted on developing and supporting flexible learn-ing, and educating academic and administrative staff to cope with it, one might be forgiven for thinking that overall there is not a lot to show for it. We might have expected more progress in twenty years. Change has tended to be evolutionary, with few institutions, particularly in higher education (HE), grasping the nettle of radical reform in learning and teaching methods, resources and support structures. Evolution-ary change driven by enthusiasts seems set to continue, albeit on a less fragmented scale and with more confidence than ten years ago.

At best there is a synergy between what can be achieved by individual initiatives, on whatever scale, and a corporate response to the need for 'a fundamental appraisal of and radical approach to problems of teaching and learning in mass higher edu-cation . . . While the scale of changes required is such that an evolutionary form of development is both inevitable and desirable, there is an urgent need to foster and introduce innovative approaches and structures and to make the most effective use of new technology' (Committee of Scottish University Principals, 1992).

I think it would be misplaced to lay the blame for slow progress on, variously, unimaginative management, a teaching profession resistant to change, or the conservative expectations of students, though they all have some responsibility. There is, however, a paradox at the heart of what we are doing in trying to develop more flexible approaches to learning. What characterizes many of the projects described in this book is that they have been designed to meet the learning needs of targeted learning groups: the 'powerful synergy of circumstances, skills, people and organiza-tions' (Chapter 5, 'Moving into the Open') has operated in relation to the specific. Flexible learning is not about producing variously deliverable learning packages or pick-'n'-mix courses to an otherwise undifferentiated mass market. It is about being prepared to configure all available resources, expertise and learning opportunities in the way that fits the learning purpose best. I suggest that for the foreseeable future, because developments are targeted and specific, change necessarily appears to be confined to pockets of activity and to be evolutionary, but the more management and the teaching profession are able to support the specific and to draw analogies between one learning situation and another and adapt accordingly, the better the chances for successful evolution. Looking for a universally applicable model of flexible learning is like looking for a static model of change. It just is not like that.

In the same way, I suggest that though progress in implementing more flexible approaches to learning may be slow, it is substantial, though often elusive because it turns out to be different from the indicators of progress which were being sought. Generously funded projects do not result in further look-alike projects in the same institution nor, necessarily, the wider uptake of the original project.

The physical assets of any project tend, towards the end, to be spirited away and, sooner or later, to resurface in other incarnations. I suggest that the same happens with the intellectual assets – the lessons learned and the expertise acquired. It may not be the most effective or timely use, but less is actually lost than one might initially suppose. The provenance of 'new' thinking is rarely traced back very far or regarded as a beneficial outcome of earlier investment.

Substantial government investment in projects such as Open Tech may not have generated (and given the impetus to continuing generation of) more open learning (OL) materials of publishable standards: the investment in occupational competence-based accredited training across the board may not, so far, have brought in its wake an enthusiastic and income-producing response to National Vocational Qualifications (NVQs). But these, and other developments, have had an impact. If a modularized curriculum works, then some of the credit must surely go to the good systems and materials designed and used to support OL students and to the skills acquired in recent years in tutoring students in heterogeneous groups. Similarly, the lessons learned about identifying and developing competence must have contributed to a concept which relies on the students' competence and need to make informed choices about study routes.

What is achievable, and then sustainable, in a complex organization tends to be less colourful than what visionaries originally had in mind. This is not to say that we can congratulate ourselves on simply maintaining the status quo and leave change to evolve comfortably without further intervention: quite the reverse. Where sustainable change takes place, rather than the sunburst display of innovation which one-off funding enables, it must be due to the commitment, imagination and ability to translate good ideas into practice, in small things as in great, of management and staff. Equally importantly, it takes the same qualities in the market served.

Some of the projects explored in this book are large-scale and have been dependent on external funding ever to come about – in other words they are in the 'sunburst' category. Others, though, are the result of a gathering groundswell of change in need, attitude and response which have not required external investment; which may attract little attention from outside but which may be equally indicative of a shift towards flexibility. John Bothams's collaborative research with an action learning set of medical directors (Chapter 12, 'Action Learning as a Means of Helping Professionals into a New Management Role') or Bruce Gillham's materials development workshops for further education (FE) teachers (Chapter 5, 'Moving into the Open') are by no means the only examples.

Irrespective of what happens within education, the context is changing around us and, willy-nilly, bringing about a sea change. The trouble with sea changes is that they do not stop when you have had enough and they are never quite what you expected. They are also influenced by winds and tides outside any institution's or government's control. Thus, the opening up of Eastern Europe has profoundly affected many UK universities' and colleges' perception of their market, and the development of satellite and cable transmission for home-based entertainment here and abroad has potentially presented HE and FE with the possibility of taking education programmes to people's homes, almost irrespective of geographical distance and at low capital cost (Chapter 11, 'Interactive Transmission by Satellite'). A few years ago neither of these would have been perceived as sufficiently realistic to influence corporate planning, but both are now.

Of course the education sector is not unique in the effect of change upon it. Mac Stephenson and Timothy Lehmann (Chapter 2, 'Managing Change: Towards a New Paradigm?') identify the following factors which affect the shape and operations of any organization. They apply to education institutions as much as to any business:

- the demands of business and the pursuit of world-class excellence
- the management of increasingly rapid change while meeting ever-rising quality standards
- the development of technology
- changed perceptions and demands from individuals as a result of the above factors and the changed employment patterns they have brought about.

The organizations which survive and succeed can identify and maintain their competitive edge, continually adapt structures and processes to meet continually changing needs, use IT to extend and accelerate opportunities, and foster a workforce which capitalizes on the strengths of individuals and equips them continually to learn, relearn and apply what they have learned to changing circumstances. All of these are evidenced in the following chapters.

A MODEL OF FLEXIBLE LEARNING

So what do we mean by 'flexible learning'? Is it just OL by any other name? And what does that mean anyway? Certainly many of the contributors, though not all, come from an OL background and make no hard and fast distinction between the two.

Bruce Gillham (Chapter 5, 'Moving into the Open') and Andrena Telford (Chapter 14, 'Mixed-mode Delivery: The Best of Both Worlds?') start by defining some of the terms which proliferate in this area. As well as specific meanings, though, terminology gains a distinctive flavour. The term 'open learning' has connotations of being about learning packages, most commonly print-based, which an individual learner could study at or in his or her own pace, time and place. In the early 1980s there was a misplaced and unfounded expectation that this would turn out to be tutor-free, increasingly technologically based, eminently portable, endlessly available and cheap. Just about all of those have created a bitter aftertaste causing, in their time, hostility in parts of the teaching profession and scepticism among college managements and corporate and individual clients.

There was always far more at issue than simply the production of learning materials, as any of the contributors would be the first to own. Perhaps the term 'flexible learning' for the time being anyway, shakes off the limited perception of what OL is and implies a wider view of the learning process.

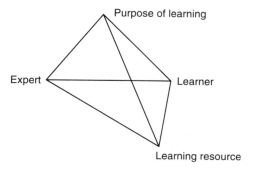

Figure 1.1 *Model of flexible learning*

Let me throw my hat into the ring. In my view 'flexible learning' is not necessarily synonymous with what is commonly understood as OL. Flexible learning encompasses the possibility of traditionally taught sessions and, if need be, of a traditional lecture delivered to a large audience (perhaps through satellite transmission to a *very* large audience) as well as individually negotiated learning activities and all points in between. Many of the principles of good OL practice articulated in the last fifteen years have informed thinking about flexible learning, and the best OL programmes exemplify flexible approaches to learning. But, for my money, flexible learning is the dynamics of the learning process which takes place between the expert, the learner and the learning resource. Precisely what the relationship is between these three is determined by:

- the *purpose* of the learning
- the *capabilities* of expert, learner and learning resource
- the *needs* of the expert, learner and learning resource.

See Figure 1.1.

Let me anticipate two possible objections to this model. First, what about organizations and infrastructures? I have subsumed those in the learning resource, for they serve no other purpose ultimately than to support learning. That is not to be dismissive: far from it. A supportive organizational structure is indispensable to sustained development and to confident performance by teachers and students alike, as Jacki Proctor and Ruth Wright tellingly illustrate (Chapter 6, 'The Development of Open Workshops: How to Make it Happen'). 'Learning resource' includes not only the obvious resources within an educational institution, but also the workplace, superior performers and learning strategies such as action learning sets. Hence the inclusion of the *needs* of learning resources in the model. While we would not normally consider a computer as having needs or a perception of its role in the learning, a student's line manager or a librarian or an administrator responsible for turning round assignments most definitely has.

The second objection is, I suspect, that the learner is not at the centre of this model. So let me qualify that. At the point of learning, whether that is in a class or laboratory, using software, using resources at work in support of a learning contract, interacting with a programme transmitted from thousands of miles away, the learner *should* be at the centre. The activity should be designed to meet purposes which the learner has negotiated or at least endorsed; start from a point that he or she understands; be expressed in terms that he or she understands; take into account his or her preconceptions, sensitivities and so on. At this close-up level too the learning purpose for the learner should be the same as the learning outcome, and that equation should be measurable.

What concerns me is that there is far more to learning than the highly focused point of learning. The danger of putting the learner at the centre, from whichever perspective we view the model, is that other things are seen as off-centre. This is not to say we think the teacher or the technology, for instance, should themselves be at the centre. It would be a brave heretic who dared to say that programmes should be designed around what the technology could currently do or the teacher felt like teaching. A model similarly skewed in favour of the learner does not attract anything like the same opprobrium but it may be equally unrealistic, because at many levels at which the purposes of learning are determined the learner is not even present. If 'learner centredness' is still emblazoned on the banner, though, somebody must claim to represent the interests of learners.

To an extent, to have sufficient knowledge of, understanding of and empathy with one's students to be able to represent them fairly is a teacher's responsibility. Politicians might claim the same. But there is a danger that many other interests get swept up in 'learner centredness': government control can appear as freedom of choice for the individual; a teacher's concern for the limited capabilities of a group of students may mask insecurity about his or her own expertise; an employer's perception about what is or is not relevant to students he or she sponsors may be more indicative of the level of development of his or her business than of a real knowledge of the students.

To those at the edge of the learner-centred model there is a very strong incentive to claim to represent the interest of those at the powerful heart.

The model I have proposed has two benefits. If other parties are freed from or denied the responsibility of representing the learner, the learner is more likely to be represented in person. Virtue Jones (Chapter 10, 'Using Audio and Community Radio') illustrates how learners were involved in the design and production of radio programmes and had a significant role in shaping the design for use. It is also interesting to see how their contributions ran alongside the university staff's professional perception of students' needs and attitudes. It is clearly possible to involve learners at an earlier stage and in a more meaningful role than we would while we assumed we knew what they wanted and how they would react.

The second benefit is that, if one accepts a model in which the dynamics of the needs and capabilities of learners, experts and resources are seen as equally influential, it becomes *allowable* for teachers, line managers, mentors and students to say what they can and cannot do, and for an honest appraisal of availability, development needs and commitment to be included in the equation. This is not a howl of protest or a bid for power, but the expression of a variable which, if not taken into account, will adversely affect the outcome.

The final danger which I see in adopting a universal model of learning which has the learner at the centre is that there is a tendency to assume that the learner's purpose is the whole purpose, which is not necessarily the case. Obviously the learner's purpose must be met, but so, quite legitimately, may the purpose of, for instance, a sponsor or a locality. John Bothams's chapter (Chapter 12, 'Action Learning as a Means of Helping Professionals into a New Management Role') gives an interesting example of the participants in an action learning set collaborating in research at the same time as tackling their own management problems, thus fulfilling their own and the university's learning purposes to their mutual satisfaction.

A multiplicity of purposes is only suspect when some are withheld from some of the parties engaged in achieving them. Continual change means we have to live with ambiguity. We do not have to live with obfuscation.

The model I propose would be straightforward if for 'expert' we could read 'teacher'; 'learner' would then equal 'student', who would also equal 'client' or 'sponsor'; and 'learning resources' would be a limited repertoire of materials and strategies. The problem is that none of these will stay in its own corner for very long: the model has to be infinitely variable to reflect particular circumstances.

First of all, what do I mean by 'an expert'? I have no problem seeing the teacher in this role as a kicking-off point. The role comprises two main elements. The first is that he or she has to be sufficiently expert in the subject to make a useful contribution to the learning process and the assessment of the learner's progress. That pretty much goes with the job. It is not the same as invariably knowing more than the learner or being a better source of information and expertise than anything else. It demands two things: being able to articulate a conceptual framework and equip learners with the vocabulary to discuss experience; and being expert enough to recognize and, within realistic constraints, make available the best and most enlightening learning opportunity for the learner in question.

The second element of the role is concomitant with this recognition of what will best meet the learning needs: the expert should understand the learning process and have a repertoire of strategies which will create or make the best use of existing learning resources so that the learner learns. More than that, the expert in this role has to be responsible for setting the process in motion, for ensuring that the learning model is dynamic and working towards the achievement of the learning purpose. This role does not necessarily have to be fulfilled by one person, though I am sceptical about being able to support learning in a context in which one is simply facilitator, with no subject expertise which would provide a valuable and relevant contribution.

The dynamics of this role in relation to the learning resource can be very varied. Gil Graham and Rod Macdonald (Chapter 9, '*Motion: A Visual Database* – Learning with Interactive Video') describe how IV is used to support learning about the concept of motion. In this case the actual teaching of the key concepts, which the students find notoriously difficult, is retained by the teacher: the IV and associated software and guide are used for experiment, data-gathering, analysis and extension of understanding.

Elisabeth Clark (Chapter 3, 'Open Learning: Educational Opportunity or Convenient Solution to Practical Problems in Higher Education?') envisages pretty much the opposite to this, where OL materials are used to 'impart information' and tutorial time is used for, among other things, more free-ranging discussion, experiment and extension of understanding.

John Bothams (Chapter 12, 'Action Learning as a Means of Helping Professionals into a New Management Role') presents a situation where the teacher, in this case predominantly in his or her role as an expert in learning dynamics, creates the situation in which Health Service managers can, to the best advantage, learn from their own experience and that of their peers. Thus the learning resource is the strategy and techniques to facilitate learning, and the source of *subject* expertise is predominantly the participants themselves.

Virtue Jones (Chapter 10, 'Using Audio and Community Radio') describes a situation where a highly charismatic teacher with the knack of conveying basic scientific principles memorably and clearly used this skill to good effect on community radio, thus becoming inseparable from the learning resource.

Problems arise when any of the players – teachers themselves, management, students, corporate clients, or sponsors including the government – see teachers or, indeed, anybody else, as ossified in one particular role, or undervalue the importance of the dynamic they represent in the learning relationship. To be as flexible in their role as the range of examples just selected highlights the fact that teachers need support to:

- build the confidence to move freely within the flexible learning relationship
- update and maintain their subject expertise which, we must suppose, is going to change at an accelerating rate for the foreseeable future
- learn how to use new teaching strategies to achieve particular learning outcomes
- feel tolerably comfortable from day to day that there is an administrative and management infrastructure in support of what they are doing.

Learning to use new strategies is most likely to involve:

- learning to recognize and capitalize on learning opportunities
- using learning resources created elsewhere
- adapting or creating learning materials
- coming to terms with unfamiliar technologies.

All of these, probably, will be 'on the job' and, if they are to be meaningful and productive, in relation to something specific.

Each of these is challenging and potentially an assault on innate professional conservatism. If the climate is such that teachers feel their contribution is of low value and dispensable, or that it would be in a proposed flexible learning relationship, then flexibility will be resisted. Although inevitably, as Jacki Proctor and Ruth Wright illustrate (Chapter 6, 'The Development of Open Workshops: How to Make it Happen'), any educational initiative is prey to whatever power struggles are currently going on, flexible learning demonstrably does not have to meet with blanket resistance. Elisabeth Clark (Chapter 3, 'Open Learning: Educational Opportunity or Convenient Solution to Practical Problems in Higher Education?'), Bruce Gillham (Chapter 5, 'Moving into the Open') and David Baume (Chapter 4, 'Staff Development in Open and Flexible Learning') are all particularly concerned with what it takes both to ensure the engagement of teachers in flexible learning and to meet their intellectual, personal and skills needs.

I said earlier that the trouble (though not a weakness) with the model of flexible learning I proposed is that nothing stays tidily in its respective corner. If an expert teacher writes a package for independent study, the essence of his or her skill goes into the learning resource. Probably the efficacy of that resource will also be dependent upon the expertise of others – text editors, radio producers or whatever. What the teacher creates and delivers, heavily supported with tutorials in one context, may be used in relative isolation as a learning resource in another institution. None of this devalues the input of the expert or, given that the content is dynamic and changing, means that that expertise is likely to be redundant because it is pooled or transferred to a particular medium.

In the same way, the learner is not simply the passive recipient of knowledge, or even the active pursuer of knowledge. He or she may be a source of expertise for other learners, or the purpose of the learning may be not to *increase* knowledge, but to learn to appraise differently what the learner already has.

By the same token, the learning resource, even an inert one, can affect the dynamics of the learning relationship. Consider, for example, Gil Graham and Rod Macdonald's account of Anglia Polytechnic University's development and use of IV (Chapter 9, '*Motion: A Visual Database* – Learning with Interactive Video'). In this case the IV was designed to be a learning resource, but what the technology made possible (watching and measuring the motion and impact of, for instance, a tennis ball striking a racquet, slowed down to single frames) changed the common perception and added to the knowledge of what actually happens. Thus the learning resource adds to the store of knowledge and expertise within the learning relationship.

EXTERNAL INFLUENCES AND THE LEARNING PURPOSE

Experts, learners and, indeed, the learning resource are affected by developments and agencies outside the context in which they are conjoined. Obviously major changes in the state of the national economy, international relations, and national and regional business failure and success have a continuing effect on the learning purpose.

As well as these easily recognizable major influences, however, there are also continual, relatively minor changes in the dynamics of the learning relationship. Mac Stephenson and Tim Lehmann (Chapter 2, 'Managing Change: Towards a New Paradigm?') would argue that it is a sensitivity to the nuances of changed demands – picking up the slightest currents in the sea change, in other words – which characterizes business survival. The same sensitivity certainly contributes to an optimum learning outcome and translates into very practical considerations. Virtue Jones (Chapter 10, 'Using Audio and Community Radio'), for instance, explores the different attitudes and prior assumptions we bring to the same aural information depending on whether we hear it on the radio or as part of a multimedia learning package. Years of exposure to radio and television mean that we bring some very sophisticated and complex expectations to the way audio and video are presented, and word-processing has rapidly raised all our expectations of the appearance of typed text. Although these influences may not in themselves represent a learning purpose, they affect how other learning purposes can best be achieved.

All the contributors demonstrate the ability to see the learner in his or her social and economic context and to recognize the effect this has at a personal level. They are also adept at identifying possible learning opportunities and resources in a given context. We see this in close-up in Chapter 13, 'Learning Contracts in Management Development Programmes'. Chapter 15, 'Supporting, Assessing and Accrediting Workplace Learning', demonstrates the same skills being applied across a range of courses for professional groups. We could take virtually any other chapter as an example of similar thinking.

I should like, however, to look briefly at the treatment of partnerships. A partnership to some extent formalizes the relationship between parties without necessarily 'freezing' it. It also implies an agreement on purpose – either that a common purpose is shared or that discrete purposes are compatible, mutually agreed to or, better still, symbiotic. Partnerships might, therefore, provide exemplars of the flexible learning model I have proposed.

Two chapters in particular explore the concept of partnership – Chapter 7, 'Working in Partnership', and Chapter 8, 'Open Learning for Health Service Managers'. In Chapter 7, Geoff Layer describes the partnership arrangements that Sheffield Hallam University has with further education colleges in the South Yorkshire region. The shared common purpose is primarily to extend learning opportunities to geographically and culturally isolated parts of the region, which have been dealt a further blow by the demise of the coal-mining industry. Second to that, the purpose is to develop a clear, consistent and readily accessible route through to HE. In this case one could argue that the university and the colleges share the 'expert' role. Equally, however, the university originally identified the colleges as a learning resource – a learning opportunity which met the needs of potential students for local centres.

In Chapter 8, Alison Baker and Euan Henderson explore possible models of partnership between FE and HE and the Health Service, created to support a management development programme. It is suggested in both Chapters 7 and 8 that the learning purpose is most fully achieved where there is a genuine sharing and a balance of interests: as Geoff Layer puts it, there is a 'need to ensure that partnership is effective, real and not a misused word for control by one organization of the delivery of another'.

Alison Baker and Euan Henderson conceive of this tension somewhat differently – as a spectrum of possible relationships ranging from exclusive ownership by the education sector to exclusive ownership by the Health Service. In between are examples of two relationships, each slightly dominated by one service or the other. Each delivers different benefits and disbenefits. Presumably, though, the nuances of this relationship offer scope for myriad variations, and the precise configuration of a model that best meets local needs would require regular monitoring and renegotiation. To do this on the basis of a shared and mutually respectful recognition of capability, need and purpose can only be healthy. Negotiation which is reluctant, infrequent and as open as a game of poker creates losers and denies the possibility of benefits beyond the accomplishment of the immediate purpose. These include opportunities for staff development; reciprocal opportunities to understand and work in different environments; the acquisition of new skills; scope for undertaking consultancy and research and for obtaining higher degrees; the extension of markets; and the opportunity to form strategic alliances which support wholly new development. These represent potential benefits to all parties at individual or institutional levels and characterize a model which is healthy and adaptive. Geoff Layer sees the very openness of the model as one of its strengths: 'a major beneficiary is the university, not in the form of any ownership but in the way it has opened up the curriculum to be challenged and debated by other educational practitioners. Such debate and challenge lead to reform and accountability: accountability both to the parties involved and to the students.'

Both chapters suggest that, if a partnership is to be more than a temporary and *ad hoc* alliance of individuals which can be undermined by the exertion of powerful pressures on any of the partners, it needs the protecting influence of a professional body or institution, and publicly visible senior management commitment. That may only be won, however, when there is sufficient interest, expertise and enthusiasm at grassroots level to *command* attention. As long as the learning purposes are felt to be worth realizing (and that is the acid test), the relationship continues to need the investment of energy and commitment by all parties at all levels. 'If partnership is to mean anything then that partnership needs to be sustained through the pain of contraction as well as the pleasure of expansion' (Chapter 7, 'Working in Partnership').

This is more than generalized goodwill: it translates into creating a supportive organizational infrastructure, deploying resources and honouring commitments to do so, expressing and demonstrating commitment even after the initial glamour has worn off, recognizing the value of work for which the institution cannot take sole credit, and allowing reasonable autonomy of decision-making to those who are outside the mainstream of activity dealing with new situations. This applies as much to business partners as to educational institutions.

A FINAL NOTE

Either lengthy contemplation of change is exhilarating or it brings on motion-sickness. It is tempting from time to time to see ourselves as a fixed point around which the world changes, but that will not do. Acknowledging that we are changed and will continue to change and that every aspect of our professional life has to be endlessly renegotiated fosters its own freedom. It is quite liberating to be able to admit that we do not necessarily know the answer and can only, to the best of our ability, share the process by which we might find out. The skills which we have traditionally valued, the ability to 'structure unfamiliar material in a way which makes sense', 'to develop several ways of explaining an idea until it is firmly grasped', and 'to encourage students to describe their current state of understanding' (Chapter 4, 'Staff Development for Open and Flexible Learning') remain indispensable to learning. So are the learner's interest in learning and the opportunity to learn.

That is one constant. David Baume sums up the other in the same chapter: 'Look for . . . the ability to develop new and better ways to learn. Look, perhaps above all, for the ability to make students, a whole group or class of them, feel heard and understood and cared about and respected.'

REFERENCE

Teaching and Learning in an Expanding Higher Education System (1992). Report of a Working Party of the Committee of Scottish University Principals. Edinburgh: Committee of Scottish University Principals.

Chapter 2

Managing Change: Towards a New Paradigm?
Mac Stephenson and Timothy Lehmann

INTRODUCTION

The Northern Regional Management Centre's (NRMC) main focus is the research and development of new approaches to management education and training, in collaboration with employers and managers. As such, it needs to ensure that it is aware of and addressing major issues facing organizations and management education. State University of New York (SUNY), Empire State College, has similar concerns, as a pioneer of contract learning and one of the USA's leading 'adult learning' institutions. The college's central purpose is to expand access to higher education for students, primarily adults, who choose alternatives to the fixed schedule, place, programme and structure of campus-based education. This purpose is met through a variety of approaches to teaching and learning, including guided independent studies, group studies, application of computer and video technologies, experimental learning and collaboration with SUNY and other organizations. The college has pioneered the use of individual plans of study, independent learning arrangements and recognition of college-level learning acquired on the job and in other life contexts for credit towards the degree. The purpose of this chapter is to sketch these issues and suggest possible courses of action. There is also a concern that even if the issues are known, they are being addressed in a piecemeal fashion. This may be justifiable 'strategic incrementalism': it may be clouding the need, *in toto*, for more radical solutions.

ISSUES: SHORT-TERM

The major issues facing employers centre on the management of increasingly rapid change while meeting ever rising quality demands. Leaving aside some of the harsh realities of this scenario – unemployment, redundancies, etc. – the development issues which need to be addressed are becoming clearer. Overall they represent some of the many facets of the challenge employers must meet if 'world-class excellence' is to be achieved.

The issues are mapped in Figure 2.1. Based on an extensive literature survey, the framework illustrates:

- major challenges managers will face over the next decade
- the 'pattern' of features of organizations regarded as being of world-class excellence
- the 'pillars' on which their excellent performance is built
- the main areas of national standards for managers, aimed at their improvement through developing competences
- examples of the immediate concerns of managers, which may need to be tackled before further development can occur.

The framework suggests that to address these components, a 'management of change and quality' process will be necessary. Given the importance of developing people in such a process (and as a component of world-class excellence), it is further suggested that the UK government initiative Investors in People could play an important role. For comparison, the framework also sets out the main features predicted for future organizations and the main features of the major US quality award, the Baldridge. Attainment of these features could be helped significantly by successfully developing the components of world-class excellence.

Of course, world-class excellence is not a static picture, but the framework should be robust enough to accommodate changes. The component 'headings' are reasonably familiar. Without going into detail there seem to be some critical issues and longer-term implications:

- Employers will need to be acutely aware of their 'competitive edge', present and future.
- The pace of change will not decrease, and continuous 'organizational' and individual learning and relearning will be necessary.
- The structures and processes of future 'organizations'/'work units' will be different.
- The context in which managerial competence is exercised will be radically different.
- Lifelong learning by qualified, empowered employees with the ability to 'learn to learn' will be necessary for the success of 'organizations'. Hence employers will need to be closely involved in the 'directed training' and support of employees' learning.
- Information technology (IT) and computer-mediated communications will have a growing impact, both increasing the pace of change and offering opportunities to address change.
- The above will apply to private and public organizations and employees, including those in higher education (HE) and further education (FE).

The cumulative effect has been described as a 'new economy': an illuminating summary is given in *America and the New Economy*, by Anthony P. Carnevale:[1]

> The new economy is distinguished from the old economy by a new set of competitive standards. In the old economy competitive success was based almost exclusively on the ability to improve productivity. In the new economy organizations and nations compete not only on their ability to improve productivity but on their ability to deliver quality, variety, customization, convenience and timeliness as well.

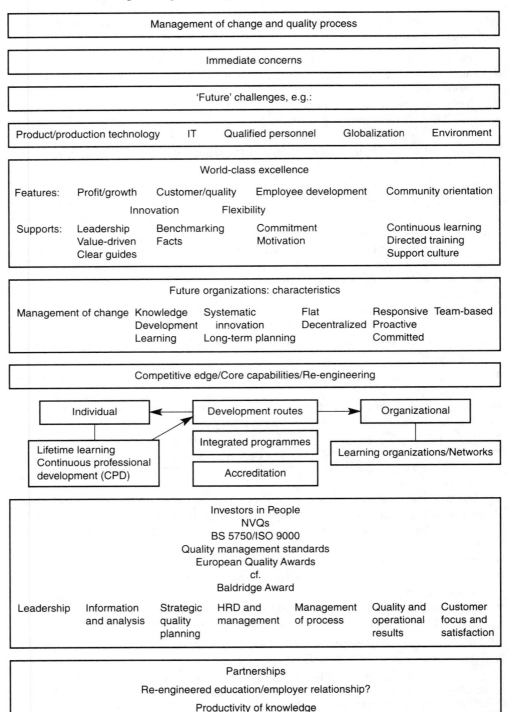

Figure 2.1 *World-class excellence: components of a development framework*

The shift from the old to the new economy results from the globalization of wealth and competition and from the introduction of new flexible technologies that allow the simultaneous pursuit of the full range of new competitive standards on a global scale.

The new competitive standards and flexible technologies of the new economy need to be housed in new kinds of organizations. Both large, top-down hierarchies typical of manufacturing and smaller, isolated and fragmented structures typical of services are being replaced by flexible networks.

The new economy is creating a new structure of jobs. Organizations are using a mix of highly skilled but fewer production workers and more service workers to meet new competitive standards.

The new economy also requires a more highly skilled workforce. Workers' skills need to be both broader and deeper especially at the point of production, service delivery and at the interface with the customer in order to meet new competitive standards and to complement flexible organization structures and technology.

(p.iii)

CURRENT RESPONSES

The foregoing issues have already had a massive impact on organizations. Their responses fall under four themes:

1. 'downsizing', with major redundancies and/or closure or divestment of business
2. 're-engineering': a fundamental restructuring of operations
3. 'empowerment': giving employees more responsibility for decision-making, supported by flatter organizational structures, self-directed work teams and networks
4. 'learning organizations': the creation of processes enabling and supporting individual learning and ensuring that the latter contributes to the sum of organizational learning. A separate strand of this theme is the recognition of the necessity of continuous professional development (CPD) and lifelong learning.

Themes 2–4 are interrelated: each demands the other if it is to be successful. These themes are underpinned by a fifth:

5. IT: the growing realization of its capability,

and are in turn themselves underpinning a sixth:

6. 'productivity of knowledge': a perception of the growing competitive importance of knowledge possession and use.

Downsizing (Theme 1)

Downsizing and its effects do not need detailing here. Suffice it to say that it will sustain a continuing demand for training and retraining and possibly a pool of labour who will be unemployable in the competitive, professional businesses of the future.

Re-engineering (Theme 2)

Re-engineering is the imprecise buzz word describing successful radical action by some leading organizations. In *Re-engineering the Corporation* by M. Hammer and J. Champy,[2] the following definition and description is given: 'Re-engineering' properly is 'the fundamental rethinking and radical redesign of business processes to achieve dramatic improvements in critical, contemporary measures of performance, such as cost, quality, service and speed'. This definition contains four key words.

The first key word is 'fundamental'. In doing re-engineering, business people must ask the most basic questions about their companies and how they operate: why do we do what we do? And why do we do it the way we do? Asking these fundamental questions forces people to look at the tacit rules and assumptions that underlie the way they conduct their businesses. Re-engineering begins with no assumptions and no givens.

The second key word is 'radical'. Radical redesign means getting to the root of things: not making superficial changes or fiddling with what is already in place, but throwing away the old. In re-engineering, radical redesign means disregarding all existing structures and procedures and inventing completely new ways of accomplishing work. Re-engineering is about business reinvention – not business improvement, business enhancement or business modification.

The third key word is 'dramatic'. Re-engineering is not about making marginal or incremental improvements but about achieving quantum leaps in performance. Re-engineering should be brought in only when a need exists for heavy blasting.

The fourth key word is 'processes'. Although this word is the most important in our definition, it is also the one that gives most corporate managers the greatest difficulty. Most business people are not 'process-oriented'; they are focused on tasks, on jobs, on people, on structures, but not on processes.

> We define a business process as a collection of activities that takes one or more kinds of input and creates an output that is of value to the customer . . .
>
> The core message of our book is: it is no longer necessary or desirable for companies to organise their work around Adam Smith's division of labour. Task-oriented jobs in today's world of customers, competition and change are obsolete. Instead, companies must organise work around process . . .
>
> This is an assertion as radical and as far-reaching today as Adam Smith's was in his time. Managers who understand and accept this concept of process-based work will help their companies lead ahead. Those who don't will stay behind.
>
> (*ibid.*, pp. 32–5, 27, 28)

SUNY, Empire State College, provides a dramatic example of possible ways of learning as a process is structured into individually designed programmes. Recognizing that college-level learning derives from purposes important to the individual and that learning occurs in various ways and places, Empire State College uses a contract mode of learning and a portfolio assessment process for prior learning to create flexible degree programmes for adults in consultation with teaching staff.

Re-engineering, with its focus on processes, encompasses the examination of an organization's 'core capabilities' or 'competences' – not just products, but those capabilities which will enable an organization to keep ahead of its competitors, and survive and respond to a changing environment. J. B. Quinn in *Intelligent Enterprise*[3] argues that these competences will be 'intellectual assets', therefore human, which should move people development into the forefront of strategic thinking.

Stalk *et al.*[4] have made a distinction between capability and core competences:

> Both concepts emphasize behavioural aspects of strategy in contrast to the traditional structural model. But whereas core competence emphasizes production and technological expertise at specific points along the value chain, capabilities are more broadly based, encompassing the entire value chain. In this respect, capabilities are visible to the customer in a way that core competencies rarely are.

As to the actual approach to be taken, Stalk *et al.* argue that:

> The starting point is for senior managers to undergo the fundamental shift in perception that allows them to see their business in terms of strategic capabilities. Then they can begin to identify and link together essential business processes to serve customer needs. Finally, they can reshape the organization – including managerial roles and responsibilities – to encourage the new kind of behaviour necessary to make capabilities-based competition work.
>
> (*ibid.*)

In relation to core competences, Prahalad and Hamel[5] argue that three tests can be applied:

- A core competence provides potential access to a wide variety of markets; for example, competence in display systems enables a company to participate in such diverse businesses as calculators, miniature television sets, monitors for laptop computers, etc.
- A core competence should make a significant contribution to the perceived customer benefits of the end product.
- A core competence should be difficult for competitors to imitate.

At the moment, the core capability/competence approach is a concept, more or less understandable, with no clearly defined process. However, the approach is clearly concerned with long-term perspectives on change and quality, and with the core competences which determine an organization's competitive edge. The 'possession' of competences and their management lie with people.

Empowerment (Theme 3)

Successful re-engineering and core capabilities/competences approaches demand empowerment of employees. If employees are not to have defined tasks, they must have latitude for action, and responsibility for decision-making. 'Empowerment' is seen as a major criterion for successful business, and its organization, in the 1990s. The nub of the argument is that business cannot compete, cannot meet the quality levels demanded by customers, cannot be responsive to customers, cannot deal with the rapid rate of change, unless all its employees believe and aspire to the best performance and customer care. To enable this, business has sought to encourage individual responsibility, through flatter organizations, self-directed work teams, mentoring, etc. In essence, this is 'empowerment': enabling individual employees to take responsibility. It is recognized that empowerment will be a meaningless concept unless there is a develop-ment process and support system encouraging less dependency on the part of employees, and less 'control' on the part of managers.

Again, SUNY, Empire State College, places full responsibility upon the adult learners for designing and carrying out a degree programme. Of course, this process is done with the teaching staff's supervision and support, but it gives the learner an enormous challenge and potential to shape an education to fit his or her present post with future educational goals and experience. Over 80 per cent of Empire's students are working, the vast majority full-time, so empowering individuals to reshape their education expectations also has substantial work consequences (T. Lehmann, 1988[6]).

The exercise of individual responsibility is the *sine qua non* for many of the approaches to quality management which are being adopted, and it underpins organ-izational re-engineering. The parallels with NVQ/competence development seem obvious.

Indeed, competence development and empowerment should be mutually reinfor-cing and enabled in tandem if they are to be capitalized upon fully. Acquisition of all competences would obviously increase a person's ability and willingness to take on responsibility. Certainly empowerment without competence, and vice versa, would seem a nonsense – a dangerous nonsense.

As a corollary, if empowerment succeeds, the context and locus of the exercise of competences could be radically changed. Peter Wickens of Nissan has long argued that managerial competences should be the competences of all employees. This may be premature for many organizations, but significant movement in this direction is occurring.

Learning organization (Theme 4)

Empowerment links to Theme 4, 'learning organizations'. To survive, an organization will need to be responsive to its rapidly changing environment, and in particular to the needs and quality levels of its customers. This responsiveness can only come from its employees: they can only be responsive if they are enabled to learn, to keep up with developments, encouraged and supported. The essence of the learning organization is individual learning, encouraged and supported by the organization and centred on its aims, so that the sum of the parts is greater than the whole. The concepts of learning organizations should be familiar to readers: *The Fifth Discipline*, by P. M. Senge,[7] and *The Learning Company: A Strategy for Sustainable Development*, by Pedler *et al.*,[8] illustrate current work in the area. More directly related to the development of individual employees, though within the context of what employers deem will be necessary competences for their learning organizations, are:

- the specification in the United Kingdom of National Vocational Qualifications (NVQs): partly paralleled in the USA by the Senate Commission on the Achieve-ment of Necessary Skills
- the specification of processes for continued professional development
- an emerging dialogue, on the implications of lifelong learning – access, support, accreditation and the skills required to 'learn to learn'.

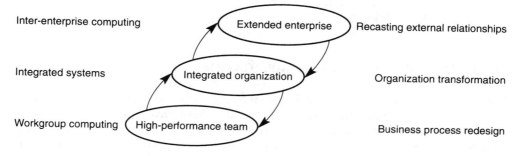

Inter-enterprise computing   Extended enterprise   Recasting external relationships

Integrated systems   Integrated organization   Organization transformation

Workgroup computing   High-performance team   Business process redesign

Figure 2.2   *Enabling effect of IT*

IT (Theme 5)

IT has stimulated the rate of change which has engendered the above responses, and is enabling these responses to be successful. In *Paradigm Shift: The New Promise of Information Technology*, by D. Tapscott and A. Caston,[9] the authors argue that three fundamental shifts are occurring in the application of IT to business, each affecting a different level of business opportunity. IT enables enterprises to have a high-perform-ance team structure, to function as integrated businesses despite high business unit autonomy, and to reach out and develop new relationships with external organizations – to become an 'external enterprise'. The enabling effect of IT is summarized in Figure 2.2 (*ibid.*, p. 15).

The IT theme need not be laboured: its application is becoming robust and cost effective. It is enabling, supporting and enhancing the processes and information flows of the 'new enterprises' – and the training of their employees, through interactive video, computer conferencing and bulletin boards, E-mail, satellite conferencing, etc.

Productivity of knowledge (Theme 6)

The orientation of new organizations, the importance of learning for their success, and the growing potential of IT to enhance their processes has led to the (emergent) sixth theme, 'productivity of knowledge'. Peter Drucker in *Post Capitalist Society*[10] argues that the single greatest challenge facing managers today is to raise the productivity of knowledge and service workers. He argues that this will determine the competitive performance of companies, the quality of life in every industrial nation, and the very fabric of society. To quote Drucker:

> while the world economy will remain a market economy and retain the market institutions, its substance has been radically changed. It it is still 'capitalist', it is now dominated by 'information capitalism'. The industries that have moved into the centre of the economy in the last forty years have as their business the production and distribution of knowledge and information, rather than the production and distribution of things. The actual product of the pharmaceutical industry is knowledge; pill and prescription ointment are no more than packaging for knowledge. There are the telecommunications industries and the industries which produce information-processing tools and equipment, such as computers, semicon-ductors, software. There are the information producers and distributors: movies, tele-vision shows, videocassettes. The 'non-businesses' which produce and apply knowledge –

education and health care – have in all developed countries grown much faster even than knowledge-based businesses.

EDUCATION: RESPONSES AND IMPLICATIONS

What are the responses and implications of the preceding issues and developments for FE and HE? It is stating the obvious to say that there have already been massive changes to education. In the main they have been impelled by government, but some have been in response to the foregoing issues – encouraging competitiveness through granting more autonomy to institutions; encouraging development of 'enterprise' attributes; encouraging greater employer involvement through Training and Enterprise Councils (TECs), etc. There are also initiatives to increase provision and access, from the creation of the Open University and the growth of open learning, to increasing modularization, with the Credit Accumulation and Transfer System. However, there is a widespread feeling that resources are not there to meet the demand and a growing concern that resources might never be sufficient – whatever the outcome of the debates on student loans, full-cost courses, etc. This concern has been paralleled by the oft-stated fear that increased numbers will threaten the quality of education – and decreasing resources make the fear more justifiable. The Committee of Scottish University Principals addressed these concerns in their report *Teaching and Learning in an Expanding Higher Education System.*[11] The report's main finding was that:

> A fundamental appraisal of, and a radical approach to, the problems of teaching and learning in mass higher education is now necessary. While the scale of the changes required is such that an evolutionary form of development is both inevitable and desirable, there is an urgent need to foster and introduce innovative approaches and structures, and to make the most effective use of new technology. These, however, can only supply part of the solution to the problems which higher education faces. The greatest challenge is to persuade a majority of those involved in higher education to see teaching as their prime activity, and as one posing intellectual challenges and offering rewards comparable to those of standard research. The development, and imaginative use, of shared educational resources, and the necessary research into learning processes and new forms of large-scale teaching, will all require new organisational structures, and the creation of supporting infrastructures at national and institutional level.
>
> (*ibid.*, p. ix)

Similar concerns were expressed at a recent US conference on Higher Education and Workforce Development, organized by Empire State College and the National Centre on Adult Learning (NCAL). NCAL has its headquarters at SUNY, Empire State College, and its primary mission is to improve the research and effective practice of adult learning. By providing faculty fellowships for innovative projects and periodically sponsoring conferences on topics pertinent to adult learning, like the recent one on Higher Education and Workforce Development, NCAL becomes a forum for new approaches to learning and work and experimenting with new practices across America. There was a consensus that new approaches were necessary; requiring 'systemic collaboration' between employers and F/HE. Pamela Tate, president of the Council for Adult and Experiential Learning (CAEL), argued that, for workforce development, 'third-wave' solutions were necessary. The 'first wave' had been recognition of adult learning; the 'second wave' meant some involvement of employers; the 'third wave' recognized that the development of the workforce is an economic imperative. Douglas Johnstone, Dean of College Wide Programmes, Empire State College,[12] argued a similar case from a different perspective. He emphasized the low level of US workforce competence and the rising cost of educational institutions. He argued for HE in the workplace, and college/corporate partnerships on these grounds:

- We are broke and need new sources of revenue.
- The people who need what we can give are out there not in here: more than 80 per cent of all the people in this country who will be working in the year 2000 are already in the labour pool.
- Industry cannot close the 'competence gap' alone: 75 per cent of our labour force currently needs complete retraining every seven to ten years. That pace is accelerating; education and training must now be continuous.
- Our 'competence gap' is a national crisis: we have a moral obligation to respond to it.

The 'bottom line' for the education system may be illustrated by the boxed news item from the *Guardian*, August 1993 – the system could virtually be ignored by business:

Car parts firm to set up skills 'university'

Unipart, the car parts company, is to set up its own 'university' in Oxford to improve skill levels in its 3,700 workforce.

Employees have been barred from speaking about the project, drawn up over the past two years under the direction of group chief executive John Neill, but one source said it represented a 'huge investment'.

Mr Neill is keeping details under wraps until the formal launch of the project by John Patten, the Education Secretary, next month. But he yesterday confirmed that a leading academic on the car industry, Professor Dan Jones, of Cardiff Business School, will be part-time principal.

Outsiders have suggested the Unipart initiative may provoke debate on whether universities and colleges of further education have done enough to meet industry's needs for tailor-made, relevant courses.

SUMMARY

While predictions of the future must be treated cautiously, many of the issues outlined are already with us – re-engineering, globalization, lifelong learning, the impact of IT – and the pace of change is increasing. Responses are being made by employers, HE and the government. Informed commentators have argued that these responses are not radical enough, because they do not reflect the importance of workforce development, or recognize the seriousness of the resource and quality issues facing HE. What can be done?

Action

Flexibility is required if increasing rapid and uncertain change is to be addressed. This has led NRMC to consider smaller 'learning units' which would be able to adapt quickly. The analogy of amoebas sprang to mind. It was used to see whether it afforded insights into alternative forms of learning support for managers – NRMC's particular concern.[13] It was suggested that in a management context a 'learning unit' or 'learning amoeba' would be, in its smallest form:

- *a manager* with X – the motivation to learn, for whatever reason(s) – and with support.

If lifelong manager development is to become possible for the majority of managers, then self-development 'capacity' and support must be affordable and accessible. Both these latter features seem feasible through the use of:

- a self-development 'backpack'
- collaborative learning
- mentors.

A self-development pack is feasible because of the number of 'artefacts' now available for diagnosis, development and support, giving the abilities to

- self-assess competence, organizational blockages, learning styles
- self-develop, considering work-based learning opportunities and using open learning materials and interactive technology
- gain relevant, in-house support through learning contracts, through action sets or by linking to networks.

Collaborative learning is feasible, and a valuable source of motivation, through in-house groups; self-support groups of small firms managers; and groups of managers from a number of firms 'hosted' by a large firm (generally, one to which they are suppliers).

NRMC is piloting a Learning Community for Management Development in the north-east of England. Its aim is to enable managers to attain world-class performance levels. It recognizes that individual managers and organizations have difficulty monitoring and acting upon change: in collaboration they will at least be able to monitor major trends. The community has brought together representatives of employers, TECs, education, and training providers. Basic information on aspects of world-class excellence is available through workshops, newsletters and an information assistant. Collaborative development is occurring in action learning groups, and through informal contacts. Computer-mediated communications are being established to record and disseminate all activities, provide up-to-date information and simple 'action guides', and encourage 'conferencing' on topics of interest.

Finally, mentors seem critical. It is mentors who could provide the continuing flexible support required for 'lifelong' individual learning. They could 'square the circle' with the culture (whether it be an organization or, for instance, a small firms market) to enable resources to be obtained and development to be healthy for all concerned. The frequency, type (academic or work-based) and costs of mentoring all need to be explored. It so happens that teaching staff at SUNY, Empire State College, who are called mentors go far beyond the traditional and narrow teaching function of classroom dissemination of information. These mentors must be knowledgeable across a wide range of academic disciplines, must understand disciplinary modes of enquiry, and must possess a repertoire of effective strategies to engage adult learners in academic issues central to their programmes of study. Mentors thus serve as expert advisers, resource brokers and curricula planners, linking adult learners to the academic and work worlds of the future.

These suggestions are direction indicators but they do indicate that 'learning amoebas' – learning units supporting individual managers in a variety of management contexts – are relevant and possible.

Following chapters illustrate other flexible learning support strategies in a variety of contexts. *In toto*, these represent the necessary 'strategic incrementalism' referred to in the Scottish University Principals' report.[11] There is still the question of more radical action which some respected commentators have deemed necessary.

Tapscott and Caston[9] argue that four paradigm shifts are affecting business (and, by extension, the educational system).

The shifts are:

- *new business environment* – open, competitive, dynamic market place
- *new technology* – new goals for IT; open, user-centred network computing
- *new geopolitical order* – open, volatile, multi-polar world
- *new enterprise* – open, networked, information-based organization.

Educational institutions must consider whether incremental approaches are adequate and speedy enough responses to these shifts.

Within this consideration and of vital importance to NRMC and educational institutions is the theme embedded in three of the paradigm shifts at least – the 'productivity of knowledge'. This enigmatic phrase may well be indicating a new paradigm, certainly for workforce/manager education, but also for education as a whole. If commentators are correct, and business is to be more knowledge-based, then education as a 'knowledge industry' must have a vital role to play. As an example, NRMC has already reaped the financial awards of 'intellectual property' and increasing the 'productivity of knowledge' by:

- communicating the same knowledge to a large number of learners, by selling workbooks
- enabling learners to apply this knowledge to their own organizations, hence generating further knowledge for themselves and their employers, through open learning programmes
- enabling mentors to support the learners and increase their own knowledge at the same time
- overall, enabling learners to learn, so they can continue to acquire/generate knowledge.

'Productivity of knowledge' could be increased by the use of computer-mediated communications, and will have to be so to deal with decreasing resources and increasing demand/lifelong learning.

When considering new paradigms, J. A. Barker in *Paradigms: The Business of Discovering the Future*[14] states that the question to be asked is: 'What is impossible to do in your business (field, discipline, department, division, technology, etc. . . .) but if it could be done, would fundamentally change it?' An illustrative answer, for NRMC and for education, could be 'audio/visual person-to-person and person-to-group contact'. This is technically feasible, though not robust enough for mass, practical application at present. Both employers and educational institutions are moving in this direction, with satellite/computer conferencing. Linked to the increasing use of IT within organizations for conducting their business, it is possible to envisage a completely different pattern of education support to employers – completely work-based, delivered simultaneously to different and widely dispersed sites, accessing leading practitioners (recorded or live) from anywhere in the world. It would be a college without walls, a corporate classroom or a university of life, drawing upon and giving lifelong access to the best of experiential and academic learning.

CONCLUSIONS

There are massive opportunities for FE and HE with lifelong learning, the importance of 'productivity of knowledge' and the potential access to learners afforded by flexible learning strategies and IT. These opportunities are not being presented to the 'educational system' alone. There is a global market which is seeing competition from training providers, publishers, media, employers and other educational institutions. Addressing these opportunities might raise the morale of educational teaching staff, increasingly depressed by rising student numbers and falling resources. It the opportunities are ignored, FE and HE could become increasingly irrelevant, certainly to workforce development.

NOTES

1. Carnevale, P. (1991) *America and the New Economy*. Washington, DC: American Society for Training and Development/US Dept of Labor.
2. Hammer, M. and Champy, J. (1993) *Re-engineering the Corporation*. New York: HarperCollins.
3. Quinn, J. B. (1992) *Intelligent Enterprise*. New York: The Free Press/Macmillan.
4. Stalk, G., Evans, P. and Shulman, L. E. (1992) Competing on capabilities: the new rules of corporate strategy. *Harvard Business Review*, March–April, 57–69.
5. Prahalad, C. K. and Hamel, G. (1990) The core competences of the corporation. *Harvard Business Review*, May–June, 79–91.
6. Lehmann, T. (1988) Fulfilling democracy's promise through education: the Empire State College experiment. In Granger, D., Education Issue of *Golden Hill*, **4**, 5–45.
7. Senge, P. M. (1990) *The Fifth Discipline*. New York: Doubleday.
8. Pedler, M., Burgoyne, J. and Boydell, T. (1991) *The Learning Company: A Strategy for Sustainable Development*. Maidenhead, Berks: McGraw-Hill Europe.
9. Tapscott, D. and Caston, A. (1993) *Paradigm Shift: The New Promise of Information Technology*. New York: McGraw-Hill.
10. Drucker, P. *Post Capitalist Society*. New York: HarperCollins.
11. Committee of Scottish University Principals (1992) *Teaching and Learning in an Expanding Higher Education System*. Edinburgh: Committee of Scottish University Principals.

12. Johnstone, D. (1993) College at work: the new imperative for American workforce development. Paper given at the Education and Workforce Development Conference, Saratoga Springs, June.
13. Stephenson, M. (1991) Learning amoeba: supporting individual managers during rapid change. Paper given at the Learning Organization Conference, Warwick University, April.
14. Barker, J. A. (1993) *Paradigms: The Business of Discovering the Future*. New York: HarperBusiness.

Chapter 3

Open Learning: Educational Opportunity or Convenient Solution to Practical Problems in Higher Education?

Elisabeth Clark

A NEW FRAMEWORK FOR HIGHER EDUCATION

The publication, in May 1991, of a White Paper establishing a new framework for higher education (HE) and setting down the government's plans for it may be regarded as a major milestone in education policy. Significant expansion was clearly one of the government's targets – whereas in 1991, one in five 18–19-year-olds enrolled on HE courses, the target of one in three was set for the year 2000. Moreover, this expansion was to be achieved through increased efficiency and without a commensurate increase in resources. The need for greater flexibility in patterns of teaching and learning was, therefore, highlighted, as was the adoption of a more market-oriented system. Greater emphasis was also to be placed on quality assurance to ensure the enhancement of the quality of both teaching and learning. Thus, the ground rules were set out for a model of mass HE.

There has since been fairly widespread discussion and debate about how to cope with expansion on the scale proposed and within the context of an overriding concern to maintain quality. While it was recognized that some efficiency gains, and hence some savings, might be achieved by squeezing more teaching into the working day and by extending the academic year, many vice-chancellors and senior managers realized that traditional patterns of education provision would not enable HE institutions to meet the expansion of student numbers envisaged in the White Paper, while at the same time maintaining academic standards and the quality of the provision. In 1993, there was a reprieve when a halt was called on the rate of expansion; but since then there have been further, significant reductions in the unit of resource. To cope with such unwelcome changes and establish sound, long-term strategies, a fairly fundamental review of existing systems is needed, including a consideration of the possible contribution of more flexible patterns of teaching and learning.

During the 1980s, a degree of awareness about flexible approaches to education was beginning to percolate through HE. This may in part be attributed to the work of the Open University (OU), which employed a number of part-time tutorial and counselling staff from within the ranks of HE lecturers. More recently, a number of institutions became involved in the hundred or more Open Tech projects that were funded by the then Manpower Services Commission. The impact of such developments was, however, fairly limited. For many HE lecturers, it was against the uncertain background of expansion and resource constraints that they first encountered any serious discussion of open learning (OL). It was, therefore, hardly surprising that the initial reaction of many individuals to the idea of exploring alternative approaches to teaching and learning was sometimes less than enthusiastic: many were fearful for their jobs and hence were suspicious of motives.

While on secondment to the Open Learning Foundation as the academic co-ordinator for Health Services, I ran a series of workshops designed to introduce colleagues to the concept of OL and explore ways of building greater flexibility into existing and new course provision. It was in this context that I initially encountered some of the resistance outlined above. It was also around this time that I began to realize that OL was perhaps being introduced to many HE lecturers in entirely the wrong way – as no more than a means of responding to government targets and of solving some of the associated practical problems currently facing HE. As educationalists first and foremost, teachers in HE are understandably and rightly suspicious of any approach which appears to spring from mere expediency rather than from a sound and principled educational foundation. Hence the importance of starting any debate about the possible contribution of OL by exploring some of the educational reasons for adopting alternative approaches to teaching and learning and by considering the possible advantages and disadvantages of particular approaches. Since my work in the OL field has mainly been in the area of health and nursing, I shall draw largely on the relevant literature in this area, whenever the points that are raised apply equally to other subject areas.

Traditionally, the organization of HE has been largely course-based, and as a consequence most educational activities have centred on the course. The past decade, however, has seen the introduction of a number of educational initiatives designed to enhance the accessibility and flexibility of HE, bringing with them a number of significant benefits for both students and employers. The main innovations include the following:

- *Modularization* – students are no longer expected to commit themselves to entire courses that may last several years. Rather, they can enrol on individual modules (each of which is likely to be between 120 and 200 study hours) and can shape their programme by selecting subsequent modules with the benefit of the experience gained.
- *Credit accumulation and transfer scheme (CATS)* – with modularization, it became necessary to develop a system that enabled academic credits to be 'banked' and recognized by other institutions, allowing students to transfer more easily between institutions than had traditionally been the case. Between 1986 and 1991, the Council for National Academic Awards (CNAA) spearheaded the development of CATS, thereby helping to change the culture of HE by enhancing flexible provision and structures. This scheme has now been adopted by many universities.
- *Accreditation of prior learning/prior experiential learning (APL/APEL)* – this increased student mobility between education institutions through CATS required, in its turn, the establishment of a formal system to assess and accredit prior

learning. Only thus could it be ensured that students received both full, formal academic recognition for previous learning, and appropriate guidance about what modules needed to be successfully completed in order to gain a particular award.

For many students, traditional programmes and methods of teaching raise enormous difficulties. Taken together, the above developments lead to an increase in accessibility and flexibility. They open up HE opportunities to a wider section of society including part-time and mature students, and remove many of the barriers of inflexible structures previously encountered by many students. As a corollary, increasing numbers of institutions are realizing the need to explore new approaches to teaching and learning, and are beginning to explore how OL materials might be incorporated into new and existing modules to enhance the flexibility afforded by modularization, CATS and APL/APEL. It is on OL that I wish to focus in this chapter. From the outset, I would like to stress the importance of looking at both the educational advantages and disadvantages and the need to acknowledge these when considering how OL might best be used within an HE context. If, as suggested above, OL is merely regarded as offering a pragmatic solution for some of the practical difficulties currently facing HE, then it is unlikely ever to be regarded as a mainstream educational activity. By contrast, Thorpe (1987) argues that open learning should be viewed as: 'an approach which, rather like the Trojan Horse, has brought back more urgently into the strongholds of institutions of education and training, a set of issues about whom we should be providing for, to what purpose and by what means' (p. 71). If it is to succeed, OL must be fully integrated into course provision and its contribution needs to be evaluated.

OPEN LEARNING: ITS EDUCATIONAL PHILOSOPHY

As we shall see, the educational philosophy behind OL is entirely in accordance with a number of educational practices which many HE lecturers would wish to support. While there are numerous definitions of OL, for the purposes of this chapter I want to extract six key concepts that are embedded in the philosophy of OL:

- a student-centred approach
- students encouraged to take responsibility for their learning
- learner choice
- opening up learning opportunities by overcoming some of the barriers to course attendance
- flexible education provision to meet individual requirements
- the use of specially prepared or adapted learning materials.

The OL approach, therefore, brings together sound educational principles and an organizational framework which is practical and suited to the needs of our times. Its success depends on the provision of effective learning materials which have been specifically designed to enable students to take responsibility for their learning. It is characterized by the flexibility, adaptability and responsiveness of organizational structures and – not least – by the reduced reliance on teacher availability at specific times and places. In all these respects, OL provides a significant alternative to conventionally taught courses within traditional HE structures.

Within a programme that uses OL materials, there can, of course, be substantial differences in the amount of openness and control offered to students. At one extreme, students may, with guidance, be allowed to make important decisions about many aspects of their learning, including:

- *what* to study – programmes, modules, sequence
- *how* to study – preferred methods of learning, preferred media, what routes to take
- *where* to study – location(s)
- *when* to study – start/finish dates, pace of learning.

In addition, students may be involved in decisions such as the kind and amount of support needed and who might provide it (tutor, colleague, manager); and whether the learning will be assessed and, if it is, how it will be assessed and when.

At the other extreme, lecturers may wish to exert far more control over the learning process, determining what is studied, broadly when it is studied (fixed programme start and finish dates), and how and when learning will be assessed. However, even when such parameters are defined at the outset, the use of learning materials which encourage active learner involvement and which can be studied away from an educational establishment may still allow students greater flexibility and control over learning than is usually possible in conventionally taught courses offered within traditional educational structures. Finally, the middle course between teacher control and student autonomy is readily achieved by the inherent flexibility of an approach in which OL is given a significant role.

At present, despite the success of local schemes, the use of OL still appears to be somewhat marginal. It is largely confined to areas where access to conventional education provision is problematic, or where a student population tends to be scattered over a fairly wide geographical area. In order to examine the case for open/distance learning, it may be helpful to explore some of the potential advantages and disadvantages. To do this, I shall focus on two different perspectives: that of the lecturer and that of the student. As we examine each of these in turn, the following list of key characteristics of education will provide a useful framework to evaluate the possible contribution of OL:

- accessibility
- availability throughout the lifespan
- responsiveness to widely differing individual life circumstances
- ability to cope with learner diversity
- affordability (for both provider and recipient)
- demonstrable effectiveness.   (adapted from McManus and Lyne, 1992).

THE LECTURER'S PERSPECTIVE

From a teacher's perspective, there would appear to be a number of potential advantages in using OL. First, the continuing move for providers of HE to widen access faces teachers with the challenge of meeting the learning needs of increasingly large, heterogeneous groups of students who may also be at different starting points in terms of background knowledge, needs and academic ability. The use of learning materials can help cope with larger student numbers while still maintaining the quality of educational provision. Taking an example from the area of health and nursing, one can look to the uptake of the OU's programme *A Systematic Approach to Nursing Care* (P553) to see how a set of learning materials written on a core topic has been used on a large scale to meet a particular education need. In just the first four years of its presentation, the OU claimed to have sold over 20,000 copies, and it has been estimated that the actual usage increases this figure by at least a factor of three (Robinson, 1989).

Since teacher contact time tends to be a relatively small proportion of total study hours (say 40–60 hours out of a total of 100–200), the use of OL materials to cover much of the core 'information giving' can free lecturers from that role, enabling them to focus more on facilitating the learning process and providing guidance and support to individual students and small groups of students. In this way, available contact time may be used to ensure that individual learning needs are met, and to focus on learning activities that cannot be achieved by materials-based learning (such as seminar work, small group discussions, etc.). Indeed, by combining the advantages of materials-based learning and face-to-face contact in mixed-mode modules/programmes, it is possible to capitalize on the advantages of each.

Published learning materials have usually been written by experts in their field, and during the developmental process are reviewed by further subject experts and groups of students (known as field testers or developmental testers), who work through the materials, providing detailed feedback regarding their relevance and usefulness from a user's perspective. With such systems in place to ensure quality, a programme that incorporates effective learning materials may offer a better learning experience than an equivalent taught course, particularly when teacher contact hours are limited. For some lecturers, however, the possibility of using learning materials either produced in-house or by major producers such as the OU and the National Extension College raises the crucial issue of the 'not invented here syndrome'. To counter this, Stainton Rogers (1987) argues that there are some

> very good functional reasons for deciding to incorporate materials produced by somebody else into your own teaching. Very often such materials will have been produced by an organisation with access to skilled staff, and considerable resources . . . for the generation of high quality text, video- and audiotape, computer-aided learning software and so on. . . . considerable time and effort has already been expended in their development.

If one is prepared to accept these arguments, the use of such learning materials can save education institutions considerable development and course planning time, although any learning materials that are used do, of course, need to be fully and carefully integrated into the overall educational philosophy and structure of the programme in which they are used. Meanwhile, the shift of emphasis for the lecturer from primarily a teaching/lecturing role to one of facilitating learning can be enormously rewarding, reminding one perhaps of halcyon days when considerable periods of time were spent with students on an individual basis or in small groups.

In addition to the use of OL materials to meet the needs of large numbers of students, OL can also enable lecturers to offer options to small groups that might otherwise not be regarded as economically viable when face-to-face teaching costs are calculated.

There is also evidence, which may surprise some educationalists, suggesting that OL materials can provide an effective means of changing attitudes (Stainton Rogers,

1986). For those HE lecturers involved in delivering programmes of professional education, this is an important consideration. The benefits of OL do not, therefore, appear to be restricted solely to the cognitive domain. The application of theoretical and conceptual issues to work experiences is also of central importance for teaching groups such as social workers, nurses and midwives, teachers and managers. Lawrence *et al.* (1988) found that through the use of carefully designed activities, OL materials can provide an effective means of helping students to relate theory to practice, thereby bridging the theory–practice gap that dominates much of the literature on professional education.

Perhaps not surprisingly, there are also some potential disadvantages. The cost of the learning materials can be high, whether they are developed in-house or bought in from an external producer. This may require pump-priming funds, or some form of loan, since in HE fees follow student enrolments, and this can make it more difficult to fund any new development that is front-loaded in terms of costs. If money is borrowed to purchase learning materials or to develop them in-house, and has to be repaid from income derived from running the programme, a sound business-planning approach is vital. There may also be additional costs incurred in adapting or augmenting the materials so that they can be used within a particular programme to ensure that learning outcomes are fully addressed. An even greater disadvantage in some areas is that suitable learning materials simply do not exist, forcing lecturers to consider whether they should become involved in developing them in-house. With just this reason in mind, the Open Learning Foundation (formerly the Open Polytechnic) was established in 1990, encouraging its 23 founder members to collaborate in the development of core learning materials that would meet their needs (see Hardy, 1991, 1992).

The change in role to 'facilitator of learning' may initially seem rather threatening to some lecturers in HE. This feeling is clearly reflected in one of the findings of the survey of OL undertaken by Lawrence *et al.* (1988): 'Teachers frequently expressed the need for training in the use of learning materials and for the development of the facilitator role. There is a sense of anxiety about the loss of control of the learning experience in many of the statements made . . . by teachers, which may reflect their uncertainty about their own future roles.' Initially, the use of OL may involve a period of considerable uncertainty for some lecturers while they adjust to the shift in emphasis from the role of teacher to that of facilitator of learning and to a perceived loss of control over the learning process. To address this issue, some producers (the Open Learning Foundation, for instance) offer their learning materials on a computer disk to enable teachers to select particular sections, adapt the text and add local examples, case material, etc., prior to reproducing the material for use with their own students, the rationale being to increase the sense of ownership. Some teaching staff will, therefore, need additional preparation to develop the skills, attitudes and confidence required to facilitate learning and to encourage students to become more self-directed. They may initially require considerable help and support from more experienced OL tutors. Initial staff development and institutional development needs can incur high start-up costs which need to be regarded as a long-term investment.

Although, in the long run, effective, supported use of OL materials within an educational programme can enable students to become more self-directed, this can take time to develop. Teaching staff must realize that, initially, some students may need considerable time and support during their early exposure to OL until they have developed sufficient confidence to work with reduced teacher input, direction and control, and patterns of independent learning have been established. In addition, lecturers may need to adopt more flexible working hours to meet students' needs, particularly those of students studying part-time (some, but not all, staff may welcome this). To sum up, for lecturers and students alike, the underlying aim and basic principle can be seen to be increased autonomy and self-direction.

THE STUDENT'S PERSPECTIVE

In some respects the student perspective has much in common with that of the tutor who is introducing the principle of self-directed learning – both may have new habits, skills and attitudes to learn! Depending on the openness of the system, OL can allow students to shape their own learning programme by defining their own learning outcomes and working through learning materials at their own pace. The use of individually negotiated learning contracts can help ensure that learning meets the specific needs of individual students, although this is essentially a two-way process. It aims to help students avoid repetitive learning and build on existing knowledge and skills. A further benefit is that students can study in ways that are best suited to their individual circumstances, and make optimum use of available time to meet their own particular learning needs. As a practical consequence, opportunities may be increased for those who, due to unsocial working hours and personal commitments, might otherwise be unable to attend a more traditional programme. In addition, there is also the important educational gain in the understanding of, and commitment to, the learning process. We have seen that OL offers flexibility and the scope for individuals to study different topics at different depths and different speeds according to specific interests and needs. The use of learning materials can allow learners to exert greater control over the pace, place and time of learning. These benefits are nicely summarized for us by the Open Tech slogan of the mid-1980s: 'OL enables people to learn at the time, place and pace which suits them best.'

Given the stages through which quality learning materials must pass during development, they can offer students exposure to the ideas and teaching of nationally recognized experts who might not otherwise be available to lecture in their local institutions. The use of good learning materials can help to ensure quality education provision that is not dependent on who is teaching, how the teacher is feeling and other factors that can affect the quality of face-to-face provision, such as unsuitable teaching accommodation and the like. If the quality and suitability of learning materials are carefully evaluated prior to their use, an OL programme can be of a very high quality. Not only may the use of such learning materials raise the morale of hard-pressed lecturers who are committed to the delivery of quality learning opportunities for their students, but they can also help to engage the understanding of students and thus motivate the learner.

Among the advantages perceived by students is also the choice of working either alone or in small groups, depending on preference and on individual learning styles. The use of learning materials need not, therefore, necessarily imply isolation. Moreover, learning materials are always available to the student for reference in a way that a teacher cannot be. As a further benefit, it can be easier to make up for lost study time if a student is absent due to illness or some other reason.

Students can also become more self-directed and begin to acquire the habit of lifelong learning that is all-important when working in environments that may constantly be changing. As noted above, it can help to empower students to take charge of their own learning through greater control and ownership of the learning process. Students who are able to organize and structure their own learning will have developed the key skills of self-motivation, self-discipline and self-management that are now required in so many work contexts.

Turning now to the major potential disadvantages, some students may experience isolation if they are not able to attend regular, scheduled face-to-face sessions during which ideas can be exchanged and the enthusiasms of others shared. Mann (1988) argues that student support by teachers is the key to motivating students to ensure that they successfully complete a programme of learning. Negotiated access to tutorial support at specified times/places is crucial, as is the installation of direct telephone lines with answerphones. A student whose interest and motivation may be failing is unlikely to persist in trying to get in touch with his or her tutor if the switchboard is always slow to answer a call, or if an individual is constantly unavailable. Due to the problems associated with isolation, students will often welcome a mixed mode of delivery, whereby OL materials are integrated within a module that includes some scheduled face-to-face sessions that allow students to benefit from the advantages of both modes of delivery. The creation of self-help groups can also provide a valuable source of peer support that can help to reduce the sense of isolation.

Students need to feel a high level of commitment and internal motivation to succeed, since much more is left up to the learner. It has to be acknowledged, therefore, that OL may not suit all individuals at the outset: some students may need considerable support initially before they begin to feel comfortable and confident with a more self-directed mode of learning. This point is reflected in one of the findings reported by Lawrence *et al.* (1988), who state that 'not everyone responds to this learning approach, it may be that some degree of preparation is needed to cope successfully with this learning method'. OL producers believe that although not all students respond well at the outset, the vast majority can be helped to understand OL and value a more student-centred approach.

POSSIBLE BENEFITS FOR EMPLOYERS

Increasingly, industrial and commercial organizations are looking to OL to help meet the education and training needs of the workforce (see, for example, Foggo, 1986; Stanford, 1990). Those HE teachers who are offering education and training programmes for either the public or private sectors should be aware of the reasons why an increasing number of employers are finding that the use of OL materials can help meet their needs. The potential benefits include:

- a means of relocating some components of education into the workplace
- an educational resource that may be shared by colleagues in the workplace – such sharing can also encourage the creation of a subculture where continuing education is highly valued

- a means of implementing work-based learning that can help to bridge the gap between theory and practice, since learning occurs while the individual is actually doing his or her job
- access to materials by those, such as mentors and facilitators, responsible for supporting the student in the workplace, which can also assist the provision of more effective learner support than might otherwise be possible for students following a conventional teaching programme, where the mentor/facilitator may have considerably less understanding of course content
- not needing to release staff from the workplace at set times and on set days
- study time that can be programmed more flexibly around the needs of the organization, enabling times of peak workload and staff absences to be more readily accommodated, while meeting individuals' professional development needs
- possible reduction of travel time, travel costs and subsistence costs, although it is important to stress that OL should *not* be regarded as education/training on the cheap.

A major issue in the minds of any potential user is that of affordability. Cost effectiveness is often assumed to be one of the main benefits of open/distance learning and, indeed, it may turn out to be highly cost effective. At present, however, there is insufficient evidence either to support or to challenge this assumption. It can be difficult to measure in any meaningful way the full costs of providing an OL programme and compare these with the full costs of an equivalent conventionally taught course. When costing any education programme, it is necessary to calculate both the fixed costs (which tend to remain constant throughout the life of an OL scheme or conventional programme) and the variable costs, which will vary depending on the number of students. Fixed costs for OL include items such as the cost of accommodation, publicity material, scheme managers and administrators, institutional overheads, and developing or purchasing the learning materials. Variable costs include tutorial time, copies of material, computers, etc. Some preliminary costings from Highland College of Nursing and Midwifery suggest that 'OL is a cost effective method of delivering continuing education to nursing when compared with conventional methods' (Wakeling, 1989). If you are interested in undertaking your own costing exercise, you are recommended to look at one at least of the following resources: the revised edition of the Training Agency's handbook entitled *Ensuring Quality in Open Learning* (Training Agency, 1990), the monograph entitled *Costing Open Learning: Factors for Consideration* (Robinson and Clark, 1992), or Section 4, 'How to estimate the costs and benefits of open learning', of Module AA, *How to Design an Open Learning System* (Scienter, 1994).

If the idea of using OL materials in your own teaching seems appealing, then you might find the following checklist (adapted from McManus and Lyne, 1992) useful, since it outlines the kind of environment in which OL might thrive:

- support from the top; management being seen to value OL
- learners and organization in agreement about the aims of learning
- provision of local support for open learners
- an education framework in which OL can fit together with other types of educational provision

- careful and efficient management of hardware, resources and support systems
- systems for evaluation and feedback
- skills in student support and counselling
- study-skills training
- teachers who regard OL as an opportunity rather than as a threat
- teachers who are ready to take on new roles in the support of learning
- time and resources to develop sound OL schemes
- skilled co-ordination of the many activities needed to develop OL materials and to set up OL schemes.

STAFF AND INSTITUTIONAL DEVELOPMENT

Finally, if OL is to become more widely used within HE, and if it is to offer a good educational experience for every open learner, we need to consider a number of key issues in relation to staff and institutional development. David Baume in Chapter 4, 'Staff Development for Open and Flexible Learning', also considers possible approaches to staff development for those using OL and the need for institutional development.

Staff development for teaching staff using OL

Lecturers will need to develop the skills required to evaluate published learning materials prior to their use within specific education programmes. They will need to distinguish between 'experienced and competent providers (producers) of OL and those whose enthusiasm outruns their competence and whose ignorant or exploitative approach to OL might bring the whole idea into disrepute' (Training Agency, 1990). Any systematic evaluation of learning materials will need to assess the extent to which they meet an agreed set of criteria, including the learning outcomes for a particular education programme. Robinson and Clark (1992) suggest that a minimum of 10 per cent of the total study hours may be required to evaluate a set of materials (that is, a minimum of 12 hours to evaluate 120 hours of learning materials). If the evaluation suggests that the materials are not entirely appropriate either to student needs or to the desired learning outcomes, then additional time and resources will be required to adapt or supplement the materials.

In addition, as we have seen, some teachers may need considerable support while adjusting to a shift in their role from teacher to facilitator of learning, as well as help in encouraging students to become more self-directed. Some may also want to acquire further skills in guidance and counselling in order to provide better student support, and to help students to formulate their own objectives and plan how these might best be met. Some teachers will also need specific preparation on the use of the learning materials, telephone tutorials and the management and administration of an OL system. Thus, a programme of staff development will usually be required to develop a critical mass within the overall population of teaching staff with the necessary attitudes and commitment to implement OL successfully. And, even if there are already significant numbers of teaching staff who are experienced in using OL, they will need time to become thoroughly familiar with the learning materials that form the basis of a specific module or programme. Recognizing this, the OU pays a staff development fee to all tutorial staff who are new to a particular programme to cover the cost of this all-important familiarization period.

Once successful OL schemes have been established both within and beyond mainstream undergraduate provision, they can be set up as demonstration projects within an institution, or even within the HE sector as a whole, to help raise the level of awareness among colleagues. The use of demonstration projects, coupled with workshops and more widespread dissemination of ideas through publications such as the *Times Higher Education Supplement* and journals such as *Open Learning*, can go a considerable way to further the debate about the potential value of introducing more flexible patterns of teaching and learning.

Regulation issues

Internal debates may be needed within an institution about the proportion of the total number of study hours that can be dedicated to OL and still contribute towards an award previously based on a fixed number of hours of classroom teaching. The concept of minimum course attendance requirements would obviously need to be reassessed. This in turn raises the question of whether it is necessary to specify minimum time periods for the achievement of particular learning outcomes. Some students may be capable of achieving specific learning outcomes in a considerably shorter time than other students and should perhaps be allowed to complete summative assessments whenever they are ready, rather than at fixed points in a module or programme. The emphasis needs, therefore, to be shifted away from specifying numbers of study hours, module/programme duration and/or minimum attendance, and towards the development of more flexible means and timescales for students to demonstrate the achievement of specific learning outcomes at predefined academic levels.

Staffing issues

In some institutions, there may be concerns about how to weight students who do not attend programmes in a traditional manner. Indeed, OL students may be weighted differently in statistical returns, making it less beneficial for staff members wishing to incorporate OL materials into their programmes for sound educational reasons. If, under a modular scheme, one student full-time equivalent (FTE) is regarded as equivalent to a student enrolled on six modules (each of 20 academic credits), then one student enrolled on one module equals one-sixth of an FTE. If the same criterion were to apply to OL students, then six OL module registrations would equal one FTE. Thus, OL students can be recognized in the same way as, and given the equivalent weighting to, any other student in the institution.

Student support

Student support is recognized to be crucial to the success of any programme incorporating OL materials. Students need to be provided with clear information about the availability of tutorial support (both individual tutorials and telephone contact) when undertaking any programme of self-directed learning: the use of OL should *not* be viewed simply as a means of reducing the amount of teacher contact or teaching hours. As already suggested, students should also be encouraged to set up self-help groups or study pairs to help reduce the sense of isolation that some may feel. In the first instance, students may also require special preparation to help them to appreciate and take full advantage of the flexibility afforded by OL and to seek tutorial or peer support when needed.

The provision of adequate administrative support

By comparison, conventional teaching requires relatively little administrative support and, as a consequence, there is a tendency to underestimate the amount of administration time needed to establish and manage an effective OL system, and the cost of providing that support. Administrative support is needed to deal with enquiries, and to ensure the availability of learning materials which need to be ordered, checked, logged in, stored and issued. If a loan scheme is in operation for the learning materials, returned items also need to be checked, and non-returned items need to be chased to ensure their availability for future students. The establishment and maintenance of accurate and up-to-date records is also essential, particularly if assessment does not occur at fixed points in the programme or at fixed points in the year, and if a large number of students have enrolled.

A crucial aspect of any OL system is, therefore, an efficient administrative system. In my experience, many course/programme leaders have, at the outset, seriously underestimated the amount of administration time needed to run a programme involving OL, and this element needs to be adequately costed (see Clark and Robinson, 1992). As OL operations develop within a school, department or faculty, it may become necessary to appoint an administrator with special responsibility for OL. Moreover, this person may be required to work flexible hours (including evenings) to ensure that adequate administrative support is available to both students and staff during periods when OL students come into the institution.

Course validation

Existing institutional validation procedures may not readily accommodate the special needs of a programme with a substantial OL component, and may need to be adapted. Members of a validation panel for an OL programme must be familiar with the specific issues that would need to be addressed in both the supporting documentation and during the validation event, to ensure that sufficient attention is paid to all aspects of the OL system that could affect the overall quality of the student learning experience. This should include the provision of flexible student support and also adequate administrative support for both students and teachers. Whenever published learning materials are to be used, evidence would be required that a systematic evaluation of the materials has been undertaken to establish their suitability for the proposed use.

In a mixed-mode module/programme (combining forms of face-to-face teaching with the use of materials-based learning), validators must ensure that the various components are well integrated, and that a consistent educational philosophy is maintained throughout and is clearly understood by all members of the course planning team.

Where learning materials are being developed in-house, it should be noted that it would be entirely inappropriate for validators to require to see all the learning materials prior to validating the course. They should, however, reassure themselves that sound procedures have been implemented, by requesting a clear description of the stages of materials development and the steps that have been taken to assure quality, together with a sample of the learning materials that have been developed. Quality control procedures should include:

- evidence of developmental testing (by a sample of students from the target audience)
- external reviewing by subject specialists
- the use of OL editors to ensure that effective learning materials are produced.

Following validation, it would be necessary to ensure that the course/programme/module evaluation tool was suitable and catered for specific issues relating to the OL system that could affect the overall quality of the learning experience. If a standardized evaluation tool is in use, then a review of the format is likely to be necessary to take account of the key OL issues which can affect the delivery of a quality learning experience for students.

Institutional development

Some education institutions will need to establish policies and set up the necessary structures and processes at institutional, faculty and school levels that would allow teaching staff to plan and deliver flexible education programmes. As we have seen, this would include the provision of staff development to ensure that all staff are adequately prepared to deliver quality flexible learning, the allocation of resources to purchase suitable published learning materials or to develop materials in-house, the introduction of appropriate course validation processes, the provision of direct telephone lines and answerphones to facilitate access for those students who do not attend the host education institution on a regular basis, and the introduction of a flexible tutorial system so that some student support is available outside 'normal' working hours. This is, of course, particularly important for part-time students who may be studying in their own time. To sum up, OL should not be regarded as a second-rate alternative when conventional educational provision is not practical or cost effective; it should not be considered only when the necessary subject expertise is lacking; and it does not provide education and training on the cheap. Rather, as we have seen, there are sound educational reasons for incorporating OL into new and existing programmes, thereby offering a flexible means of meeting student learning needs in an environment that is increasingly market-oriented and in which responsiveness to customer needs is paramount. While there has in the past been a definite divide between distance education universities throughout the world and campus-based universities offering face-to-face tuition, White (1992) claims that 'the most significant step forward in education in this half of the century has been the burgeoning of the distance education mode of teaching and . . . that just as significant *in this decade* will be the mixing of the distance teaching mode with the face-to-face mode' (my italics). As we have seen, a mixed mode of educational provision can offer advantages for teacher and student alike. And, *if* OL is to become firmly accepted as part of mainstream HE, we must continue to study systematically and to record the specific costs, benefits, possibilities, limitations, challenges and opportunities that it affords – the potential for research is enormous.

BIBLIOGRAPHY

Clark, E. (1989) Hybrid courses in continuing professional development. In Robinson, K.M. (ed.) *Open and Distance Learning for Nurses*. Harlow: Longman.

Clark, E. and Robinson, K. (1992) *Good Practice in Open Learning within Nursing, Midwifery and Health Visiting*. Monograph prepared for the English National Board for Nursing, Midwifery and Health Visiting. Sheffield.

Coughlan, R., Rounds, C. and Scriber, M.C. (1991) Access and individualisation: Empire State College's response to dispersed adult learners. *Open Learning*, **6** (2), 50–5.

Foggo, T. (1986) Open learning in ICI. *Open Learning*, **1** (1), 13–15.

Hardy, D. (1991) The Open Polytechnic. *Open Learning*, **6** (2), 55–9.

Hardy, D. (1992) The Open Learning Foundation and the new framework for higher education. *Open Learning*, **7** (3), 56–8.

King, B. (1993) Open learning in Australia: government intervention and institutional response. *Open Learning*, **8** (3), 13–25.

Lawrence, J., Maggs, C. and Rogers, J. (1988) *Interim Report on an Evaluation of the Use of Distance Learning Materials for Continuing Professional Education for Qualified Nurses, Midwives and Health Visitors*. London: Institute of Education, University of London.

McManus, M. and Lyne, P. (1992) *Mainstream or Margin? Open Learning in the Changing World of Nurse Education*. Monograph prepared for the English National Board for Nursing, Midwifery and Health Visiting. Sheffield.

Mann, S. (1988) Why open learning can be a turn off. *Personnel Management*, January, 41–3.

Open University (1984, rev. 1989) *A Systematic Approach to Nursing Care: An Introduction*. Milton Keynes: Open University Press.

Robinson, K.M. (1989) Open learning: the current scene. In Robinson, K.M. (ed.) *Open and Distance Learning for Nurses*. Harlow: Longman.

Robinson, K.M. and Clark, E.H. (1992) *Costing Open Learning: Factors for Consideration*. Monograph prepared for the English National Board for Nursing, Midwifery and Health Visiting. Sheffield.

Scienter (1994) Module AA, *How to Design an Open Learning System*. London: PALIO Project.

Secretary of State for Education and Science (1991) *Higher Education: A New Framework*. Cm 1541. London: HMSO.

Stainton Rogers, W. (1986) Changing attitudes through distance learning. *Open Learning*, **1** (3), 12–17.

Stainton Rogers, W. (1987) Adapting materials for alternative use. In Thorpe, M. and Grugeon, D. (eds) *Open Learning for Adults*. Harlow: Longman.

Stanford, N. (1990) Opening up learning in the Prudential. *Open Learning*, **5** (1), 19–23.

Thorpe, M. (1987) Adult learners in open learning. In Thorpe, M. and Grugeon, D. (eds) *Open Learning for Adults*. Harlow: Longman.

Training Agency (1990) *Ensuring Quality in Open learning: A Handbook for Action*. Rev. edn Sheffield: Training Agency.

Wakeling, C. (1989) Highland Health Board: a coordinated scheme. In Robinson, K.M. (ed.) *Open and Distance Learning for Nurses*. Harlow: Longman.

White, V. (1992) Response to Greville Rumble's article 'The competitive vulnerability of distance teaching universities'. *Open Learning*, **7** (3) 59–60.

Chapter 4

Staff Development for Open and Flexible Learning

David Baume

A SYSTEMATIC APPROACH TO DEVELOPMENT

Staff development

To the extent that staff development for open and flexible learning is a matter of training staff in certain reasonably well-defined skills, attitudes and approaches, then a conventionally systematic approach to staff development can be applied. These conventional steps, briefly, are:

1. Identify the staff to be developed.
2. Identify the overall aims and then the detailed intended outcomes of the training.
3. Devise a training and development regime under which the staff being developed can learn the underlying philosophy and the basic skills.
4. Obtain or develop materials and resources to support this learning process.
5. Provide a series of cycles of guided practice and feedback until the desired outcomes have been shown to be attained.
6. Include an outer loop of evaluating and modifying the training strategy and materials. (Baume and Baume, 1994).

However, a model of the learning process seems to underlie, at no great depth, 'staff development' as defined in this way. The model suggests that skills (or attitudes or approaches) are first learned, and then applied. I consider this view to be rather simplistic, for three main sets of reasons, and I shall go beyond this simple model to suggest one which I consider richer and more developmental.

Objections to 'staff development'

John Holt, in his sadly neglected *Instead of Education* (Holt, 1976), attacks the distinction between 'learning' and 'doing'. 'Learning', he suggests, is mainly 'doing' with an intent to improve the skill of the doer. The erroneous separation of 'learning' from 'doing' he finds wholly unhelpful, leading to much of what he finds wrong with education, including the alienation which many learners experience from the process of schooling to which they are subjected.

Holt was concerned mainly with education in schools. However, many staff developers have also experienced the alienation of a group of staff who have been gathered together to be 'developed' in some direction which they do not necessarily wholly embrace. The first objection to a simple model of 'learn, then do' is that it does not always meet with the wholehearted support of the learners.

The second objection to the simple model of first acquiring and then practising skills is that 'doing' does not follow in an unproblematic way from 'learning'. Learning from experience, to work from Kolb's helpful account, is a cyclical process: planning an activity, undertaking it, evaluating the success of the activity, and then finding or making explanations for the specific successes or otherwise of the activity, and thus devising new approaches to the task which offer increased chances of success the next time we go round the cycle. Learning, in this account, does not result from any single step of the cycle, but rather from moving round the cycle in a reflective and analytic way.

What does this have to do with staff development for open learning (OL)?

I am not suggesting that staff should learn to write or deliver OL just by writing materials or running courses, and then revising their approach on the basis of student feedback. Experiential learning is more than learning from mistakes and successes. But learning must be an active process. And, given the need for staff development work to be as efficient as possible, the learning should be focused on the particular educational task – in this case, on developing the particular skills required for the particular OL project. This may sound like a narrow approach; training rather than education, perhaps. I am only suggesting that training should start with a narrow focus on the particular project. Breadth comes later, in the processes of reviewing the effectiveness of first pieces of work and in accounting for their effectiveness or lack thereof.

The third objection to the simplistic separation of 'learning' from 'doing' is that, even if learning were as straightforward as being taught and then applying what one has been taught, as the simple staff development model may imply, this would still not be appropriate for staff development for OL. Why? Because each OL project is in important ways different from every other.

This inconvenient fact could be accommodated by a staff development regime which taught a generic body of skills and approaches, and then helped the newly trained staff steer or adapt these common skills to the particular project. But such an approach has drawbacks. By starting from the general and then going to the particular, it increases the chances of the newly developed OL people producing generally rather than specifically appropriate materials or courses. It may require some unlearning of skills recently learned as work starts on the project; there are very few OL principles and practices which should never be discarded under particular circumstances, and starting from the general again makes such acts of imagination and originality less likely. And, perhaps most important and worthy of a little more space here: the kinds of excellent teacher we want to become involved in writing and using OL materials are generally at their best, their most appropriately creative, under the same conditions under which they do their best teaching; namely, when they are responding to the particular challenges of a particular project, devising teaching approaches and materials which best meet the challenges of the particular learners and the particular skills and content to be taught.

This section started by describing the conventional approach to staff development as the development of skills to be applied later as 'simplistic', and promised a richer and more developmental model. This is outlined below.

Educational development

Much of the necessary development work associated with OL should be seen, planned, undertaken and reviewed as educational development rather than staff development. 'Educational development' implies people working to solve educational problems and meet educational challenges. In the case of OL educational development implies the process of devising a complete system for defining learners' educational needs, producing materials and support systems to contribute to the meeting of those needs, running the OL scheme, conducting evaluation activities to identify necessary changes, and making those changes. If the brief is more constrained; for example, if the learning outcomes are specified and the size and form of the materials defined; then educational development still means working within those constraints to produce the best possible materials – which in turn implies some prior work to define what is meant in this context by 'best'. A similar account could be given of the educational development challenge associated with devising an OL delivery system.

'Educational development' is thus very different from staff development. Educational development implies the whole business of undertaking a project. How does it relate to staff development, to the development of skills? The roles of 'staff developer', 'project manager', 'new writer' and the rest change somewhat. These people become collaborators, rather than trainer and trainees. They still have different skills, and these differences will be acknowledged; I am not suggesting introducing some false egalitarianism into what will have to be a tightly managed project. But it will become easier to harness the talents and creative energies of all. The 'trainees' will have a much clearer view of how the skills they are developing fit into the project as a whole, and they will be clear what contributions they can make from the start. Staff development will be not just a bolt-on activity, and not just a precursor to the project, but an integral part of the project. Staff development will embrace all project participants, as it includes a process in which everyone associated with the project processes their recent experiences of it, and offers insights, developed individually and jointly, which can feed the further development of the project and of the individual capabilities of all participants. Educational development does not replace staff development, but it embraces it and fits it more naturally and constructively into the project process.

Staff development revisited

I suggested at the start a model process for staff development. There were six stages to this model: identifying the staff to be developed, identifying the learning outcomes, planning the training, devising or obtaining support materials, providing alternating periods of guided practice and feedback, and, as an outer loop, reviewing and changing the staff development process. The subsequent critiques of the concept of 'staff development' do not invalidate this model; rather they provide a context in which 'staff development', whether for the staff who produce OL materials or for the staff who use this material in their teaching, should be undertaken.

STAFF DEVELOPMENT FOR PRODUCING OPEN LEARNING MATERIALS

Train whom?

A variety of functions can be identified in the production of open and flexible learning. These can include client, project manager, writer or producer of materials, OL editor, text editor, content or specialist editor, designer, referee and field tester. I consider the issue of function and role in this chapter on staff development because clarity over these various roles and role boundaries is essential if staff development is to be effective and economical of effort. (Such clarity over roles is also essential to the success of the OL project itself!)

I shall concentrate on developing the skills of OL writing. I do so because the demand for staff development for OL editors is likely to be small given the smallness of their numbers, and anyway editors tend to develop their skills either as general editors moving into OL, or as successful OL writers moving into editing. But, in planning staff development for writing OL, as in planning any other form of training, it is necessary to start with a clear view of who is to be trained and with the intended outcomes of the training, which in this case means starting with the clearest possible account of the job description, role, responsibilities – call it what you will – of the people to be trained.

What are you looking for in a potential producer (usually writer) of OL materials? (Apart, of course, from proven expertise in producing successful OL materials of a form very similar to that which the project will require!) You will be looking for an appropriate level of *subject expertise*; appropriate, that is, to the project. I suggest 'appropriate' rather than 'high'. As with face-to-face teaching, so with OL writing, massive subject expertise can lead to the wish to explain and communicate all that the teacher or writer knows. All-knowing subject experts can become good OL writers, but they need additional personal qualities and skills, such as restraint and a willingness to be guided by their editor.

You might expect that the next quality to look for is proven *writing ability*. Yes – but there are many kinds of writing. A writer of academic papers will not automatically be able to write good OL material. As is stressed elsewhere in this book, effective OL materials are characterized by a direct, engaging, personal style. When you are auditioning possible new writers, ask them to show you some of their less formal writing.

Rather than writing ability, I suggest that you look for *teaching ability*. Good OL material is teaching on paper – a 'tutorial in print', in Derek Rowntree's valuable phrase (Rowntree, 1992, p. 134). Look for the ability to structure unfamiliar material in a way which makes sense to new learners; to develop several ways of explaining an idea until it is firmly grasped; to devise frequent appropriate questions and activities which students can use to develop and prove their understanding. Look for a teacher who constantly encourages students to describe their current state of understanding. Look for the ability to use student misconceptions and confusions as bases for moving their understanding forwards, and the ability to develop new and better ways to teach. Look, perhaps above all, for the ability to make students, a whole group or class of them, feel heard and understood and cared about and respected.

It may not be easy for OL materials to include all these qualities of good teaching. But teachers who can do these things well face-to-face with their students have most of the skills to teach well by OL. It will be much easier to help such teachers translate their considerable teaching skills into writing than to help some other kind of writer develop all these skills of teaching.

Aims and outcomes

The emphasis on the value of educational, rather than staff, development recurs here, when starting to identify the learning outcomes required for the training of those who will write or produce the materials. The learning outcomes for the training of the writers will depend on the details of the particular OL project. The writers should have been involved in determining the nature of the OL materials to be written. If this planning process has been undertaken in a rigorous and collaborative way, which explicitly addressed the skills needed of the writers at the same time as considering their current capabilities, both in the subject and in OL writing, then the writers will have been helped to define, and will thus be very likely to accept, their own skills needs.

However, some more specific guidance on learning outcomes for training OL writers can be given, as long as it is accepted that each of these outcomes is subject to modification and clarification to fit the requirements of the particular project. The examples below are edited from a training pack on basic OL.

Choosing OL as a topic for the examples should both exemplify the meaning of each of the learning outcomes, and add further suggestions on training for OL.

OL writers should be able to do the following:

1. Describe the *aims* of the materials they are to write; describe what the training is intended to achieve. (*Example*: the aims of this training are to introduce you to some key features of open learning; to help you explore a range of possible approaches to the open learning writing task you are planning; and to help you to select an appropriate approach and produce a first draft which you are willing to show to your editor.)
2. Specify the *learning outcomes* for the materials; describe what the students should be able to do after they have worked through the materials. (*Example*: on completion of this training you will be able to plan, and produce a first draft of, open learning materials on [the specified topic] to the specification provided.)
3. Describe the *audience* for the materials, and any assumptions which the materials will make about the *capabilities or limitations* of the users of the materials. (*Example*: this open learning training has been designed for academics who are good teachers of their discipline and who are very familiar with the content which is to be the subject of the materials, but who have no previous experience of writing open learning materials.)

4. Describe the *rationale* for the OL materials; describe the reasons why the student should be willing to devote time and energy to working through the materials. (*Example*: the rationale for this pack on open learning is that, taken together with the specifications you have been given and the workshops and the regular support from your editor and co-writers, it will help you to develop the necessary skills of open learning writing and to write the materials for which you have contracted, quickly and to a high standard. Using the pack will also give you some first-hand experience of studying by open learning – this should help you appreciate the point of view of those who will use the materials which you are writing!)

5. Describe in detail the *content* of the pack. (*Example*: this pack includes material on writing aims and learning outcomes for open learning materials; describing the audience and their capabilities; writing a rationale for the materials; describing the contents; specifying study methods; writing questions and activities; giving responses to likely student answers; describing information sources to be used in conjunction with the materials you are writing; writing assessment tasks; and evaluating the success of your materials.)

6. Describe the *study methods* to be used. (*Example*: work through this pack. Keep to hand the specifications for the materials you are to produce, and the reference materials on open learning writing [see point 9 below]. In doing so, you will plan and produce a first draft for the materials for which you are contracted.)

7. Devise appropriate *questions and activities* for students using the pack. (*Examples*: does the statement of aims you have written give a clear overview of what the pack is intended to achieve? If a student has attained each of the learning outcomes which you have specified, do you feel this would constitute attainment of the aims of the pack? Check that each of the final assessment questions maps clearly and explicitly onto one or more of the specified learning outcomes.)

8. Give *reactions* to likely student answers. (*Example*: the pack asked you how far through the text which you are writing you would place your first student activity. You say that you have planned to include the first activity after ten pages of content. This approach can be satisfactory in a textbook. However, it rarely works well in open learning material. The underlying idea of open learning is to keep the student very active. See if you can plan that section again, with an appropriate activity on every double-page spread. The learning outcomes you wrote earlier should give you some suggestions on possible activities.)

9. Specify additional *information resources* for users of the materials. (*Example*: as well as this pack you should have to hand, and make frequent reference to, the overall description of the open learning project, the detailed specification for your section, and copies of . . .)

10. Devise appropriate *assessment tasks and criteria* for students. (*Example*: critically evaluate the readability of the first draft materials using the Gunning Fog Index, and edit the materials to bring the Index within the project readability specification.)

11. *Evaluate* the materials. (The evaluation methods will normally be part of the project specification rather than within the control of the individual writer. However, as an *example*: watch one student work through the first draft materials. Make notes on which aspects of the materials appeared to work well, on where the student experienced difficulties, on the nature of the difficulties, and on suggested improvements.)

A training and development regime

A detailed specification of the learning outcomes, such as that suggested above, makes the planning of the staff development much easier. It would be possible to devise a one- or two-day introductory workshop for new writers in which they worked through each of the eleven steps described immediately above (using another writer as evaluator at point 11) for a small section of the materials which they were to write. Such a workshop should allow a great deal of time for the new writers to work together, using each other as consultants and sounding boards. This is a much more productive approach to development than having a long series of workshops each concentrating on one aspect of OL writing. By the end of one or two days of the kind suggested here, the new writers would have tried, and received feedback on, each step of the writing process, and, if the event had been skilfully and supportively facilitated, would feel some confidence in their ability to continue the writing task which they had already started.

The training and development regime must also include support for and communication with writers between workshops. The better the project team members have come to know each other during the workshops, the more they will be able to support each other during the writing process.

Subsequent workshops can go into more detail on any one of the 11 topics suggested above. Detailed planning of these workshops should be left until the writers, and the editors seeing early drafts, form a view as to where these subsequent workshops should concentrate. It is very likely, however, that further work will be needed on specifying learning outcomes, on devising questions and activities, and on assessment. It is important that these subsequent training workshops work very closely on the writers' and editors' concerns, and on the actual materials being written. The writers will be developing more general skills of OL writing, but the focus has to be the particular project.

Resources for staff development for producing open learning materials

The list of learning outcomes and the associated examples above could readily be translated into a guide to writers. The bibliography at the end of this chapter lists some excellent sources on writing OL. Writers also need a very clear specification of the materials they are to write, and a clear outline of the project as a whole to provide the context into which their work must fit.

Practice and feedback: tutorial support and consultancy

The ideal support for new writers is an ever-available (not ever-present – that might feel oppressive), sympathetic, supportive and expert coach, adviser and friend. In the absence of this, I would suggest some negotiated combination of peer support from other writers, the encouragement of frequent contact by post, telephone, fax or E-mail, news of progress by other writers and on the project as a whole, and regular meetings which may be combined with further training sessions.

Evaluating the training

A large-scale systematic evaluation questionnaire for each training event is not needed, unless the client insists. However, reflection on the training, on its highs and lows, and on possibilities for change should be a regular component. The new writers will develop their skills of OL writing very quickly. The timetable for an initial training event, however well it worked, will not necessarily be appropriate for subsequent training. The best evaluation uses powerful but simple questions. 'What features of this training worked well for you?' 'What worked less well?' 'How should the next training event be different?' These questions will provide most of the necessary information.

STAFF DEVELOPMENT FOR USING OPEN LEARNING

This section is much shorter than that above on staff development for writing OL. This is not because devising schemes for using OL is easier than writing it. In many ways it is much more complex. But the same principles apply to training design whatever the content of the training. This section assumes that you have read the previous section, and accepted the underlying approach. The comments at the start of this chapter about the value of educational development rather than simply staff development apply with even greater force to the use of OL than to the writing of it. The project team will need to devise an OL delivery and support system which meets the particular needs, circumstances and resources of the institution, the department, the subject, the learners, the course approval system, the accommodation, etc. In doing so they will also need to define and then develop the necessary skills. Staff development will be very closely integrated with educational development. The aim of this section is to help ensure that the development of the necessary skills is given sufficient attention during the usually hectic process of planning and implementing an OL system.

Train whom?

Implementing a successful OL scheme needs very high levels of education, administrative and team-working skills. Members of the OL project team should between them possess all these. Some of the administrative skills may best be found in administrative rather than academic staff. In what follows, I shall focus on the skills and training regimes, without specifying each time whether the staff concerned are academic or administrative. However, I shall focus on the training of the team rather than of individuals.

Aims and outcomes

The aim will be that the team as a whole has the necessary skills to implement the OL project. The precise skills required will depend greatly on the nature of the scheme. However, the following overall principles apply:

- Some degree of specialization within the team is necessary. However, duplication of skills is essential – it is not safe to devise a scheme dependent in any crucial respect on just one team member. Two, three or more should be able to carry out each function.
- The scheme should be thoroughly documented, and every team member should have a complete and current set of the documentation. Good documentation can reduce the need for training, by making procedures and their rationale explicit. Good documentation certainly reduces the need for memory!
- One skill which every team member needs is skill in team-working. Fortunately, this skill can usually be developed very powerfully in the process of devising the OL system. However, when staff join the team when the scheme is in operation, their induction will need to give attention to team-working.

A training and development regime; practice and feedback; tutorial support and consultancy

The training should be planned as an integral part of the project planning process. The emphasis should always be on the project, on the schedule which must be achieved if the project is to succeed on time. Training will be an adjunct to this. At the end of each working session of the project team, some time should be devoted to identifying the new skills which were used during the session, or the skills which turned out to be missing or insufficiently developed. As the next working session is planned, attention should be given again to the skills which will be needed. Most of the staff development needed for the project will come about through peer support and explicit attention to skills.

Unlike OL writing, where members of the team will spend the great majority of their time working alone, members of an OL delivery team will spend much of their time working together. Some tasks – writing the student handbook for the scheme, developing a roster for staffing the OL centre, preparing publicity material – may still be solo ones. However, the team will meet together much more often – outline plans or documents will be agreed by the team, written up by an individual and then brought back for the approval of the group. (The group can usefully include one or two of the students who are to use the scheme.)

Different roles are possible for the staff developers in such a project. They can provide some initial input on the operation of OL schemes; give feedback on early drafts of documents and plans; even undertake research into practice in other institutions. But their major role is likely to be that of facilitators of planning sessions: helping the team to clarify exactly what it is trying to achieve, suggesting working methods, taking some responsibility for time-keeping and process management while the team gets on with the work. It is essential that staff developers help the team develop skills and good practice in team-working, so that, once the staff developers have completed their work, the team can continue to function effectively, reflectively and in a way which is acceptable to all its members. Even when the team is running well, an occasional short session facilitated by the staff developer can help its members reflect on and improve further the way they work as a team.

At the end of each phase of the project – for example, when the planning is complete, or after the first semester of operation – a half-day or day, with a facilitator external to the project team, can usefully be devoted to reviewing the achievements of the project to date, the need for further development, and the technical and interpersonal skills of the team as revealed by the successes and difficulties of the project and the needs for further training and development. Such sessions require considerable openness on the part of the project team, but can lead to a very clear account of what should be done next.

Evaluating the training

Because it is such an integral part of the project, the training will best be evaluated by much the same means as are applied to the evaluation of the project itself. The questions suggested above for the evaluation of training on writing OL work as well for training on its use. 'What features of this training worked well for you?' 'What worked less well?' 'How should the next training event be different?'

INSTITUTIONAL DEVELOPMENT

The distinction between staff development for producing and staff development for using OL works well on clearly specified open learning projects. The approach which I have called educational development leads to a much closer integration of purpose and product between writers of OL and those planning systems to enable students to make use of it. However, when the decision is made that a department or a whole institution will move to greater use of OL, then a still broader approach can be adopted; I shall call this institutional development. How might a programme be developed to help a university whose senior management had decided to make a substantial commitment to OL? The overall aim of the work is to provide a rapid expansion of the university's capabilities in producing and using OL materials, taking OL quickly to the heart of the university's curriculum and helping the university to achieve its targets for expansion of numbers, increased access, and closer working with local colleges and employers.

The university's strategy for OL might be based on an OL centre with staff on part-time secondment from faculties. They would then work with a selection of major courses across the university on the selection and development of materials and on devising OL implementation systems. This strategy could be supported by four parallel sets of staff development activities:

1. training the staff of the OL centre
2. working with selected course teams on the development and introduction of open learning
3. helping institution managers to stay abreast of development and work through the institutional implications of OL
4. ensuring that staff across the university as a whole are at least aware of the developments which the selected course teams are making.

Let us look at each of these possible staff development activities in more detail.

Training the staff of the open learning centre

Staff will need to be trained in the skills of OL writing and editing, and also in the skills of acting as a change agent within the university. After an initial intensive, perhaps two-day, workshop on OL writing and implementation, a series of workshops at two-weekly intervals during one term would be interspersed with support by post, telephone and fax. A final workshop would concentrate on the skills of training other staff.

The emphasis throughout would be the skills which would be required to work in participants' own schools, as OL writers and editors and as facilitators of development. Another important aim of the staff development work with the OL centre staff would be to help them become able to work together as a team, providing mutual personal, professional and technical support.

Working with selected course teams

A similar pattern could be used: an introductory two-day workshop, then a series of one-day workshops supported by consultancy and feedback on drafts. The OL centre staff would play an increasing role in these workshops and consultancies as time passed. The workshops would not be 'about' OL and course development to embrace it – they should be seen as part of the development process, with staff spending a good part of each day developing materials and implementation systems. This approach reflects the view expressed earlier in this chapter that educational development, rather than staff development, is usually the most productive approach.

Other elements could be planned to increase the effectiveness for the university as a whole of the development of individual course teams. A member of staff from each other department in the school could be invited to attend the workshops, as could a member of staff with responsibility for course validation and review. If the workshops were run as away-days, and if two course team events were run at the same time and venue, then the social time could lead to valuable sharing of ideas and experience between members of both course teams, and the formation of further working links between staff about OL.

Working with institutional managers

At the same time as the previous two sets of training, work should also be undertaken to ensure that the managers – including heads of department and schools, academic support services, academic registry, and senior management – were aware of the developments undertaken by the OL centre and the course teams. Managers would also be helped to work out the implications for their own areas of responsibility (often substantial) of the OL developments which were taking place. Briefing events with inputs from course leaders and staff of the OL centre are appropriate for this purpose.

Awareness raising

With intensive development work being done in the OL centre, with some course teams and by senior management, there is a danger that the majority of the staff of the university who are not directly involved in these developments might feel left out, and might come to harbour suspicions. A series of short, school-wide workshops could be planned, aimed to reach most of the staff of the university. As well as explaining the underlying ideas of OL, these would also provide input from the course leaders in the schools involved in OL developments and from staff of the OL centre.

CONCLUSION

Many of the really successful and innovative OL projects work in the way I have suggested in this chapter. One underlying principle is to combine clarity of development goals and individual roles at any one time with a willingness to negotiate and agree changes as circumstances require or as new opportunities present themselves. OL writing can be a horribly solitary activity; the good project manager will ensure that communication, by telephone, fax, E-mail and meeting, figure large in the budget. Good communication within the project breeds good team-work. And, not by coincidence, projects which are experienced and spontaneously described by the participants as team efforts are also the most rewarding on which to work. They often produce excellent OL. And, in doing so, they require and support all members of the project team to develop and celebrate their individual and team skills.

BIBLIOGRAPHY

Baume, David and Baume, Carole (1994) A systematic approach to the evaluation of staff development.

Brew, Angela (ed.) (1995) *Directions in Staff Development*. Buckingham: Open University Press.

Holt, John (1976) *Instead of Education*. New York: E.P. Dutton.

Rowntree, Derek (1992) *Exploring Open and Distance Learning*. London: Kogan Page.

Chapter 5

Moving into the Open

Bruce Gillham

INTRODUCTION

Openness is a much-vaunted concept: we hear of open government, open systems, open faces, open colleges – but while it is universally valued, it has almost universally been treated as a romantic illusion.

Being open necessitates taking risks, and these frequently seem more sizeable than what are interpreted as philosophical gains. Undoubtedly, it is extremely difficult to set up and operate open learning (OL) systems within bureaucratic, highly regulated structures. It is part of the necessary and ongoing battle between the need to control and the need to permit creative freedom. Control sets up standards and regulators that permit monitoring, remedial action and effective financial management. Freedom encourages and releases creativity, generates feelings of ownership, and – at the same time – enriches the process and enlarges choice and variety.

The balance between control and freedom in educational institutions is of crucial importance in the development of OL systems and materials. Such provision must be, by its very nature, targeted to precise groups with precise needs. Indeed, even issues like corporate house-style and structural decisions about the design of learning materials can prevent effective operation.

This chapter is about a collaborative endeavour in which four partners worked to shift teaching in tertiary education into a more open mode. The programme lasted for two academic years. It involved funding from the Technical and Vocational Education Initiative (TVEI), the commitment of management and staff, support and resources from Wearside Tertiary College, OL expertise from the University of Northumbria, and the production and design services of Formword Ltd, an OL development company based in the north-east. TVEI interest centred on exploring and exploiting what they termed the 'flexible framework' for teaching and learning, and they already had a committed member of the Wearside College staff working on their behalf. The college was itself besieged by a range of problems: by large numbers of additional students, by strapped budgets, by the need to reduce unit costs, by quality issues, and by the need to upgrade and enhance the teaching and management capacities of their staff through systematic staff development. The University of Northumbria had been involved in OL for many years, and had been responsible for launching the North East Open Learning Network during the mid-1980s. The network involved a number of other active partners in the further education (FE) sector in the north-east and proved a valuable consolidation of a number of parallel developments within the partner institutions. Several former staff of the university who had operated as senior consultants for Open Tech and for the National Council for Educational Technology (NCET) had also set up or taken over companies which rapidly began to establish reputations in the region and beyond. North East Training Services (1986), OTSU Ltd (1986) – created from the ashes of the Open Tech Training and Support Unit – and Formword Ltd (1983) were three such companies.

It was this powerful synergy of circumstances, skills, people and organizations which permitted the development described in this chapter.

TOWARDS A DEFINITION

There is much confusion in the terms we use to describe the situation in which students are seen as active agents in their own learning. Four phrases which hit the ears regularly, and which are frequently used in a way which suggests an easy interchangeability, are 'independent learning', 'distance learning', 'open learning' and 'flexible learning'. If these terms are to be useful to us, we need to be clear that they are not coincident in meaning.

Independent learning simply implies that the learning can be done largely by learners on their own, in any way that fits their own personal style. Thus, any book is a vehicle for independent learning and all students study independently for projects, working in libraries or workshops and frequently setting their own agendas. This sort of independent learning is a widespread phenomenon and has been a feature of 'real education' ever since individuals began to study, research and seek to understand on their own account. It is at the heart of learning, for, in the final analysis, all education is self-education. Consequently, whatever educational structures we set up, this sort of learning is bound to go on spontaneously and productively. On the other hand, it is perfectly possible for colleges, schools and other educational establishments to build on what comes naturally, and enhance the independent learning capacities of their students.

Systematic *distance learning* appeared on the scene a long time ago. At first, it consisted simply of correspondence between experts and their distant admirers as acts of friendship. Then, as the efficacy of the approach was realized, it developed more formally into a relationship between a tutor and a student. Many teachers enhancing their qualifications forty years ago will remember presenting themselves at the examination rooms of the University of London, clasping their distinctively coloured Wolsey Hall course notes to their bosoms. Since then, Wolsey Hall has identified more lucrative markets, and distance learning has achieved its greatest expansion ever through the development in the early 1970s of the Open University (OU). This massive investment of public resources moved distance learning into a new era of sophistication, using tutor support and multimedia approaches like radio, television and interactive computer programs. It was also revolutionary because the university used the term 'open' in its title. And indeed, the opening up of opportunity by the OU was enormous. It tackled several problems which had long bedevilled higher education (HE). Britain's female population, discriminated against for generations, represented an untapped pool of talent. Suddenly, with the advent of the OU, the opportunity was opened up for women of all ages to engage in university study. This could be done conveniently at a distance, with support and in a way which made it possible to overcome financial constraints, and match the demands of academic work with other family and occupational responsibilities.

However, the OU – in order to remain credible and maintain the structure necessary to accomplish its mission – was forced to erect some barriers to access. In particular, courses generated at Level Two and above had to operate at a level which was demonstrably equivalent to what other universities were providing. Consequently, some of the possible concessions which might have helped students could have been interpreted as intellectual dilution, and had to be avoided. Despite this, the message of 'openness' was taken on with enthusiasm, and the notion of more comprehensive, adventurous and welcoming educational programmes was pursued with vigour.

By the mid-1970s, the use of the term *'open learning'* was beginning to emerge. OL was concerned with equal opportunity, and preached the message that whatever training and education individuals required and wished for should be accessible to them. In other words, education should be designed to match more closely the aspirations of learners. Education was to become 'learner-centred'. OL came to imply any situation in which all those features and characteristics of learning programmes and systems which reduce opportunity and access are identified and modified to avoid closure.

I have elsewhere defined OL in precise terms which seek to show how far it is necessary to go in order to avoid closing down educational and training opportunities:

> an open learning system is one which puts the individual learner at the centre of things. It is sensitive to the learner's motivations, anxieties, convenience, preferred study mode and language capacity. It is flexible, in terms of organisation, workload, work pacing and timing. The learning materials which accompany an open learning system are precisely targeted at particular learners, are learner active, personal, friendly, and conversational in style. In addition, the open learning system is one which tries to create learning materials which circumvent the communication trap posed by subject expertise and takes steps to tackle the unhelpful legacy of buildings, structures, procedures and assumptions passed on by tradition.[1]

The more recent term *'flexible learning'* appears to be a way of recognizing the myriad possibilities open to educators, as new ideas, new procedures and new media appear. It pushes the idea that, in order to maximize educational opportunity and achievement, we need much more than a teaching force prepared to be flexible. It is increasingly necessary to create structures, organizations and management styles which can construct a flexible learning framework within which a wide range of opportunities exist and can be accessed by learners.

POTENTIAL GAINS AND ASSOCIATED FEARS

Adopting the flexible and open approach to teaching and learning can offer real rewards to any college brave enough to install the necessary management and develop or buy in the support required. OL and flexible learning, by eliminating barriers to access and applying the principles of OL provision, can:

- extend the geographical reach of courses in terms of the hinterland for recruitment
- increase the penetration and take-up rates within the local market area
- ensure higher success and retention rates among students once enrolled
- maximize the use of existing physical and human resources
- enable tutors to handle more students without appreciably increasing their workload
- improve the quality of the student learning experience, and thereby the reputation of the providing institution
- enrich and enhance the nature of the tutor's job through variation, open procedures and more creative approaches to assessment.

The overall promise is therefore to reduce student unit costs while, at the same time, improving the quality of the service and raising staff and student morale.

Such an array of claims will undoubtedly be viewed with some scepticism by anyone who has sought to introduce innovatory practice at any but the most mundane level! There are certainly problems to overcome. Institutions consist of an uncomfortable truce between people and structures. Those who already occupy powerful or personally satisfying roles within the existing structure will undoubtedly wish to preserve the status quo. Radical change always tends to increase workload before it eventually rationalizes and controls it. Individuals at all levels are made uncertain as time-honoured skills and procedures are called into question. In addition, even those who support the changes know that it is always the new departures which receive the sharpest critical analysis, and they worry about the consequences of failure. Many teachers in FE and HE fear that the new methodologies being advanced will replace them and make them redundant. Such doubts and reservations cannot be ignored. It is a fact that relatively few manage to set their sights on the beneficial consequences of a shift towards more open approaches – a different kind of job, more rewarding, more creative and more supportive of students. OL is designed to improve the quality of learning and access to it, not to dehumanize it or to shake out dedicated staff. Any careful analysis of what a successful OL system involves soon convinces educational managers that following the principles of OL will produce excellent value for money, but does not come cheap.

A MODEL FOR ENHANCEMENT

The task facing the originators of the Wearside College scheme lay in devising and operationalizing a development project which could maximize the virtues of open approaches while defusing the most serious problems and fears. TVEI, with its encouragement of networking between schools, colleges and businesses, its penchant for student-centred active learning, its keen interest in technical and vocational areas, and its willingness to back these predilections with support in a variety of forms, provided a powerful launch-pad for this development. Derek Wallace, the TVEI co-ordinator at Wearside College, was interested from a number of points of view. He was aware that:

- the teaching methodology used within the college was frequently passive and tutor-centred

- the OL centre at the college and the technical support available already provided a focus of expertise for development
- the college needed to compete effectively with other local providers in terms of quality provision
- the need to recruit meant exploring new markets
- the staff were nervous, insecure, doubtful and frequently cynical. Indeed, many new developments – including this one – were perceived as threats rather than opportunities.

Twenty years ago, J.D. Nesbit[2] suggested that there were four main consequences of innovation:

- an increase in *workload*
- a period of *acute anxiety*
- feelings of *confusion and disorientation*

and, looming in the background

- the threat of an evaluative *backlash*.

Certainly in the area of changes in curriculum delivery and teaching methodology, this analysis remains valid, except that increasingly, innovators have had to deal with a fifth consequence:

- the manifestation of disbelief and cynicism about the innovation and the motives of those concerned with it.

It was clear that any programme to develop and institutionalize OL and flexible learning would have to deal with these issues. Whatever was presented during the initial staff development input, it must provide real benefits within a realistic context. Accordingly, the initial experience was presented to staff in the form of a one-day practical workshop.

The first of these initiating workshops operated in late 1991 on a trial basis. It was designed to take account of the four concerns identified by Nesbit, plus the additional dimension posed by cynicism. Before the workshop, a sheet containing a set of objectives and expectations was distributed to the self-selected group of staff (Figure 5.1). No pressure was put on any member to participate. Also, before the workshop, the programme was circulated (Figure 5.2).

Addressing concerns about personal workload

Worries about workload were generally manifested as *time sensitivity*. This problem was tackled in several ways. Firstly, it was essential that the day in itself should be perceived as time well spent. Accordingly, the short formal inputs on background, principles, features of materials and techniques were related directly to the practical analysis and critique of learning materials, design activities and working directly on the product which each workshop member had elected to develop. Of the six hours available – excluding lunch – three hours and five minutes were spent on practical activity.

Secondly, producing a first-draft, eight-page package within two hours and 35 minutes – designing, planning and writing – was emphasized as being within the realms

Objectives and Expectations

Objectives

1. **Clarification**
   You will be clear about what open learning and flexible learning imply, and understand their likely contribution to tertiary education.
2. **Reflection**
   You will reflect on what high-quality open and flexible learning materials and procedures are like, and the sorts of feature which they possess.
3. **Action**
   You will employ a planning proforma and a 'fast-write' technique to produce a first draft learning package of around eight A4 pages.

Expectations

1. Participants should arrive with an intention to produce an eight-page open learning unit for independent use within the time frame of the workshop. You could come with:
   - the idea only (*difficult*)
   - the idea and some resources which will help (*easier*)
   or
   - something you have used for teaching and wish to convert or enhance for future use (*best strategy*).
2. It is anticipated that at least 30 per cent of those present will have completed, in longhand and cut-and-stick, a first draft of their learning unit by the end of the workshop.

Figure 5.1 *Workshop objectives and expectations*

of the possible. In fact, in all six runs of this workshop at Wearside College, at least two participants completed their drafts within the day, and others finished and submitted copy in the following few days.

Thirdly, the structured use of a design proforma, a page-spread model and a 'fast-write' procedure were intended to help participants to achieve within the pressured time constraint.

Fourthly, the fact that time was allocated by the college and funded by TVEI was seen as real support, and the follow-up design and refinement service provided by the company involved meant that participants felt their time was being maximized by a set of empathetic collaborators.

Programme

9.00   Arrival and coffee
9.15   *Introduction and background*
          Input; discussion and self-assessment (document)
9.45   *What are the principles of designing self-study and flexible learning materials?*
          A model for supported self-study (document); building on the principles (document)
10.15   **Evaluation activity**
          Product evaluation: incorporates coffee/tea at 10.30
          Testing the principles; using an evaluation checklist (document)
10.45   *Features of open/supported self-study/flexible learning materials*
          Structural elements of the materials (document);
          The planning process using a proforma (document); discussion: your own planning
11.30   **Planning activity**
          Designing your product
12.20   *Developing a house-style*
          A definition (document); an example . . . and fonts too
12.45   Lunch
1.45   *Fast-write introduction* (document)
2.00   **Writing activity**
          Group and/or individual work
          Planning and writing
3.45   *Future directions and process review*
          Intention to progress; preparing materials for DTP
          How do you feel?; what next?
4.00   *Finish*

Figure 5.2   *Workshop programme*

Dealing with a range of anxieties

Anxieties about 'working oneself out of a job' and concerns about an unwarranted rejection of traditional wisdom and approaches were defused by the workshop tasks. Participants saw how labour-intensive the development of flexible learning materials and systems would need to be. Discussion of matters like high-quality learner support, editing, updating and developing new courses and materials for new target groups all delivered a similar message. A personal anxiety about capacity to design, write, resource and create open, active, student-centred learning materials was also addressed directly through involvement in the process. The realization that powerful support was at hand to help produce materials, and that peer and team editing were readily available, helped to defuse this worry.

Reducing feelings of confusion and disorientation

Confusion is commonly associated with developments and ideas only just appearing on personal horizons. The distribution of official reports and printed materials and the formal delivery of dense, technical explanations do little to reduce these feelings. Indeed, the documentation designed to help frequently engenders panic reactions and a retreat into safer ideas. Confusion and disorientation do require the presentation of ideas, but only within a context in which their practical implications can be worked out, discussed and mulled over. In this workshop structure, principles (theory) spilled over immediately into product evaluation (practice); structure and design (theory) translated into product design (practice); house-style considerations and 'fast-write' (theory) led directly to planning and writing (practice).

Defusing the fear of an evaluation backlash

Fear of some awful judgement was reduced by the informality of the workshop activity. It could not be expected that every participant would experience the same level of success. There were no retributions to be faced. Attitudes to new styles of teaching were expected to change, but often the benefits were departmental rather than personal. Progress in the Wearside College Construction Department, which embraced the ideas enthusiastically, built up a knowledgeable and positive team and delivered some solid achievements. Nevertheless, not everyone in the department felt like, or wished to be, a writer. The evaluation which did take place involved interactions between peers and within departments. Only the workshop providers felt some legitimate unease about evaluation!

Rescuing the development from doubt, cynicism and hostility

Fast change in recent years has made many teachers feel defensive and unsure about the validity of what is happening. This response to educational change was modified by clarification and by exemplification. There should be no pretence, and while the workshop itself had to be good of its kind, the learning materials it brought to the attention of the participants during the evaluation activity had to be carefully selected across the full quality range. Poor, hastily designed and relatively inadequate materials were an essential element in the evaluation activity. Workshop participants realized that a simple contrast between 'good' and 'bad' materials was not the point of the exercise. Quite rightly, thinking turned to improving materials, enhancing their effectiveness, and building on their virtues. The lack of planning – obvious in some published materials – made points about time, the level of resource availability, or both.

The first workshop stirred many reactions. The working products which resulted with professional support were being used in classrooms within a matter of days. These

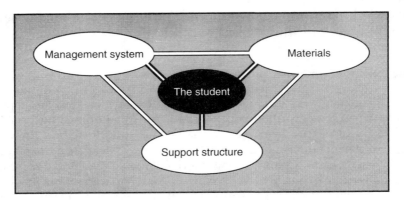

Figure 5.3   *Support structure needed for student-centred approaches*

materials raised aspirations, gained adherents and fuelled the process. In all, the first workshop and five repeats – each involving about sixteen participants – meant that about a hundred college staff had been through the process by the end.

One model used in these initial workshops proved very powerful in picking up the structures necessary to support student-centred approaches (Figure 5.3). At one level, it was seen as a micro-model for the development of one learning product – it implied generating materials which incorporated support and management. At a macro-level, it was seen as a model upon which a college might base its management structure. At this point, the methodology begins to move beyond the ambitions of individual writers and their creative, student-centred learning materials.

The last of the six initiating workshops ran in January 1993, and the key participants at Wearside – Peter Eagle, assistant principal, and Derek Wallace, the TVEI co-ordinator – began to respond to a demand for two higher-level workshops. Clearly, at this level, it would be possible to address in more detail the options open to potential producers and users:

- *the level of production*: from generating new products, through customization and enhancement of existing materials, to 'buying in'
- *the media presentation*: exploring media choices from paper, through audio, video, interactive video and computer-based to mixed-mode
- *the selection of assessment mechanisms*: self-assessment, peer assessment, mentor assessment, tutor assessment, computer-based assessment, work-based assessment, and the measurement of competence and performance.

It was also possible to clarify, explore, suggest and discuss in an increasingly open-ended way – for example, beginning to generate a typology of study guides; teasing out what is meant by an assignment briefing; deciding on the nature of worksheets or handouts; creating quality criteria for learning materials, and much else besides.

Increasingly, the development was moving in ways which were as creative as they were unanticipated. Inevitably, intermixed with all this creative thinking was a complex web of political interactions. The truth is that educational innovation, while possessing its own kind of chaos, has also to respond to turbulence within the system, the management, and the personalities involved. Innovations are never straight-forward, but even chaotic butterflies flapping their wings can cause storms, and storms can distribute the seeds of good ideas.

CONCLUSIONS AND REFLECTIONS

This chapter has explored a particular case study in which a group of partners set out to win over a group of realistic tertiary education teachers to a powerful learning methodology. Understandably, the latter were anxious, confused and fearful for the future, and very doubtful about the merits of moving into the open.

The Wearside College *TVEI Annual Review* produced by Derek Wallace in January 1994, under the heading 'Teaching and learning styles', summed up these develop-ments in the following words:

> With the introduction of incorporation there is a greater emphasis on study hours rather than teaching hours. This has resulted in a variety of modes of learning being explored, introduced and delivered within learning programmes. This flexible approach to learning will continue to expand as most students are now producing individual action plans and where appropriate follow individual programmes of study.
>
> There has been an increased demand for flexible learning facilities within the college. In order to accommodate this, an additional Flexible Learning Workshop is being con-structed within the Tunstall Centre. This is in addition to the current provision of a Flexible Learning Workshop at each centre.
>
> A comprehensive staff development programme has been delivered to ensure that staff understand the philosophy of flexible approaches to learning, and appreciate the reasons for its introduction and development. It was initially difficult to assess/establish the needs of individual tutors and level of support required. Therefore, it was necessary to offer a range and level of flexible learning workshops such as An Introduction to Flexible Learning, Flexible Learning Resources, Writer Workshops and Desktop Publishing. As a result of these programmes staff have produced high quality flexible learning resources and are using them effectively within their programmes of study.

So in the end, the college has created something which is likely to be effective, efficient and economical, while at the same time matching the fast-moving circumstances in which we all find ourselves. Open and flexible methodologies may, in the end, prove the only way in which we can all deal with our elastic futures.

NOTES

1. Gillham, B.A. (1990) Open learning: an introductory perspective. In Potter, F. (ed.) *Reading, Learning and Media Education*. Oxford: Blackwell.
2. Nesbit, J.D. (1975) Innovation – bandwagon or hearse. In Harris, A., Lawn, D. and Prescott, W. (eds) *Curriculum Innovation*. London: Croom Helm.

Chapter 6

The Development of Open Workshops: How to Make it Happen

Jacki Proctor and Ruth Wright

DEVELOPING FLEXIBLE LEARNING SYSTEMS

The buzz words have been around a long time. The development of 'flexible delivery systems' for curricula, intended to provide opportunities for the 'independent learner' to use 'alternative learning strategies', has been an objective for providers of education since the 1970s. The rationale for such development has changed, as the government and its policies and priorities have changed, but the need for the development was indicated in the first place by demographic, economic and social trends which have not changed and which continue to challenge education organized on traditional lines.

Generous funding has been available to developers from national government under a number of development initiatives intended to:

- increase the responsiveness of colleges
- extend access to non-conventional students
- provide off-the-shelf curriculum modules.

These funds were either 'earmarked' and channelled through local authorities, or awarded by direct tender to institutions. Additionally, funding could be sought from the *European Social Fund*, under initiatives which were not intended to change existing education structures but were primarily related to increasing access to training perceived as ameliorating social conditions and complementing social change.

There have been variations in the rationale for government funding. In the 1970s, it was an egalitarian 'access to education' rhetoric. During the 1980s, as unemployment figures rose, there was an unprecedented focus on further education (FE) and the development of youth training schemes and 'work related non-advanced FE'. The early 1990s have seen a shift of emphasis towards higher education (HE) and work-based learning: 'investing in people for increased productivity and profits'.

These variations have made it possible for all political shades to identify the development of flexible learning as a 'good thing'. However, project funding has not been integrated. 'Pump-priming' money has been available to disparate initiatives, while the reservoir needed to maintain education provision has been slowly drained.

Changes in employment, the economic recession, the fluctuation in birthrates and changing populations all indicate the importance of flexibility in educational provision. Over the years, government initiatives adopted to foster the development of flexible delivery systems have focused successively on:

- physical resources: particularly investment in information technology (IT)
- the control and management of provision: centralizing control and targeting funding onto administrations supporting flexible learning
- curriculum development: the production of open learning (OL) packages
- academic and administrative staff development.

Taken together, the funding and implementation of these strategies might have been expected to lead to significant progress over the past twenty years. This has rarely been the case.

In contrast with other colleges, Bradford and Ilkley Community College (formerly Bradford College) has succeeded in establishing, maintaining and extending flexible learning systems, but without fully achieving radical and ambitious development plans. An analysis of the continuing and largely successful development of the Communication Workshops, a centre for OL, is used as an example to reveal some of the factors which may create resistance to change or influence its pace in educational institutions.

THE BRADFORD OPEN WORKSHOPS

A Mathematics Workshop and a Communications Workshop were established at Bradford College in 1975. The definition of 'open workshop' at that time is given in Lewis and Pates (1987):

> The term 'flexible open workshop' is used . . . to describe a location in which learners, individually and/or in groups, can pursue their own learning programmes. Learners may attend the workshop on a timetabled or drop-in basis. In a flexible workshop:
>
> - learners generally work at their own pace from
> - resources designed for self-study use;
> - teachers back up the learning materials as required, for example, offering guidance and counselling;
> - access to the workshop is at times convenient to the learner.

Additionally, at Bradford, the workshops were to offer the diagnosis of individual learning needs, and a prescribed learning package to meet those needs. There was, even then, a recognition that the 'drop-out' rate from further education was unacceptably high. It was expected that individual learners who might seek this support would include those having difficulty in meeting the demands of mainstream programmes, as well as those working independently to improve their life chances. In further support of the delivery of college programmes, the workshops were to provide a resource base for class teachers.

The development of the workshops was seen as essential to support the achievement of college equal opportunity policies, designed to ensure that the college resource met the needs of the urban multicultural community within which it was situated. It was recognized that literacy and numeracy skills were basic to success in the job market and at every level of post-school education, although it must be said that, at that time, the concern was to remove barriers associated more with gender and class than race.

This chapter will not describe the Mathematics Workshop since such descriptions have been published many times (Lewis and Pates, 1987; Sands, 1984; Spencer, 1980). An earlier paper contrasts the different rates of development of the two workshops during their first five years (Proctor, 1985). This chapter focuses on the Communication Workshops and, from a consideration of its history, identifies factors which are essential to the development of flexible learning systems.

THE COMMUNICATION WORKSHOPS: A HISTORY

The development of the Communication Workshop began in 1975. Initially, it was a low-tech, paper-based, remedial centre. It was given generous accommodation on the main campus, although this was not easily accessible. It had a full-time academic manager and, from the outset, was allocated an administrative assistant. As was fashionable at that time, the college organization was a matrix structure. The workshop was located, as a resource, within a 'faculty' and not, as a base for courses on which students were registered, within a 'school'. It was expected that workshop staff would develop techniques to diagnose difficulties with written English experienced by individual students, and that they would design and prescribe structured learning packages, to meet students' needs and to open, and widen, access to credentialling examinations at several levels. However, in its first five years of operation, although its contribution was useful, this did not happen. No students were registered to use OL as their sole means of studying English language. The workshop continued to be seen, by English teaching staff, mainly as a resource intended to support class teaching. Albeit unintentionally, college staffing procedures prioritized class teaching to the extent that the workshop manager found difficulty in facilitating development since continuity in workshop staffing was not assured. In some instances, the staff who were allocated to the workshop were 'making up' their timetables when their other duties fell short of contractual norms.

Furthermore, the demands made on workshop resources by college staff teaching 'English' were often incompatible both with one another and with the development of workshop practice. There was little consensus about the concept of Communication Workshop. During the first five years it was used as an effective but pragmatic response in support of other curriculum development concerns. Over this period of time, the physical space and resources were used by class groups doing projects, or timetabled for literacy, personal, communication, study or life skills. The individual learners who used it were a small minority. Some found it on their own initiative and were able to exploit its resources to their advantage. Some, most often with multiple difficulties, were sent there by tutors unable to meet their needs during class teaching. This variation in use was matched by a lack of clarity in determining the direction the accumulation of resources should follow. In attempting to meet the interpretations of what the workshop might offer, the workshop manager tried to develop an all-purpose communication centre, all inclusive for literacy, oral, aural, media and word-processing advice. Yet the space, the resources, the funding, and the staffing available made the fulfilment of this optimistic definition extremely problematic. While broadening the perspective of some curriculum development initiatives, it remained an expensive addition to class teaching.

Between 1981 and 1982, there was a change in the leadership of the college, accompanied by the introduction of a linear management structure. A School of Open Learning was created to focus the development of flexible delivery systems. It accommodated cross-college functions: the library, research and development, a unit for multicultural education and the OL workshops. Communication and Mathematics Workshops were grouped together to form a Department of Open Workshops. At this time, there was a vision, yet to be achieved, of a 'workshop wing', with additional workshops (including keyboard skills, electronics, the social sciences, and art theory), open seven days a week all year round.

The Communication Workshop was given a small increase in its full-time staffing. At the same time, a diverse group of interested staff agreed a policy for the teaching of English across the college, which was approved by the academic board. The policy affirmed the Communication Workshop as the key central agency co-ordinating English-language teaching and included in its function the establishment of a resource network to enhance provision. The purposes of the workshop were then described as the provision of:

- alternatives to class-based teaching as a way of taking recognized examinations
- flexible modes of learning, in terms of time, method or materials, to meet special needs
- a study area open to individuals
- a centre for testing in English language and communication skills in terms of development of tests for college use, advice on the development of tests, and storage of tests developed for use within the workshop or elsewhere
- a resource centre for associated learning materials and media equipment.

This led to the first sustained initiative to introduce accurate diagnosis of English-language difficulties and provide structured materials for the development of literacy skills. The development focused on reading and writing skills. The workshop model was aligned to distance learning and was paper-based. At that time, aural and oral skills were relatively unimportant in accreditation systems and the production of materials to support their development was temporarily shelved.

An analysis of the skills which contribute to competence in reading and writing English was made. Modularized learning packages, which could be 'pick-and-mixed' to meet a variety of learning needs, were produced. This meant that the individual learner was enabled to work to improve spelling, punctuation, comprehension, business letter, essay and technical report writing, and the like.

A major effect of the co-operative tutorial work needed to place reading and writing skills within a structure, and to design materials to facilitate their development, was a change in the nature of the workshop. Gradually, through a period of intense interpersonal debate, the workshop became an intellectual centre, a learning community. the staff involved had widely divergent approaches to the English curriculum, but they gradually developed a shared understanding. They were excited by their progress and their excitement drew in other staff. The workshop became a staff development facility, supporting staff learning at the same time as student learning.

The most significant outcome of the materials and staff development was that a number of modes of attendance and attachment were agreed. Some students were registered as OL students and could pursue programmes leading to a recognized qualification (including GCSE, AEB tests in Business English, City and Guilds Report Writing) without attending classes. Additionally, mainstream taught classes were accommodated in the workshop as tutor-led study groups supporting individual rates of progression. For the first time, the expense of the resource could be measured against conventional audit systems, since there were now registered student hours. The efficiency of workshop delivery of courses can be gauged by the fact that prior to workshop registration there were 214 student places available to those wishing to prepare for GCE examinations in English language, the only main campus offer in language development at that time. Student registration to the workshop made possible the enrolment of many more of those wanting to return to, or continue, studying and, in 1991, 758 students were registered to the workshop: an increase of 254 per cent.

In 1986 the structure of the college was 'fine tuned' and the function of the School of Open Learning relocated in course-based schools. A-level mathematics courses were only available through the Mathematics Workshop and, as a consequence, the Department of Workshops was relocated in the School of Science and Technology. In 1988 the Communication Workshop was moved to more accessible accommodation. It was allowed more space and was asked to incorporate an existing computer-based Keyboard Skills Workshop. Additionally, changes in the GCSE regulations increased the importance of oral competence and its assessment. This effectively reintroduced the wider definition of 'communication' previously jettisoned. In recognition of this, the developing suite of accommodation became known, in the plural, as the Communication Workshops. The availability of cheaper computers and educational software led to a gradual integration of high-tech delivery of learning into the workshop, although it remains predominantly paper-based. The college was awarded Education Support Grant funding (ESG XXXI) to develop OL provision for basic skills in both literacy and numeracy, bringing basic skills into the mainstream of the city centre campus while maintaining community-based provision. It chose to locate this project in the Communication Workshops.

Most recently, the Communication Workshops have been relocated once more in the structure of the institution. The Schools remain predominantly bases for the delivery of learning programmes, but, in addition, most have taken specific responsibility for an element of cross-college activity. Since 1993, the Communication Workshops have been separated from the Mathematics Workshop and have joined the Department of General Education, located in the School of Adult Education. As a part of its function, the department brings together those involved in the provision of English-language and English-literature teaching across the college. It supports class teaching of English literature and English as a foreign, or second, language, and the Communication Workshops. Nevertheless, the first development plan for the department avoids predicting how bringing together strands of English teaching will benefit curriculum delivery overall. The strength of the evolved 'workshop method' is described in the final report on the ESG Adult Literacy and Numeracy Project, Wright (1992):

> The workshops operate on a system of supported self study with a strong emphasis on initial assessment, frequent negotiation, re-assessment and adjustment of the learning programmes of individuals. On-going enrolment and negotiation of attendance patterns are also of great benefit to adult students. Each student has an academic counsellor who is responsible for the student's learning programme and its development. . . . Meetings of

staff to discuss and assess provision are held regularly. Working in open learning workshops means that tutors meet and interact more frequently than they would in class-based situations. Timetabling ensures that tutors and support staff new to the workshops will be teamed with more experienced staff. Team support is strong; interaction is both organic and formalised through meetings of basic education staff and of team leaders of all strands of workshop provision.

TURNING INNOVATION INTO CHANGE

Organizational factors which affect the development and maintenance of flexible learning systems are considered below. These factors interact: a certain amount of repetition is inevitable.

Some movement away from a traditional understanding of what educational institutions do is necessary if flexible learning delivery systems are to be accommodated within established educational organizations. Each stage of the development project must be accompanied by corresponding institutional adjustment if achievements are to be established and continuing development facilitated. The reality is that these adjustments are not totally predictable. They are a series of pragmatic shifts made in response to changing perceptions of how the return from the human and physical resource invested in the project can be maximized and tensions between conflicting interest groups eased.

LEADERSHIP

Although the literature on organizational change is often contradictory, it is consistent on one feature: that executive leadership matters. Thereafter there is a divergence about what aspect of leadership matters. The variations include:

- individual management style
- whether 'leadership' should be directly equated with 'management'
- the degree of management commitment necessary to change.

Nadler and Tushman (1990) distinguish between charismatic and instrumental leadership and claim that both are necessary if organizational change is to take place: 'Charismatic leadership is needed to generate energy, create commitment, and direct individuals towards new objectives, values or aspirations. Instrumental leadership is required to ensure that people really do act in a manner consistent with their new goals.' In 1981, Bradford did see a change from a predominantly charismatic principal to a predominantly instrumental principal. This might have been a factor ensuring that the Open Workshop innovation of 1975 was stabilized within the organization in 1981. Continuity of approach to the provision was assured by a vice-principal concerned with the development from the outset.

The nature of an educational organization, as a community of professionals with shared competence and conflicting interests, disposes it against a dependence on one leader. As Louis (1989) writes: 'In academia there is hardly ever one leader in a change process, which usually produces a number of competing interest groups.' Rauch and Behling (1984) define leadership in such a way that it is possible to see that 'leadership' and 'management' may not be one and the same thing: ' "Leadership" is defined as the process of influencing the activities of an organized group toward goal achievement.' During the 1980s, pressures on FE and HE provision (which included greatly reduced day-release student numbers, reductions in the numbers of teachers in training, changes in funding, changes in assessment procedures, and so on) increased the militance of professional organizations. In such situations 'power' does not reside solely with management. Articulate staff members, seen to be representing the interests of other staff accurately, become leaders. Masland (1985) describes such people: '[they] are important to an organisation and often represent ideals and values in human form. . . . [they] exemplify behaviour suitable to the College. They are role models, set standards and preserve what makes the organisation unique.'

At Bradford, from 1980 onwards, a powerful member of the professional association took on this form of leadership and identified with the open workshops. There can be no doubt that this identification had some positive effect. Staff not yet committed to OL methods were attracted into the development. OL tutors saw that they had a representative with a political presence in the institution as well as the instrumental executive support already reported. The negotiation of resources, particularly academic and administrative staffing, and the protection of their areas of concern seemed assured. On the negative side, the subsequent appointment of that staff member to a management post, without relinquishing the position of professional association leader, was a concern to some staff, who saw this dual role as ambiguous. Although his political acumen was still admired, the trust he enjoyed from representing the interests of tutorial staff was significantly reduced and some were deterred by the ambiguity of his position from engaging with the development.

A distinction between what it is that managers, as opposed to leaders, do was provided by Pfeffer (1981): 'the activity of management is viewed as making what is going on in the organization meaningful and sensible to the organizational participants, and furthermore developing a social consensus and social definition around the activities being undertaken.' The commitment of the executive to a development initiative must be expressed, incorporated in policies, and re-expressed, if change is to occur. A major factor in the success of the Bradford developments was that, even with changes in the executive, management commitment to the concept of OL delivery of courses was demonstrated in a continuous partnership, described by the senior vice-principal, Peter Chambers (1992): 'Management's task is to support the vision, provide insurance against the risks and commit the resources. The teaching staff's task is to understand the financial and planning restraints that operate in delivering the courses so that quality criteria are met and the progression contexts are recognised.'

Initially, the 'vision' was of a 'comprehensive college' developing the strength of FE, as described by Anthony Crosland (1967): 'the leading technical colleges, by their capacity to provide for students at different levels of ability and attainment (and that is why I call them comprehensive), provide a chance for students of these kinds not only to tackle degree level work part-time or full-time, but also to develop their latent capacity to do so.' The later 'vision' of the 'community college' was shaped by the 'New Training Initiative' of 1981: 'we must open up widespread opportunities for adults, whether employed, unemployed or returning to work, to acquire, increase or update their skills and knowledge during the course of their working lives.' This intention was coupled with local sensitivity to rising levels of unemployment, which were being experienced disproportionately by those of South Asian and African-Caribbean origin. These 'minority' ethnic groups formed 39 per cent of the 16–19 age group by 1986. The college policy sought 'to equip all members of the community, including those from sub-groups, both to play a full role in their own community and to achieve fully within the majority culture'.

The development of OL was essential in both the comprehensive and the community college. Economically and practically, the achievement of policies aiming for equality of access to learning was dependent on the flexible and responsive delivery of programmes. Management, including both the executive and the workshop manager, ensured that workshop delivery was incorporated in subject-teaching policies, in student support policies and in policies for particular learners (including bilingual students).

The development of flexible provision continues to attract government funding and senior workshop staff are regularly invited to take part in staff development programmes for other institutions. In order to disseminate progress in OL development among Bradford staff, they organize similar programmes in the college. All members of the executive have attended and taken part in these in-house staff development programmes, pointing up, by their presence, the level of their commitment. Additionally, the executive repeatedly stresses the importance of OL in meetings with consultative groups of staff. In expressing commitment to the development of OL, the executive is committing the institution to organizational change. In periods of stabilization or contraction, the introduction of another system threatens the boundaries of those already established. The executive will find themselves arbitrating between interest groups, and those associated with traditional delivery tend to be more powerful in terms of their social relationships within the institution. Arbitration is time-consuming and can be uncomfortable. Certainly, development at Bradford has not been achieved without pain. 'Commitment' implies a reiteration of consultation, exhortation, adaptation: balancing the aspirations of individuals and facilitating fresh groupings of staff to motivate further development.

STRUCTURES

In the late 1970s, the Further Education Unit (FEU) promoted an organizational matrix structure which allowed for maximum flexibility, and, by reducing the sphere of influence of senior members of staff seen as antipathetic to change, facilitated rapid implementation of new policies. However, there are disadvantages, listed by Theodossin (1984):

- possible staff responsibility to two or more leaders, with consequent possible disorientation
- a feeling of lack of identity (as can happen in a department)
- the lack of a feeling of security
- apparent structural complexity
- the engendering of frustration caused by the primacy of the course leader, with the subject leader in a supportive role.

Although the matrix structure introduced at Bradford in 1975 supported rapid change, some of the staff affected did not see this as an advantage, and the disadvantages of the structure were apparent to almost all. Primacy was given to course development, and the development of the Communication Workshop was possibly impeded as those staff necessary to the initiative were scattered through the structure and developed strong allegiance to those courses which provided their teaching hours. McAleer and Mc-Aleavy (1989) comment: 'Teachers who agree to reduce their commitment to teaching in order to participate in initiatives designed to enhance institutional change may be entering an area of considerable professional risk.' This risk is greater when there is any prospect of staff redundancy.

A hierarchical structure does not accommodate cross-departmental initiatives easily. In giving advice on the implementation of OL policies, in 1986, the FEU stated: 'There are examples of open learning being successfully used in institutions with traditional departmental structures. However, experience demonstrates that, in some cases, schemes have been more effectively operated as the result of some organisational change – for example, the establishment of extra-departmental units.' On the reintroduction of a vertical departmental structure at Bradford in 1982, the concept of a horizontal cross-college school, the School of Open Learning, was compatible with this idea, current at the time.

Speaking of any institutional structure, departmental or faculty, Janes *et al.* (1989) comment: 'The structure has a natural tendency to divide the college into separate and largely independent units, encouraging attitudes of competition and regard for growth rather than attitudes of cooperation and regard for quality.' This may be overly negative: competition is just as likely to result in departmental excellence, probably more likely, at times of retrenchment or minimal growth. At Bradford, it rapidly became evident that the Schools, vertical groupings of departments, needed to administer research and staff development funds related to their specialisms. The disbanding of the School of Open Learning in 1986, in theory, made the development of open delivery systems the concern of every department. In practice, keeping the Department of Open Workshops intact and locating it in the School of Science and Technology kept the group of English staff strongly identified with the Communication Workshops small. The most recent, 1993, separation of Communication from the Mathematics Workshop and its relocation does bring together English teaching staff and may ameliorate this difficulty. However, relocation in the School of Adult and General Education may separate Communication from the direct delivery of vocational courses. If this location implies 'enriching' and 'remedial' education, rather than vocational training, it may carry a slight danger that, at some future time of even scarcer resources, the workshop may be categorized as an optional extra rather than an essential element in the delivery of all courses.

CURRICULA

Reference has already been made to the variations in the definition of 'Communication' which hampered the early development of the workshop. The teaching of English language in FE encompasses more than one culture. There are divides between concepts of English-language curricula. One particularly polarized example contrasts the views of the traditionalists, to whom English language is seen primarily as an approach to the study of English literature, with those others who regard English language as essential to life chances and a movement towards equality of opportunity in access to education, training and employment. At one extreme, the former define 'standards' of spoken and written English in terms of received pronunciation and of the classics. At the other, the latter group value ethnically diverse literature to support language teaching, and dialects are regarded as enriching as opposed to eroding the quality of spoken English.

The provision for those whose mother tongue is not English is also divided. One side is characterized by high-status provision for foreign students. The increase in fees for overseas students ensures two things: that these students are eagerly courted and tenderly treated by colleges, and that usually they are from wealthy and privileged backgrounds. The expectation is that staff and resources will be generously available to these students and that their curriculum will reflect the traditional values of English culture. On the other side of this divide are those indigenous students speaking English as a second language. Many of these have already been rejected by, or have rejected, the British school system. They may have experienced the devaluing of their own culture during their education. The 'standards' they aspire to are the credentials which will assist their entry to the job market.

In *Learning Workshops*, Lewis and Pates (1987) commented: 'First, what curriculum areas will be provided? Some subjects lend themselves immediately and obviously to a flexible learning workshop – for example mathematics, business studies and some aspects of languages.' One of the major achievements of Bradford workshop staff was the creation of a structure for a literacy curriculum which included all those skills necessary for credentialling examinations and to which teaching staff from more than one English 'culture' could ascribe.

STAFF: THE PEDAGOGUES

Curriculum orientations do not exist in isolation. They are the property of individual members of staff. Committed staff will proselytize their view of the curriculum, gathering converts and creating groups of staff with a shared understanding. A sufficiently large, articulate or well-placed group, or those united behind a curriculum seen to be of importance to the achievement of institutional objectives, will gain political power. In many colleges, English-language staff do not share a view of the curriculum or a consistently held common purpose. There is no common understanding of the most effective processes by which their goals may be attained. This inability to speak with one voice results in relative political impotence. It seems probable that the development of the Communication Workshop was delayed because the English staff at Bradford found it difficult to combine into a cohesive pressure group.

The pedagogy most strongly associated with the teaching of English has been the pedagogy of example. Some academics find it difficult to give up a tradition of charismatic teaching, of inspirational lectures and allowing students to absorb skills by immersing themselves in the observation of an ideal model. This pedagogy is that most often associated with the 'English for the sake of English literature' approach and also with the 'great teacher' and 'missionary' movements of liberal adult and basic education. For those who have practised such pedagogy, a change to OL delivery would entail learning new skills and abandoning a professional role habitual to them and with which they are comfortable. Academic staff need to see the practical and educational advantages of developing OL systems. They need to have confidence that the curriculum for which they are responsible can be transmitted effectively through OL. They need the professional confidence to work alongside, and in full view of, other staff. They must appreciate the advantage to students, enjoy contacts with individuals as opposed to classes, and feel the satisfaction of meeting individual needs.

Another reason for pedagogues to resist the development of OL lies in the suggestion, implicit in the development, that the increased allocation of administrative and technician staff to support OL delivery would be accompanied by a decrease in the number of academic staff required. In considering the deployment of support staff to OL, Dixon (1987) mentions their contribution to the development and delivery of OL materials and the difference in their rate of pay and working conditions:

> The task-oriented team approach used in large scale development projects involves different kinds of professionals whose contributions to the task are all essential but who are on different salary scales and working under different conditions of service. . . . the professional inputs from a graphic designer can affect the learning process as much as the inputs of the subject content writer . . . support staff engaged involved in the operation of open learning workshops . . . play a 'front-of-house' role in reception and enrolment. They have a greater degree of direct contact with learners, and they assist in the maintenance of progress records. . . . librarians provide first-level tutorial support – in the form of counselling, encouragement, motivation and study skills – leaving second-level support in the form of advice on subject content and assessment to tutorial staff.

Paradoxically, on the very bottom line, academic staff may adopt an initiative if the alternative to not doing so is redundancy. Initially, it was the fear of possible redundancies which led to the adoption of workshop delivery by the majority of mathematics staff at Bradford.

The stabilization of an innovation, embedding it within an organizational structure, appointing a manager and full-time staff to it, may limit further development. Handy (1985) speaks of the stress associated with innovation:

> The major role problem encountered by people responsible for innovative activities is that of conflicting priorities. In general the power centres in the organisation are in favour of the status quo – this will impart a high degree of ambiguity to the manager of an innovative function – is he or is he not supposed to innovate? He will also find considerable conflict between the routine administrative aspect of his job and the creative side – two types of work with different psychological demands, hard to combine in one person.

The appointed manager of a flexible learning system may well limit stress by ceasing developmental work. At Bradford, the persistence of the workshop manager and senior staff, and the continuing involvement of a member of the executive with the Communication Workshop, have prevented this happening.

The stabilization of innovation may also deter adoption by other staff. The innovation no longer presents such an attractive arena of personal opportunity. Staff with ambition may seek an alternative development which they can engage with and 'own'. Again, there is a paradox in that the stabilization of an innovation may also motivate a 'second wave' of staff to adopt the new approach. It becomes a respectable and secure part of education. New job descriptions include reference to its co-ordination, continuing development and establishment. Posts are created in several institutions and an examination of the level at which they are advertised is a sure indicator of the value attached to the approach. A new route for career progression may be opened up.

There are also gender influences on the development of OL workshops. The majority of FE lecturers are white males and they dominate management roles. In developing flexible learning systems, they are mostly associated with the introduction of IT and with higher-level vocational curricula. Women in FE, however, are still generally associated with the delivery of 'women's work' courses, of general education and learner support. It is mainly women who have carried out the production of paper materials to support the OL delivery of general education curricula. This has an effect on the perceived status of the work within the institution. At Bradford the majority of Communication staff are female.

Where the group of staff associated with OL is small, any movement due to retirement, or promotion, can affect the development adversely. The Communication Workshop at Bradford has been fortunate in keeping a nucleus of staff and in being able to make some permanent appointments from among part-timers. The availability of staff development 'time' and the nature of the work have continued to attract staff, not all of them English-language teachers, from other areas of the college into the Workshops.

THE PEOPLE MAKE THE PROCESS

FE is people, and making it happen is entirely related to people. For the change to take hold, the expectations of each group of people involved in learning transactions must include OL delivery. Interactions within and between these groups of people are, at the same time, the only way to carry development forward and the greatest potential impediment to change.

Students' conceptions of learning and their expectations of educational institutions have tended to be developed within traditional organizational contexts which, while they may provide contacts with inspirational teachers, may also control, and direct, and encourage conformity to the values and rate of learning of a particular group. Students may expect class teaching and will need support as they learn to become open learners. In a report on standards in education published in 1991, Her Majesty's Inspectorate expressed concern about mature entrants to HE:

> the limited success of open and distance learning methods with students with little experience of post-16 education needs to be noted. It seems to be the case that such uncertain entrants to HE need frequent contact with good, lively teachers to help them maintain commitment to their studies. If that is generally true, it is clear that such methods will not in themselves be a satisfactory solution to the difficulties inherent in widening access.

Evidence that students were not succeeding would be sufficient to invalidate the development. However, workshop delivery, with tutorial assistance 'on tap' and careful tracking of individual students, provides a high level of student support.

OL delivery, if it is genuinely open, may present a disturbing anomaly within an educational institution, creating problems for central administrative staff. The work practices of most groups of non-academic staff are affected by the development of workshops. In the registrar's office, established patterns of work have accommodated enrolment, examination entries, invigilation and posting out the results with the same sequential certainty as night follows day. In the finance office, management information systems are most often founded on the expectation that the monitoring of institutional performance relates to a fixed academic calendar. Increased access for students means that new security and cleaning systems are necessary. The production of paper materials makes demands on the print service and the internal post. The understanding and co-operation of central administration in adapting central systems is necessary if flexibility of provision is to be enhanced and maintained.

Administrative staff associated with a workshop take on a more demanding, potentially more satisfying, role. They work in partnership with academic staff managing workshop systems, and, in direct contacts, provide support to both learners and academic staff seeking advice about workshop materials. This increased status carries considerable responsibility. Administrative posts are necessary to OL delivery; the level at which those posts are established should 'fit' appropriately into the administrative establishment of the institution.

AND FiNALLY . . .

This chapter has considered institutional elements, leadership, structures, curricula and staff, which have had an identifiable effect on the implementation of OL development policies at Bradford.

The single most significant factor has been that OL delivery systems have remained essential to the achievement of college objectives. Although they have changed over time, there has always been an equitable educational purpose expressed in the college mission statements. A clear rationale for the development of OL, based on ideals of social justice, could be identified locally. Flexible learning was promoted by central government in terms of increasing the responsiveness of FE provision. At Bradford these objectives were inextricably related to increased equality of opportunity.

Although there have been leadership changes, both in the executive and in workshop management, there has been a consistent approach to the development of OL which has kept a high profile in institutional development plans. The number of students registered with the OL workshops and following mainstream courses has continued to grow, reaching high levels, and examination success rates have been satisfactory. The workshops show up well in internal audit and quality control systems. There has been a willingness to adapt internal procedures and systems to the needs of OL delivery.

However, this chapter presents a retrospective view of stages in the development of an open workshop and, since the development has been largely successful, the representations are predominantly positive. It may be that the reality of development work has been obscured. There have been resistances to change, some of them endemic to innovation, and the process of overcoming them often disappears from consciousness as the development is successfully implemented.

Development takes place within an institutional culture and, if successful, will disrupt the existing form of that culture. The commitment of the executive to an initiative will ensure that it is not ignored, but change will only occur if, and as, attitudes and behaviour change. The creation of consensus about the change agenda is rarely achieved without conflict. The process is potentially uncomfortable and stressful. Giving up a particular work practice may lead to a sense of loss and disaffection. Personal relationships supporting established patterns of work are strained. The acceptance of items on the agenda which do not threaten the vital core of a work culture may be presented by interest groups as a demonstration of their responsiveness to change while the essential purposes of the development are pushed to the periphery of the organization. These processes are pervasive. The argument of this chapter has been to note that the successful development of the workshops in promoting flexible learning as a key element in curriculum delivery has been achieved by overcoming resistances. During the past twenty years, various interest groups of staff have tried to isolate the innovation from high-status mainstream curricula; have tried to associate it only with perceived low-status staff and less powerful, gender-related, supporting activities; and have played on the lack of cohesion in the pedagogy and values of the staff involved in the development. Even among those adopting the innovation, conflicting interest groups have formed, in some cases competing for the credit for, and ownership of, phases of the development, and in some cases maintaining involvement in the development while arguing for a return to the traditional sources of teacher satisfaction through an increase in the direction and control of learning. Executive support, strong opinion leadership, imaginative and determined staff and high profile commitment have eroded resistance. The workshops are now embedded in the heart of institutional culture and the institution-wide network of involved staff, which will keep them in that position, is being strengthened.

OL delivery systems are crucial within the provision of FE if institutions are to be responsive, both to local clients, employers and individuals, and to national financial imperatives. Specifically, the funding formulae adopted by the Further Education Funding Council may, once again, prioritize the development of flexible learning systems. As we have indicated, changes in social structures and understandings of culture accompany changes in educational transactions. As a major step towards a change in the culture of FE, the future training of FE lecturers must recognize the need for greater flexibility in delivery methods and build in the practice of the necessary skills.

BIBLIOGRAPHY

Chambers, Peter (1992) Bilingual students in education and training: resourcing the provision. Paper given at the Conference on Bilingual Students in Education and Training. Bradford: HMI.

Crosland, Anthony (1967) The structure and development of higher education. In Robinson, Eric (1968) *The New Polytechnics*. Harmondsworth: Penguin.

Dixon, Ken (1987) *Implementing Open Learning in Local Authority Institutions: A Guide for Institution Managers and Local Authority Officers*. London: Further Education Unit and Manpower Services Commission.

Handy, Charles B. (1985) *Understanding Organizations*. 3rd edn. London: Penguin.

Her Majesty's Chief Inspector of Schools (1991) *Standards in Education: The Annual Report, 1989–90*. London: HMI/DES.

Janes, Fred, Havard, Bob and Kershaw, Noel (1989) Managing flexible college structures 1: the current scene. *Coombe Lodge Report*, **21** (2), 105–59.

Lewis, Roger and Pates, Andrew (1987) *Learning Workshops: A Manual of Guidance on Setting Up and Running Flexible Learning Workshops*. York: Longman for Further Education Unit.

Louis, Karen Seashore (1989) Surviving institutional change: reflections on curriculum reform in universities. In Pazandak, Carol H. (ed.) *Improving Undergraduate Education in Large Universities*. New Directions for Higher Education No. 66. San Francisco: Jossey-Bass.

McAleer, John and McAleavy, Gerry (1989) Action research: paradigm for individual development or organisational change in further education? *Educational Management and Administration*, **17** (4), 214–24.

Manpower Services Commission (1981) *A New Training Initiative: An Agenda for Action*. Sheffield: MSC.

Masland, Andrew T. (1985) Organisational culture in the study of higher education. *The Review of Higher Education*, **8** (2), 57–68.

Nadler, David A. and Tushman, Michael L. (1990) Beyond the charismatic leader: leadership and organisational change. *Californian Management Review*, Winter, 77–96.

Pfeffer, J. (1981) Management as symbolic action: the creation and maintenance of organizational paradigms. In Cummings, L.L. and Staw, B.B. (eds) *Research in Organizational Behaviour. Vol. 3*. Greenwich, CT: JAI Press.

Proctor, Jacki (1985) Curriculum development and servicing areas in further education. *Journal of Further and Higher Education*, **9** (1), 3–10.

Rauch, C.F. and Behling, O. (1984) Functionalism: basis for an alternate approach to the study of leadership. In Hunt, J.G., Hosking, D.M., Shriesheim, C.A. and Stewart, R. (eds) *Leaders and Managers: International Perspectives on Managerial Behaviour and Leadership*. New York: Pergamon Press.

Sands, Trevor (1984) The Bradford mathematics workshop. In Lewis, Roger, *Open Learning in Action: Open Learning Guide. Vol. 1*. Coventry: Council for Educational Technology.

Spencer, D.C. (1980) *Thinking about Open Learning*. Coventry: Council for Educational Technology.

Theodossin, Ernest (1984) *Management Restructuring in an FE College*. Management in Colleges Series. Bristol: Further Education Staff College.

Wright, Ruth (1992) *ESG XXXI Provision of Open Learning Centres for Adult Literacy and Numeracy. Final Report*. Bradford: Bradford and Ilkley Community College.

Chapter 7

Working in Partnership

Geoff Layer

INTRODUCTION

For many years the traditional pattern of studying in higher education (HE) has been for intelligent 18-year-olds from a middle-class background to complete their A levels successfully and to go away to university to study for three years. At the end of that three years, after much hard work, they are rewarded with an honours degree. Very little has happened to shake that particular pattern. There have been considerable attempts to break down some of the barriers to HE, but little progress has effectively been made. The concept of HE is still that of going away to study for a period of three years after completing A levels in the sixth form.

Much has been written of the changes that are likely to take place in HE due to demographic decline, changing social attitude, raising the aspirations and horizons of people traditionally excluded from post-16 education, and greater demand for part-time study. All of these struggle to compete with the established pattern of HE.

This chapter seeks to identify the changing face of HE which is influenced, slowly, by some of the factors referred to above. The chapter will examine the ways in which those changes can be put in place within a region through collaboration and partnership between the university and other educational providers. It will address the issues by examining such relationships, the benefits to a community, the change in learning strategies, and the future.

FACTORS THAT INFLUENCE REGIONAL COLLABORATION

Many of the universities and colleges that now exist within the higher education sector started off life with a particular local ethos. Its degree varies with each institution and takes into account the traditions of the civic universities serving the citizens of the city, and the former polytechnics which were established and maintained by local education authorities (LEAs). Although that local commitment will have developed and changed over the years, it is still there in most institutions in one way or another. With the exception of the extramural departments of the old universities, it has been former polytechnics which have trail-blazed the concept of regional partnerships over the last twenty years. This commitment vested in regional partnership is due to a number of factors:

- the effectiveness of local authority representation and pressure on and commitment to HE institutions
- the commitment of the polytechnics to the Robbins principle of 'HE for all who can benefit'
- the Crosland concept of an alternative HE system
- many former polytechnics having had substantial numbers of part-time students dating back to day-release courses when they were colleges of technology; this part-time commitment has inevitably led to a greater local input into the institution
- the development of extramural departments within the older universities, which has to some extent placed the responsibility for regional collaboration with that department itself rather than the university as a whole
- many of the 'new' universities being part of the same educational structure as colleges of further education (FE) when they were all part of the LEA
- the commitment of some universities to second-chance education.

The designation of colleges of technology as polytechnics in the late 1960s and early 1970s led to significant transfer of work between colleges of FE and the new polytechnics within and by the LEA in the immediate locality. Much of this meant that HE became more concentrated within the new polytechnic. The Further and Higher Education Act 1992, which abolished the 'binary divide' and established independent FE corporations, has led to many institutions reviewing their strategic plans and mission statements. In many cases this has led to closer collaboration between colleges and universities seeking to ensure that a new binary divide between FE and HE is not now created. In essence the familiarity between these institutions led to a natural foundation for partnership and collaboration.

As HE institutions began to review the strategic plans, many committed themselves to the widening of participation. This was undoubtedly based to some extent upon a belief that demographic change would reduce demand for HE, and therefore new markets needed to be sought. In other cases there was a major commitment to the widening of participation through attracting those who are traditionally underrepresented.

Many universities soon realized that they would be unable to widen participation on their own. They did not have the background, the network and the understanding to penetrate the relevant communities. So they sought partners within FE whose local community was smaller by definition, and then worked with those colleges to make links in the communities. While many of the colleges recognized that their contacts with these target sectors of the community were not as developed as they would wish, they were significantly better than those of the universities.

Initially there was a great deal of scepticism from both partners about the value of such links and the resources required. Certain types of relationship have been developing since the late 1970s with the advent of Access to HE courses, which enabled adults to undertake one-year part-time courses leading to HE. They were predominantly aimed at those returning to education who had left with few formal qualifications, in order that they could progress into a degree or a diploma course. Many of these courses were developed through negotiation between staff at a college of FE and staff teams within HE. In the majority of cases these will have been developed on an *ad hoc* basis with little institutional co-ordination from either partner, but with the goal of ensuring opportunities for adult students. The arrangement developed through a common level of commitment at a relatively low level within the institutions. The success was achieved through that shared understanding, not through glossy statements by institutional heads.

In the mid- to late 1980s a new pattern of co-operation began to emerge through the development of HE courses within local colleges of FE. A number of colleges already provided HE courses, but the expansion that came was as a result of partnership with a university. Much of this expansion was around the first year of a degree or a diploma course with progression to the second year in the universities. The resource model was based on the government's strategy of expanding HE to one in three of the school-leaving population. This strategy was achieved through trebling the tuition fees from a base of £500/700 to £1800/2770 in the space of two to three years. These tuition fees were paid by central government through local government, and meant HE could expand on the basis of tuition fees payments for new students. All students therefore had a 'voucher' on their heads.

This mechanism saw a rapid expansion of HE in all institutions. A number of universities expanded at a phenomenal rate, whereas others grew at a much more conservative pace. The 'voucher' effectively meant that colleges of FE could afford to deliver HE courses on the basis of the tuition fee.

THE COLLEGE PERSPECTIVE

It is very difficult to generalize on the college perspective, as there are so many colleges of FE. They were traditionally maintained by the LEA, with funding coming from four major sources:

- the local authority Rate Support Grant allocation (latterly known as the Standard Spending Assessment)
- the Employment Department and Training and Enterprise Councils (TECs) through work-related FE
- local authority allocations to promote particular educational policies
- the European Economic Community Funding.

The colleges were serving a local market and trying to meet the needs for vocational education, return to study and second-chance education. Some colleges had developed a national reputation in a particular subject area (normally a vocational area) and would attract students from far afield. The college, however, is a local institution serving specific local needs. In many cases a particular industry will have shaped the role of the college through training and apprentice schemes. Consequently those near the steel industry provided a number of apprentice training courses and those in the once buoyant mining areas provided mining engineering courses. It is not unusual within South Yorkshire to see plaques on college walls identifying the college as originally having been created to serve the needs of the mining community, and to hear the institution being referred to as a mining college.

Because of changing patterns in the economy, these colleges have had to diversify and review their role. The various changes and the effect that they created can be seen as:

- *reduction in numbers* – many of the apprenticeship and training schemes no longer exist and the subsequent day release to gain a technical qualification from a major employer has also declined rapidly. This meant that the college had to address new markets and new, untapped communities.
- *planning base* – colleges have been traditionally subject to planning control by the LEA, the Employment Department, and the Regional Advisory Councils. The introduction of the Local Management of Colleges gave some freedom to colleges to take more responsibility for their own affairs.
- *incorporation* – incorporation of colleges took place in 1993 and so all colleges, like the polytechnics before them, became separate legal entities responsible for their own affairs but subject to the funding regime of a national funding council, the Further Education Funding Council.
- *expansion* – a major shift took place in government policy, alongside incorporation, which showed a desire to increase the numbers within FE by 25 per cent over a three-year period, with a small increase in funding.
- *competition* – the much-vaunted entrepreneurial regime is often referred to within colleges as being a major change in their culture. Undoubtedly the financial structures and the ability to cover costs are far more important to colleges than they had been. They are now responsible for deficits and this has necessitated a change in approach. However, the areas in which colleges can compete with each other are relatively small and apply to only a small percentage of possible students. This is due to the local nature of the college and the fact that many of the students they seek to attract cannot or will not travel significant distances. It is only therefore on the fringes of their activities that colleges actually compete.
- *tertiary education* – a number of colleges have been established as tertiary colleges providing a broad range of education for all those over the age of 16. In many cases these have been established by LEAs where there has been a desire to see a much more comprehensive approach to post-16 education and also where numbers in sixth forms have declined rapidly. This has led to a new breed of college, one that teaches a significant number of full-time A-level students. Traditionally colleges provided A-level retake classes for those who did not pass first time. These new colleges are providing full-time A-level studies for those who left school at the age of 16 as well as for adults and for people wishing to retake. Alongside that A-level provision sits the whole new era of General National Vocational Qualifications (GNVQs) and other full-time vocational courses. This has undoubtedly changed the culture of some colleges, as they faced an influx of full-time students where previously they had predominantly served part-time needs. Additionally there is an element of competition between remaining school sixth forms and tertiary colleges over recruiting the most full-time A-level students in order to demonstrate their success.

- *unemployment and training* – the 1970s and 1980s saw major changes in the way in which training for the unemployed and school leavers took place, from the early days of the Youth Opportunity Programme to the current Youth Training and Employment Training. The role of colleges within such schemes has changed dramatically over the years and the culture of training and supervising work experience with managing agents is now deeply rooted within FE.

Colleges responded to these challenges by targeting new markets. An early target was that of adults who left school at the age of 16 with few formal qualifications, and who in their mid-thirties, possibly after raising a family, wished to exploit educational opportunities. Instead of taking A levels, which are effectively designed for a 16-year-old who has just finished GCSEs over two years, the adults would follow a one-year programme designed to equip them with necessary basic skills and raise confidence in the individuals through basing work on their experience of life. These Access courses started in a very piecemeal manner and blossomed to such an extent that in the White Paper, *Meeting the Challenge*, they were referred to as the third route into HE. The link between HE and FE was essential to ensure the success of the courses and that opportunities existed for the adults. In most arrangements, students on the Access course were at least guaranteed an interview by the HE institution. The courses originally tended to be oriented towards the public sector through teacher training, social work and health-related areas, then tended to broaden out to cover other subject areas.

This, however, served only some of the needs of the local community and, as the concept of franchising began to develop, the relationships between FE and HE became closer, and many colleges sought to build on a burgeoning Access programme through the development of HE work. In some cases the colleges would already have provided some HE courses, normally in specific vocational areas. They now sought to expand that provision in order to ensure that it had a broader base, served more needs within the community, was able to expand, and could demonstrate to local employers that they had the ability to offer and provide specific, high-quality training programmes at an advanced level. Most importantly, colleges sought to demonstrate to 16-year-olds just completing their GCSEs that, as they had HE within the college, this must say very positive things about their A-level provision, which is thus more attractive than that in the school sixth form.

After a number of years of discussion, the early 1990s saw a massive growth in HE in colleges. In the majority of cases this was based on close collaboration between a university and a college.

THE STUDENT PERSPECTIVE

The student may well have a very different perspective on such arrangements. The 'traditional' model of access to HE course was that the initial return to learning took place in the college, and the HE component was delivered by and in the university. While that may well be an effective arrangement in large cities, in metropolitan areas and for those with good transport links, it did not serve the needs of a whole range of other communities. This is most marked if one looks at geographical areas like the south-west and north-west of England. These are very rural communities where the transport links between the local college and the university effectively mean that individuals could not progress their study if they could not get to the university. The issue is about access to whom and for what. It led to the Universities of Central Lancashire and Plymouth developing different types of partnership arrangement and building on Access course links to try to ensure that HE could be delivered more locally.

Similarly, geography is important in terms of the culture of communities. While the area of South Yorkshire and West Yorkshire is often seen as having good transport links between the major cities and towns, there are cultural barriers to negotiate. In many of the small mining communities where the tradition has been that the men work in the pit and the women work in the village, the concept of travelling just a few miles to a university is completely alien. Although transport links are available, people will not travel. During the miners' dispute in the mid-1980s and the establishment of the Women Against Pit Closures movement, a significant amount of awareness raising and lifting of horizons took place. Consequently many women wished to pursue educational opportunities but were unable or unwilling in many cases to travel. This led to local colleges and Sheffield Hallam University developing partnership arrangements whereby HE could actually be delivered within the local college.

There are now two types of student utilizing the HE opportunities within local colleges. One is the 18-year-old who has left school having completed A levels but not having achieved the grades required to enter university. Many colleges have used their HE provision to attract such students. This has raised many issues for the students who were conditioned and prepared for an experience within a university and have taken up a course within a college where the HE provision is a significant minority of the college's work. However, the adult group, the second main group of students on college-based courses, were perfectly aware of the courses and experience that they were about to embark on. It is more likely that the latter group's expectations are those that are met.

THE SOUTH YORKSHIRE EXPERIENCE

The experience of the partner colleges and the university in South Yorkshire is not significantly different from that of other institutions in many areas in the country. Lessons have been learned from all involved in such developments concerning the need to ensure that partnership is effective, real and not a misused word for control by one particular institution of the delivery of another.

It is interesting to note that in the majority of the areas where true collaboration has taken place, there has been the development of credit accumulation and transfer schemes within both FE and HE institutions. Such schemes provide a whole range of opportunities for learners to return to education, and to make sure that their learning is recognized and that they achieve a qualification through the process.

South Yorkshire Open College Federation (SYOCF)

The SYOCF was established in 1985 after a couple of years of research and lobbying within the area. It was based on the work of the Manchester Open College Federation, which was established in 1981 to provide an accreditation service covering four levels of education from adult basic to preparation for HE. The SYOCF was established at Sheffield Hallam University and staffed by a mixture of secondments from the university and colleges in the region. It has been enormously successful in raising the profile of the value of accreditation for learning which takes place outside the perceived 'standard' provision of a college. Accreditation by the SYOCF means that a whole range of learning provision can be given a credit value, which people then use to seek progression within the education system or, indeed, in employment. There is no desire by the SYOCF to compete with other validating and accrediting bodies. It is effectively designed to take accreditation to those areas it has not yet reached. It is part of the National Open College Network (NOCN), where open colleges nationally have come together and agreed broad aims, credit levels and definitions of credit. The aims of the NOCN are:

- to improve the quality of available provision
- to facilitate access, and in particular, progression through existing and new provision
- to encourage change in organization in the interests of learners
- to improve the flexibility of available learning opportunities.

It can be seen from those aims that the major goal is to improve the opportunities for the learner and to make sure that organizations change to reflect the interest of those learners.

As the SYOCF continued to develop and began to be recognized by many of the colleges as forming a positive route towards the recognition of learners' interests, and the staff development priorities that needed to go with it, greater recognition by college principals began to emerge. In the first few years the SYOCF, like many 'bottom-up' adult-learner forums, tended to draw support from those at the grassroots level within a college and adult education service and to receive little attention within what was perceived to be the mainstream of the college's work. It is important at this stage to recognize the value of the LEAs in supporting the development of such an accreditation framework.

Once the SYOCF had achieved the status of being the validating 'body' for access to HE courses within the South Yorkshire region, its future was effectively established. This enabled it to have more meaningful dialogue with the management of colleges over resources and to ensure that many of the curriculum discussions required for the development of access actually took place. Sheffield Hallam University was actively involved in the support of the Federation and many staff within the university committed time to the accreditation processes and staff development activities. The SYOCF has now recognized the achievements of its 10,000th learner and is registering in excess of 4000 learners a year. The language of credit has become actively used within colleges and is a means of entry into HE. In all the discussions over a partnership between the local colleges and the university, a major contributing factor is the collective support for the SYOCF.

One of the main achievements of the SYOCF has been to ensure that the curriculum is more clearly defined within the course it accredits, is structured towards the needs of the learner and has a clear rationale for teaching and learning methods, alongside the assessment strategy. It is generally recognized within colleges that this has enabled greater articulation with the local community of the opportunities available and progression arrangements, simply because it is more open.

Sheffield Hallam University

The University introduced an institution-wide credit scheme in 1988, based on very similar concepts to that of the SYOCF. The scheme was effectively an internal curriculum device to force change throughout the university and to introduce flexibility in the programmes of study offered to students. Inevitably it has raised issues concerning the process of change and the accountability within the curriculum.

As the university and the colleges have become more aware of issues around credit accumulation and transfer, the existence of two schemes which are different but similar has facilitated collaboration that would not have taken place otherwise. It was important that this occurred at senior management level when discussing partnership, but also that the credit debate was bubbling away at the grassroots level in both colleges and the university. It was in effect a pincer movement based to some extent on different ideologies and concepts that came together for the benefit of the learner and also expanded the opportunities available. It led not only to expansion but also to clearer statements in respect of the curriculum, the flexibility offered and the different ways in which it could be delivered.

The extent and nature of collaboration

Collaboration takes place at a range of levels between colleges, the SYOCF and the university. Initially it appears to be an *ad hoc* approach, but this was important to ensure common ownership. The extent of collaboration would have been far less significant if it had come as part of a strategic, top-down proposal.

Access courses

Access courses are now developed in local colleges through discussion with appropriate academic colleagues in the university and the SYOCF. Programmes are then put forward for recognition and accreditation by the SYOCF, involving university staff in the actual accreditation process. One of the issues involved is the progression arrangements into HE. The process is effectively looking to see what dialogue and curriculum planning has taken place between the university and the proposing college. That dialogue should indicate progression routes for students which have been designed to meet the needs of a very specific community in the region and also to prepare them for study within the university. Much of this curriculum discussion has been around:

- the nature of study skills
- confidence building
- requirements for numeracy and writing skills
- the need to have experience in the assessment patterns adopted within target courses at the university.

Essentially the curriculum discussions are about laying down a curriculum path that facilitates the taking of an educational opportunity into the community and provides preparation for that group of people to enter HE. The number of students now entering the university through Access courses has risen dramatically as a result of this collaboration. The awareness of Access courses within the university is such that very little debate now takes place around their concept and role. There is more about how we can support the students on the course before and after entry into the university.

Foundation programmes

These courses are a relatively new development within the region, having started life as Higher Introductory Engineering Conversion Course (HITECC) courses in the mid-1980s in the area of engineering. The courses were originally designed for humanities A-level students to have an additional year to 'switch' to engineering degrees. This route is also being used for mature adults to give them a preparatory course before entering Level 1 of a degree programme. The course effectively works as an extended degree course, with the extension taking place at the start of the degree programme. It has introduced a Level 0 year into HE. In the south Yorkshire area the university has developed foundation courses with partner colleges in the areas of construction, science, engineering, social science and humanities. These are developed on the basis of joint planning teams between colleges and the university to establish the factors to be covered within the curriculum doing that Level 0 year. The course is then validated as part of the degree for a specific type of student. Many of the students are identified as coming from the local community, having few if any former qualifications, but being able to benefit from the degree course on which they enrol. As the students receive a mandatory award for the foundation year, it has proved to be relatively attractive. Three hundred students enrolled in 1993/94, and that number could have expanded considerably if student number limits had not been laid down.

The important aspect of the foundation course is that it is collaboratively owned by the partners, all of whom are involved in the design of the curriculum, and the assessment and moderation of those programmes. There are many examples of students having come through those foundation courses and achieved excellent degrees and employment as a result of the opportunity they have been given. One of the major benefits to all the parties involved has been the debate and discussion around what a student needs to know and to be able to do to enter Level 1 programmes in a particular curriculum area. Much of this has been around the concept of learning outcomes, which has resulted in the production of shared material for teaching and assessment purposes, and this has enabled a greater level of consistency of approach and preparation for the students involved.

Franchise courses

This is where the university and the partner college come to an agreement whereby the partner college delivers a university course, in its entirety or only the first year, within the college. This enables the college to offer an already tried and trusted curriculum locally. There is considerable liaison and discussion with the unit tutors at the university to ensure consistency of approach and assessment. It is an ideal way for a college to develop the expertise and experience to provide HE programmes of a particular kind. The majority of the courses that are operated under such a franchise arrangement are the first year of degree courses and in some cases complete Higher National Diplomas (HNDs). There are some examples of postgraduate provision in particular target groups, but the emphasis is upon undergraduate work.

Within a relatively short period the partners have developed the collaboration further. This was achieved by the colleges and partners coming together to discuss and liaise over the curriculum for the franchise courses and to begin to plan them in a more consortium-based approach. In some cases this involved the consortium planning, designing and preparing learning materials to be taught across the entire course in all colleges. For the students who were recruited on to such courses, predominantly from the college's local catchment area, the advantages were of a local curriculum which had been tried and tested within HE. Of course, some of the experiences of the university were not applicable to the college environment, and indeed in many cases were challenged as part of the discussion, which led to an enrichment to the curriculum.

Validation

This is where the college (or group of colleges) prepares a course for validation by the university. It means that the curriculum is designed to meet the specific needs of a target community and is not merely adapted from that on offer with the university. The validation by the university ensures that quality assurance arrangements are in place and that the college has the capability of delivering that particular programme. Although validation is a relatively new move for the partners, it is likely that the bulk of future collaboration will involve colleges having gained the expertise to deliver HE, then designing the curriculum and seeking validation. In many cases we will see franchising declining and validation increasing.

Issues

The major challenge for the partners is to ensure that partnership is the real message. Recent changes in government policy have introduced constraints on HE numbers. This particularly hit the collaboration between universities and colleges to provide a locally based HE. If the partnership between the partners is to mean anything, it needs to be sustained through the pain of contraction as well as the pleasure of expansion. The relationship between the partners should be so important that the vagaries of government policy do not actually affect its commitment and delivery of objectives.

As a means to ensure that a partnership continues to thrive, the partners have started to establish the concept of an associate college structure. Although such titles have been around for a number of years and were part of the Polytechnics and Colleges Funding Council (PCFC) planning system, the concept envisaged here is markedly different. It is not about merely franchising HE numbers to colleges; it is about the realities of different types of institution working closely together in partnership, each knowing the others' objectives and goals. Consequently the rationale for an associate college is to seek jointly to:

- widen participation in education
- develop an institutional relationship and formal association between staff
- collaborate on franchise, validation and accreditation programmes, offering the potential for an exclusive relationship with the university for a particular curriculum
- co-operate and collaborate in research, consultancy and staff development activities
- enhance quality assurance in HE and FE
- facilitate joint ventures
- bid for new course provision.

Where associate colleges are created there are many benefits for the partners. In the first instance these are envisaged as being:

- *staff development opportunities* – this enables staff to move between different types of institution, provides opportunities for higher degrees, and ensures both greater debate and discussion over curriculum issues, and that HE learns from the development of quality assurance processes within FE which do not necessarily have highly bureaucratic origins.
- *curriculum development* – this enables more debate to take place over the curriculum design within FE and HE to ensure that progression routes are available and understood. A major achievement would be the spelling out by HE of what it actually is looking for in respect of the personal skills and aptitudes of students and what it expects them to have learnt prior to entry. It will also include a regional credit framework through which students will become more accustomed to collecting credit as they move through all levels of post-16 education and are aware of the meaning of that credit and the level which has been achieved.
- *collaboration with employers* – many employers are unaware of the distinction between FE and HE in terms of the level of the curriculum. True partnership through the associate college framework enables the employer to deal with any partner and to have the opportunity of utilizing both FE and HE expertise in the delivery of anything from a short course to longer programmes of training and learning. Rather than employers ending up with a course which does not exactly fit their needs or being passed from one institution to the other, the collaboration enables a much more responsive education system.
- *resource-based learning* – undoubtedly one of the next steps is to build on the initial development of learning materials that has taken place between the partners for particular courses, and to ensure that all courses are based on some form of resource-based learning. The collaborative design and delivery of such packages facilitates broader take-up among the community and will include those who are

unable or unwilling to attend educational institutions to raise their educational achievement.

CONCLUSION

What can be seen within the experience gained to date is that there is commitment at all levels among the partners to make collaboration work for the benefit of the students within the community. Many of the community do not see themselves as students yet, and that is the challenge that faces the partnership.

In a very short period the partnership has grown, has become embedded into the way of working for the organizations, and is regularly seen throughout the region and nationally as an indication of strength. There is no desire from either type of institution to merge or take over another; rather there is a desire to have a regional framework for education. The university's aspiration is to work with its partners to create a regional university, progression and entrance into which can take place anywhere, with achievement being obtained anywhere, but where the student and the organization concerned feel part of that partnership.

A major beneficiary is the university, not in the sense of any form of ownership but in the way that it has opened up its curriculum to be challenged and debated by other education practitioners. Such debate and challenge leads to reform and accountability: accountability both to the partners involved and to the students envisaged taking up a programme. Consequently, although it is a difficult process to manage, an enormous amount of energy goes into sustaining the associate college framework. It will lead to radical curriculum change, not only in content but also in the learning style. But isn't it time for a change?

BIBLIOGRAPHY

Department of Education and Science (1987) *Higher Education: Meeting the Challenge*. Cm. 114. London: HMSO.

Chapter 8

Open Learning for Health Service Managers
Alison Baker and Euan Henderson

INTRODUCTION

In the mid-1980s it became apparent that there was a need for a management development programme designed specifically for the National Health Service (NHS). The NHS had gone through a process of change aimed at introducing a managerial culture right across the service. Increasing numbers of clinical professionals, professions allied to medicine and administrators were moving into posts that involved significant management responsibilities. The generic management courses available in further and higher education (FE and HE) often failed to address the values and issues of the NHS. Short in-house courses did not satisfy the demand for certification in a service where qualifications have traditionally determined career advancement.

THE *MANAGING HEALTH SERVICES* PROGRAMME

Against this background the NHS Training Directorate decided to commission a set of study materials which could be delivered through local open-learning (OL) centres and through distance learning, and which would both help NHS managers to enhance their effectiveness at work and offer them a nationally-recognized qualification.

The learning materials

The original version of the *Managing Health Services* materials was developed by the Open University's (OU) Open Business School in collaboration with the Institute of Health Services Management (IHSM). They consisted of ten workbooks, designed for independent study over a period of 6–12 months with local tutorial support, together with associated readings, audiotapes and videotapes. Assessment was through in-course assignments and an end-of-course examination.

Modes of study

Managers who wish to study *Managing Health Services* by distance learning are able to do so through the well-established processes of the OU, with local tutors offering face-to-face and telephone tuition and with a weekend residential school.

The OL centres were established and accredited through the professional body for health service managers, the IHSM. It had an existing framework of professional qualifications which could accommodate the new programme. It also has an extensive network of members at all levels in the NHS who were mobilized to champion the course and act as mentors and in some cases tutors. The decision to involve HE and FE in the delivery of *Managing Health Services* arose from discussions with the IHSM, which had experience of partnerships with FE and HE and believed these could be usefully extended to embrace this course.

Accreditation of learners

An important aim of the OL delivery system is to enable training staff in Health Service organizations to offer a high-quality programme leading to a national qualification while retaining Health Service ownership of it. This is partly achieved by making materials available which have been developed using a range of academic and managerial experience that could never be available to a single OL centre. It is also achieved by a balanced relationship between the NHS and the FE and HE system in the process of assessing learners, moderated by IHSM as a professional body.

Managers who complete their studies through an OL centre are awarded the Certificate in *Managing Health Services* by the IHSM. Those who complete their studies through distance learning are awarded credit within the OU's structure of management qualifications. There is full transferability of credits between the two routes.

OPEN LEARNING CENTRES

Managing Health Services is now offered in over seventy OL centres across the UK. About three-quarters of these are based in Health Service organizations, with most of the remainder based in institutions of FE and HE. A number of the Health Service centres involve staff from FE and HE in the design, delivery and/or assessment of their programmes.

The development of open learning centres

Once the OL delivery system had been designed, attention turned to establishing it in Health Service organizations – district health authorities as they were then, units and occasionally regions. In the late 1980s, the comparative unfamiliarity of managers and trainers in the NHS with the concept of OL proved a major hurdle. The NHS was characterized then, and still is to some extent, by a tradition of sponsoring individuals on college-based courses and complementing these with short in-house training sessions. NHS trainers needed to recognize that their role in delivering *Managing Health Services* would be to facilitate learning, rather than to convey concepts, theories and models.

FE and HE probably experienced even more difficulty in using OL materials. There was inevitably resistance to the idea of using materials developed elsewhere and a tendency to try to incorporate them into a traditional lecture-based programme, or to supplement the materials with further theoretical input rather than focusing on transferring learning into the workplace.

The IHSM rapidly initiated a programme of support and training for programme managers to introduce them to OL.

For many learners from professional backgrounds, *Managing Health Services* was their first exposure to OL and to management development, both of which place heavy emphasis on the learner taking responsibility for his or her own learning. Learners whose professional training had been strongly curriculum-based, rigidly paced and well structured needed help in adapting to a new approach to learning. It was recognized early on that delivery centres would have to be able to support this shift in learning style.

Many centres based in Health Service organizations needed advice on assessment and quality assurance. Those based in institutions of FE and HE needed to gain a better understanding of the NHS and to appreciate how the programme could be adapted in response to the specific cultures and agenda of local health authorities.

The organizational development dimension

Managing Health Services had been primarily intended as a means for individual managers to develop their managerial effectiveness and acquire a management qualification. Access to learning opportunities had been a key rationale for using OL. There are no restrictive entry qualifications, and many delivery centres are at the individual's place of work or nearby. Individuals do not need to take extended periods out of work to study, and the programme is designed to be helpful to learners with non-standard work patterns.

It soon became apparent that a number of the features of the programme made it suitable not only to benefit individuals but also as a vehicle for organizational development. At the same time, the NHS was beginning to develop greater interest in linking management development to organizational objectives. OL offered opportunities to tailor the supporting tuition to local concerns. This enabled learning to be quickly consolidated through workplace experience, and organizations soon began to notice the benefits.

In many centres, change management and fostering a management culture became the theme for tuition; in others the professional/managerial interface or quality were the dominant issues. Senior managers were brought in to run workshops, providing a useful forum for a focused exchange of views. In some centres self-help groups or learning sets were established, which not only provided peer support for learning but also proved to be enduring vehicles for multidisciplinary communication within organizations. In addition, mentoring became a means of developing a cohort of people within the organization who were actively reflecting on management issues and exchanging ideas across traditional departmental and professional boundaries.

Health Service organizations have increasingly wanted to exploit the flexibility within the *Managing Health Services* delivery system to develop a programme tailored to their own concerns. This shift to a concern with organizational development as well as individual development potentially posed a threat to the continuation of OL centres based in institutions of FE and HE, which were perceived as being unlikely to be able to offer this organizational focus.

Accreditation of open learning centres

Each OL centre is accredited by the IHSM. A prospective centre approaches the Institute for advice about setting up a delivery system. When the centre is ready, a written plan for delivery is submitted to the Institute and scrutinized by a panel. Most members of the panel are practising managers in the NHS who have a particular interest in management development and experience of mentoring or as visiting lecturers at local colleges or universities. Before a centre is accredited there is a site visit by the panel.

The aim of the accreditation is to establish national standards for the delivery of *Managing Health Services*, while allowing for some variation in tuition and assessment arrangements. There are, for example, minimum standards concerning the experience of the tutorial team, support for learners and quality assurance systems, but centres have some flexibility over how much tuition they offer and in what form. The in-course assignments are set and marked locally, though they must comply with national guidelines. The end-of-course examination is set and marked by the IHSM centrally.

Quality control in assessment

The IHSM appoints an external assessor to each delivery centre. Assessors may be practising managers or they may be drawn from academic institutions. They are required to have previous experience of assessment and a good understanding of the NHS. Sharing experience between assessors from FE and HE and those who are practising managers has proved to be a fruitful way of ensuring that assessment is imaginative and relevant to the needs of Health Service managers, as well as being comparable with standards elsewhere in FE and HE. Each assessor works with four or five centres and his or her primary responsibility is to ensure that the in-course assignments are designed and assessed to appropriate standards. In practice, external assessors have often become a valued source of advice to programme managers about all aspects of delivery.

The Examination Board is composed of academics and managers. The fact that there is considerable overlap between the membership of the IHSM's Board and the OU's Board helps to ensure the credibility of the qualification. *Managing Health Services* has been given a credit accumulation and transfer scheme (CATS) rating by a university. This was negotiated on behalf of all the OL centres by the IHSM, which remains accountable to the university for the standard and quality of assessment, and is another important factor in giving standing to the qualification.

MODELS OF DELIVERY

The fact that *Managing Health Services* enables large numbers of NHS managers to achieve a recognized academic qualification has required the development of a variety of relationships between the NHS and both FE and HE. There has been an evolving role for the IHSM as a professional body in mobilizing and supporting these relationships.

Four main models of delivery have emerged, along a continuum from the point where FE or HE plays the role of the sole provider to the point where the Health Service has this role.

Model 1: Further/higher education as sole provider

Where an institution in the FE or HE sector delivers *Managing Health Services* as sole provider, the main benefits offered are a depth of expertise in the subject matter, curriculum design and assessment. Such institutions normally have systems in place for the development of programmes, tutorial support and quality assurance, whereas OL centres based in Health Service organizations often need to set these up from scratch.

A survey of what learners perceived as the benefits of studying in a college-based OL centre showed that they particularly value the safe environment, away from work, where management issues could be discussed openly. This aspect of openness is often overlooked in designing OL systems. Where management development is becoming increasingly tied into organizational objectives and culture, the opportunity for learners critically to explore concepts and alternative approaches to management is especially important. The same survey showed that learners also enjoy the opportunity to study alongside their peers from other organizations and backgrounds. Thus openness of access creates benefits in the type of learning environment which it creates.

Model 2: Involving the Health Service as client

Model 1 suffers the disadvantage of being seen as remote from the practicalities of management. The institution of FE or HE adopts the role of purveyor of wisdom; the onus for transferring learning to the workplace rests with the learner.

To counteract this criticism, some college-based OL centres have set out to involve Health Service managers and trainers in designing the programme, training mentors, facilitating work-based projects and evaluation, and commonly as guest tutors. In this model, the academic institution retains control over the programme but involves its clients to improve quality and marketability. The Health Service gains some influence, but the extent of this influence is determined by the provider.

This model works well when the academic institution finds imaginative ways of facilitating Health Service involvement. Managers do not always have the skills of programme design, for example, and their contribution has to be through opportunities that are provided in a structured way rather than simply offering a blank sheet of paper. The skills of managing client involvement will become an important part of FE's and HE's repertoire.

Model 3: Involving further/higher education as partner

Further along the continuum is the model where the locus of control over the OL programme lies firmly with the Health Service. The Health Service organization is the provider, but the expertise of FE or HE is bought in to fill gaps in skills available within the Health Service.

This model has sometimes been the basis of a genuine partnership between the Health Service and FE and HE. Instead of simply selling their services to OL providers within the NHS, tutors from FE and HE have worked alongside Health Service trainers in a way that has facilitated a mutual exchange of knowledge and skills. Trainers, for example, have enhanced their understanding of assessment processes, and tutors have developed their understanding of how the transfer of learning into the workplace can occur.

Model 4: The Health Service as sole provider

At the furthest end of the continuum from Model 1 is the model in which the Health Service is both purchaser and provider of OL. The programme is designed to suit the host organization's needs and to reflect its culture. In this model, though learning may be open in terms of access and availability, the context of learning is comparatively closed.

The demands of partnership

The criteria adopted by the IHSM in accrediting OL centres have generally discouraged centres from adopting models at either extreme of the continuum. However, developments in the culture of the NHS and the more performance-based management systems emerging in FE and HE may make it more rather than less difficult to create productive partnerships. Health Service organizations are giving increasing attention to fostering their own organizational culture; development programmes, particularly for less senior staff, are becoming more internally focused. FE and HE are coming under growing pressure to provide services in a way that can easily be translated into costs and prices. Neither of these trends is supportive of forging partnerships where skills and knowledge are exchanged across boundaries.

Yet delivering services through partnerships seems set to remain a significant theme for many parts of the public sector throughout the 1990s. It is an approach which challenges the model of expert-led services which has dominated both the Health Service and FE and HE in the past. It calls for a redefinition of the role of the corporate client from passive consumer to full member of the delivery team. This creates new requirements for team development, to support people in what are often unfamiliar roles.

Partnerships have to be managed. They require an investment of time and effort which needs to be repaid with tangible benefits including, for example, extended markets, more effective learning, increased skills or strategic alliances.

Partnerships flourish where there is an appropriate organizational infrastructure. There has to be sufficient flexibility for resource flows and reward systems to be adapted to cross-boundary working. Members of the team need sufficient autonomy to take decisions without constantly referring back to their respective hierarchies. They also need the commitment of senior managers to the venture. The partnerships developed through *Managing Health Services* have sometimes been vulnerable to changes in the policies or priorities of participating organizations. The support of senior managers offers some protection against this.

OPENNESS

The models described above raise a number of issues relating to the openness of OL, which have been a continuing part of strategic thinking about *Managing Health Services*. The concept of 'openness' has raised expectations among learners which have not been entirely met.

Assessment issues

Some of the limitations on openness have been inevitable consequences of the regulatory framework imposed by the IHSM, both in its role in guaranteeing quality and comparability with academic standards and as a professional body. Learners are required to complete the programme within a fixed period. Also, although there is flexibility for delivery centres to devise their own in-course assignments, these are primarily individual rather than group-based and have to be of types that will facilitate external moderation.

The end-of-course examination has been criticized as inappropriate for a programme where the most important learning objectives are related to practical outcomes and where a high proportion of learners have no recent experience of examinations. Fear of failing the examination both inhibits access to the programme and reduces the flexibility for learning within it. The IHSM is currently addressing this by piloting project-based assessment and introducing a competence-assessed route.

But the introduction of a competence-assessed route, based on the Management Charter Initiative's (MCI) Management I Standards, may create limitations on openness in another way. Learners will need to be in jobs with a sufficiently broad management content to enable them to collect evidence at work to demonstrate their competence across the full range of the MCI standards, and they will need the support of their line managers to do so. This will be the case even if their OL centre is based in a college or university. The style of learning is also likely to be less flexible and more dominated by the need to put together a portfolio to demonstrate competence.

Cost issues

The need to maintain a high quality of delivery leading to a credible qualification requires a Health Service organization wishing to offer *Managing Health Services* to make a considerable investment of time, and sometimes money, in tutor development, administrative systems and a supporting infrastructure.

The requirement for this investment, together with the comparatively high cost of an externally moderated qualification, has restricted access in some cases. This problem may become more rather than less significant if delivery centres want to use project-based or competence assessment, both of which are more costly and more demanding on tutors than traditional forms of assessment.

Individual needs versus organizational needs

Another issue relating to openness arises when the programme is closely linked with performance management within a Health Service organization. When learners come on to a programme because their management development needs have been identified through an appraisal process, it is an advantage that they have clear learning objectives that are supported by their managers. However, the link with appraisal has resulted in some learners feeling obliged to join the programme, and the pressure to succeed then lies in external rather than internal motivation.

As a professional body which is not accountable to any one employer within the Health Service, the IHSM has been keen to preserve the opportunities for independent management development which an OL programme should provide. The involvement of line managers in supporting the learning of their staff is welcomed, but there is a fine line between support and inhibiting learning through focusing too narrowly on organizational cultures and priorities. Learners must be able to explore views which are critical of their organization and to develop management styles which reflect their personal histories and preferences. The tendency in the NHS to foster exclusive corporate cultures may inhibit discussion within groups drawn from different organizations. The ability to create an OL environment in which groups of learners can develop and sustain a high degree of trust is an important skill for tutors from FE and HE.

Being able to use an OL programme to develop a management style which is personal to the learner is particularly important for women and people from ethnic minorities. Managing diversity involves providing development opportunities which allow for variation from, and challenge to, accepted management models. When a single set of learning materials is used as the basis for tuition and assessment, there is a danger that openness to alternative ideas will be limited. Some learners have reported experiencing the materials as closing down options rather than opening them up, and this is an important issue for tutor development.

THE BENEFITS OF THE PROGRAMME

The establishment of *Managing Health Services* as an OL programme has brought a range of benefits, both anticipated and unanticipated, to the NHS and to those institutions of FE and HE that have participated in various ways.

Benefits to the NHS

Besides enabling significant numbers of NHS managers to obtain a nationally recognized qualification, the programme has enabled many NHS trainers to develop their expertise and their confidence. The process of preparing an application for centre accreditation was designed to be developmental and trainers have obtained support and advice from their own organizations, from the IHSM and from FE and HE. For many trainers, this was the first time that they had designed a programme to run for a period of months, set up assessment systems and given serious attention to formalized monitoring and evaluation. In some cases, trainers have used this new-found expertise to apply for accreditation of other programmes. Once *Managing Health Services* became established, the IHSM encouraged programme managers to network among one another and set up meetings and a newsletter to facilitate this. Trainers have also benefited from access to the management expertise which is encapsulated within the learning materials.

A further benefit to the NHS has been the involvement of mentors and line managers in supporting learners. This has been encouraged by the production of guidelines for mentors, induction events for mentors organized locally and by the IHSM, and regular contact between programme managers and learners' line managers. Line managers have also been involved in local evaluation of *Managing Health Services*, giving them greater insight into its objectives and achievements. The participation of mentors and line managers in an NHS-based management development programme has enhanced their understanding of management development and consequently their willingness to embed a learning culture within their organizations. A significant culture change has taken place in some NHS Trusts, which have supported a number of cohorts of learners, with line managers, learners and mentors all adopting a more managerial approach to their work.

Delivering a national programme through local centres within the NHS has raised the profile of management development in the organizations hosting it. Trainers report having more regular contact with senior managers, who in turn have gained a better understanding of how management development can support organizational object-ives. There have also been examples of organizational benefits from projects com-pleted by learners as part of their in-course assessment.

Benefits to further/higher education

A survey of universities and colleges which have been involved in the programme showed that the main benefits lie in opportunities to get closer to the NHS and thus to keep in touch with developments in the Service. As one of Europe's largest employers, the NHS represents a major market for education providers. An OL programme with clear links with Health Service objectives provides a forum for tutors in colleges and universities to establish partnerships with NHS trainers, in which the specialist expert-ise of FE and HE is exchanged for a better understanding of the cultures and structures of the NHS. The involvement of colleges and universities in supporting mentors and line managers provides the basis for establishing networks within the NHS, which can be used to market other educational services and as a resource for research projects to draw upon. Surprisingly, these latter opportunities have not so far been much used by academic institutions.

There have also been opportunities for colleges and universities to provide consult-ancy to Health Service Centres which are designing OL programmes for the first time, especially to provide training in assessment techniques. Additionally, credit transfer systems can be used to ensure that learners from the programme can move easily into higher-level courses in FE and HE.

The learning materials have proved to be a source of development for tutors: using them has increased their understanding of how interactive study materials enhance learning, and this understanding has been transferred into other programmes. Tutors have also found a wealth of examples and activities in the materials which they can use in other courses.

Managing Health Services has enabled colleges and universities to develop partnerships with the NHS of a variety of kinds. Some of these have challenged existing skills and attitudes, for example towards traditional approaches to marketing and costing and accepted concepts of expertise. The involvement of IHSM as a professional body which has a strong commitment to the NHS as well as sharing some of the values of FE and HE has helped to facilitate the development of these partnerships.

THE FUTURE

The experience of *Managing Health Services* has been, broadly speaking, a very positive one both for organizations within the NHS and for those in FE and HE that have been involved. Over 6500 managers enrolled in the programme between 1990 and 1993. Its success has been such that, in 1993, an updated and expanded version of the materials was launched.

The NHS Training Directorate and the Social Services Inspectorate have also commissioned a further suite of learning materials, the *Health and Social Services Management Programme*, directed towards the needs of middle and senior managers in the health and social care sector. These materials have been developed collaboratively by the Open Learning Foundation and the OU's Open Business School. They are being presented in both OL and distance learning modes. OL centres for the new programme have been able to build on the experience of the IHSM in establishing OL centres for *Managing Health Services*.

Chapter 9

Motion: A Visual Database – Learning with Interactive Video

Gil Graham and Rod Macdonald

INTRODUCTION

Motion: A Visual Database is a Laservision interactive videodisc containing some two hundred examples, filmed in slow motion, of moving objects in the laboratory and the real world, and intended to provide students with material for the study of kinematics and dynamics. The disc is packaged with unique motion analysis software, and there is a user guide, which explains the principles and procedures of such analysis along with a number of suggested student investigations tailored to encourage independent study. The package has been used successfully to address the specific learning needs in this area of study of the increasing number of *ab initio* students in science and engineering, and is equally applicable in other disciplines such as sports science and dance.

This chapter describes the capabilities of the Laservision system, and its applicability to flexible learning generally. It then considers the benefits provided by *Motion* in physics education, as well as some of the pitfalls.

INTERACTIVITY AND THE MOVING IMAGE

There is nothing new about interactivity. Human interaction at different levels has always been a feature of instruction and learning. The equivalent of some simple forms of this interaction is provided by traditional computer-based learning materials which offer a branching pathway through what is to be learned, providing additional information and examples to clarify a point which the learner is having difficulty in grasping. But in such a system the learner is constrained by the program into pursuing predetermined learning outcomes, unable to follow a path stimulated by his or her own interest or curiosity through the material on offer.

Equally, there is nothing new about the use of photography, film or video to show or demonstrate to learners processes or activities to which they could not otherwise gain access. Access might be impossible for several reasons: for example, the phenomenon might be a one-off; it might be invisible to the naked eye, because of its size and/or speed; it might be too dangerous to allow students to get close enough to it to observe it; or it might be prohibitively expensive to repeat it for every new cohort of learners. Almost from the moment it was invented, film has been used to record such phenomena, in social sciences such as anthropology as well as in the physical sciences.

However, film and videotape suffer from the disadvantage of being forwardly linear in their delivery. Playing the film or tape enables the viewer to observe the phenomenon, and perhaps to reach some qualitative conclusions about it. But without expensive equipment it is difficult to reverse a film or videotape or to stop it at a specified point to examine the phenomenon in detail, to step through frame by frame to study and analyse quantitatively how the phenomenon changes through time, or to move rapidly and accurately to a different section of the programme. None the less film does permit the time-base of observations to be changed, by filming with a camera running at higher than normal speeds to produce slow motion, or at lower than normal speeds to produce speeded-up motion or time lapse.

LASERVISION: THE INTRODUCTION OF INTERACTIVITY

The Laservision videodisc, developed by Philips in 1977, provided for the first time at a reasonable price a device which made each frame of video (or film transferred to video) as accessible as the pages of a book. Interactive video (IV) technology is described here in some detail because the *Motion* project depends on specific features of Laservision for its operation, particularly as a flexible learning application. (There are also non-interactive (linear) videodiscs and players: references hereafter are to IV discs and players unless specified otherwise. Interactive videodisc players will play non-interactive discs, but not vice versa.)

Interactive videodiscs are made to one of two standards: on a PAL disc (the standard used in the UK and most other European countries) one second of video consists of 25 frames; on an NTSC disc (the system used in the USA and Japan) one second of video consists of 30 frames. A PAL interactive videodisc carries about 37 minutes per side (discs may be double sided) of 'full motion' video or up to 56,000 still frames, or a mix of stills and moving images. The disc is 12 inches in diameter, much larger than a CD, and IV players also tend to be larger, and more expensive.

In this context 'full motion' means that each frame is recorded on the disc in its entirety and is played at the correct frame rate. This is more space-consuming on the disc than is the technology used in Philips' more recent product CD-I (Compact Disc Interactive), where some frames ('key frames') are recorded in their entirety, but others are recorded by encoding only those parts which differ from the previous key frame. These 'differenced' frames can be accessed, but only by building them up from the previous key frame. On a videodisc every frame has a unique number (its 'address') and can be accessed directly. The maximum access time, to jump from frame 1 to frame 56,000, is about three seconds.

An IV disc may be played forward or in reverse at normal speed, in slow motion or speeded up; or it may be stopped at any frame. The quality of the still-frame is excellent, with none of the instability often observed in tape-based systems. Because it is 'read' by a laser there is no physical wear on the disc even when it is left in still-frame mode for a very long time. Laservision discs can also carry two audio tracks.

Depending on the source material, sound and vision can be of broadcast quality. The videodisc player can be controlled by a simple hand-held remote control, with Play, Reverse, Still, etc., buttons, and a numeric key pad on which the user taps in the frame number to which he or she wishes to jump.

This simple configuration, of player, screen and remote control, is often referred to as Level One IV, following a classification system devised by the Nebraska Interactive Video Group in the early 1980s.

As well as sound and vision, it is possible to encode software on the disc itself, to be used with a more sophisticated player which has some on-board programmable memory. This is a Level Two system. However, because such a system has only limited capacity, and because the on-disc software cannot be altered once the disc has been pressed, few IV applications exploit this possibility.

In a Level Three system, the player is connected to and controlled by a computer. As personal computers (PCs) have become cheaper, more powerful and more widely available, IV applications have tended to be designed at this level. Once the player is connected to a computer with the correct interfaces installed, it becomes possible to view the images from the disc full-size on the computer's screen, to overlay computer-generated text or graphics onto the image, and to use the computer to 'steer' the disc. The structure imposed by software on the learner's progress through the disc may be designed to be more or less flexible, and may incorporate assessment. *Motion* is an example of this use of IV.

Players can also be linked to a bar-code reader, which can be used to 'swipe' codes with a light pen to steer the disc, to play through specified sequences of frames, and answer pre-set multiple-choice questions.

EDUCATIONAL APPLICATIONS

A number of educational applications immediately suggest themselves for the basic videodisc player with just a hand control. The disc could be filled with still pictures, for example, providing a large and rapidly accessible collection in a virtually indestructible format. A simple printed catalogue, listing the contents of the disc frame by frame, would provide users with sufficient information to enable them to navigate easily across the disc in response to their own interests, making their own connections and creating their own structure for the material (what in the context of the good old-fashioned book one would have called 'browsing'!).

More elaborately, the printed text might include suggested pathways for the student to follow. Recent discs from the Musée d'Orsay and the Louvre exploit the technology in this way. Each museum has produced a disc which gives a linear full motion 'guided tour' of the museum on one side, supported and expanded by an interactive collection of images of the museum's holdings on the other. The discs are accompanied by a printed transcript of the narration of the guided tour, which gives cross-references to frame numbers on the interactive side of the disc where the user can find more pictures of the works seen on the guided tour, as well as of other works in the collection related to them.

This offers users, in the case of the Musée d'Orsay disc for example, one interpretation of the development of French art and art collections in the nineteenth century, while at the same time leaving it open to them to come up with a different view, based on the same information. And the physical organization of this wealth of information in itself permits users a number of choices, depending perhaps on the extent of their current knowledge of the subject, and the depth to which they wish to explore it: whether to begin with the guided tour, for example, or whether to disregard it and its transcript completely, and to concentrate entirely on the collection of stills.

These examples demonstrate the inherent flexibility of interactive videodisc, and its natural affinity with independent styles of learning. The main practical constraint on this independence is that the learner needs access to hardware which in the UK at least is widely perceived as expensive in terms of what it delivers, and is more likely to be found within academic institutions than in the home. Like most technologically delivered forms of learning, IV requires a large enough number of workstations to cope with the number of learners likely to require simultaneous access. This raises questions of cost which become even more problematical when we consider computer-controlled videodisc systems.

FAILURE OR SUCCESS?

Despite all its potential power and educationally attractive features, however, readers in the UK will be aware of the relatively small impact IV has had on education (as opposed to industrial and commercial training) here. To many educationalists at every level IV's history must appear to be one of 'lofty promises, low levels of adoption, and even lower levels of use' (Latchem *et al.*, 1993). The reasons for this failure have much to do with the marketing and pricing of IV, which have limited its spread. While by the end of 1991 there were videodisc players in 29 per cent of US schools with, by the end of 1992, over 2000 educational IV titles available, the figures in the UK are very much lower.

There are some 2500 IV systems in UK schools (equivalent to one machine in every ten schools), but as Looms reports, 'a significant number of . . . systems are no longer in use' (in Latchem *et al.*, 1993). An IV system costs at present (January 1994) about £3000 for an integrated PAL-only system, or about £3700 for a dual standard system. The comparable system in America (NTSC only) would cost under $3000.

There has been some public funding of the production of IV material for education at all levels, including *Motion*, but the number of titles published in this way scarcely reaches double figures. Few commercial publishers have undertaken major IV projects here: the best known are the BBC's Domesday Project, which introduced IV to the compulsory education sector in the early 1980s, and Evergreen Communications' series of six MIST (Modular Investigations in Science and Technology) discs. While the huge American catalogue of discs is most enticing, American discs, being NTSC, will not play on UK PAL players; the more expensive dual standard PAL/NTSC player is required. And by the same token, UK and other European PAL discs cannot find a market in America because the total range of generic disc titles produced in Europe is not large enough to create a demand for PAL players in America, quite apart from the problems of language which may occur. Also, many of the producers of generic discs lack the resources to produce and market their discs in the US. (There are a few exceptions: the Musée d'Orsay and the Louvre discs, for example, are available in both formats.) This then is the context in which *Motion: A Visual Database* has been produced.

MOTION AND MOTION ANALYSIS

> I often say that when you can measure what you are speaking about, and express it in numbers, you know something about it; but when you cannot express it in numbers, your knowledge is of a meagre and unsatisfactory kind; it may be the beginning of knowledge, but you have scarcely, in your thoughts, advanced to the state of Science, whatever the matter may be.
>
> Lord Kelvin

This has become a *sine qua non* of scientific education, as applicable today as when the words were first attributed to Lord Kelvin in the mid-nineteenth century.

Motion analysis is fairly firmly lodged in that part of the curriculum which we know as Physics. Physics is a rigorous discipline and is generally referred to as a 'hard science'. It is a study of the way in which systems interact with each other and the establishment of the laws and principles involved; above all it is a quantitative science. There is plenty of opportunity for qualitative discussions within the discipline, and it is used to great effect, but in the end it is the quantitative nature of the subject which distinguishes it.

Traditionally, this emphasis on the essentially numeric nature of the subject has led to teaching and learning strategies which self-select a particular kind of student, namely one who enjoys abstraction, positively revels in mathematical methods and will carry the torch for physics into the future. It may be that, in the end, this is the right strategy, but it rather depends on the objectives involved. If we are preparing young people for a research career in physics or engineering, then the rigour involved in traditional methods is necessary at some stage. If, on the other hand, we are trying to produce an educated and scientifically literate population, we need to examine our methods. Increasingly, this alternative objective is being accepted as the proper one for introductory physics.

There is a danger, of course, that by addressing a different audience we may be tempted to dilute the message to the point where, according to Lord Kelvin, it ceases to be science. The subject is and always must be quantitative, and however we approach it we must keep this in mind.

WHY STUDY MOTION?

The study of motion is a paradigm for the whole of physics education. Key concepts are introduced, units to make measurement are defined, observations are made, laws are formulated and principles are determined. The accumulated knowledge and understanding enables us to design practical working systems and predict their performance. But it is not only for such explicit applications that motion needs to be understood. It is essential in the life sciences, athletics, sports science, dance and any number of leisure activities ranging from weight-lifting to hang-gliding. Practitioners in these areas have rarely spent much time studying fundamental concepts, but they are often expected to embark on complex analyses of the motions involved.

We might expect that, because we have all watched things moving all our lives, we would have a thorough natural comprehension of motion. Curiously, our gifts in this respect are limited. Every teacher of physics knows what a limited perception the bulk of the population has of even the simplest motion. The educated view of motion, essentially the Newtonian description, is not the common default description; the popular perception is more closely related to early Greek notions of 'natural' motion. The psychology of perception, although fascinating, is not the subject of this chapter, but it does seem that most people need to be shown how to study moving things and helped in their understanding of motion.

There is a very good and well-known example of universal incorrect perception of a very common motion. From the evidence of paintings, prior to the early 1870s no one seems to have had much idea about how horses galloped. Almost every painting showed galloping horses in what has been called the flying gallop or rocking-horse position. It has been argued that the artists did know how the animals moved, but that they were using an agreed convention which was largely dictated by the expectation of their clients. This may be so, but why did every horse in every painting move in this phase-locked way? What changed things was the published work of the ingenious photographer Eadweard Muybridge, who invented a photographic method of recording the sequence of motion of a galloping horse. Multiple sequential images were recorded by an array of cameras triggered by trip-wires. The knowledge gained from this brilliant work showed that the received wisdom of the time was simply wrong. A new medium had revealed new knowledge.

MOTION IN THE LABORATORY

Motion: A Visual Database is a latter-day Muybridge technique. It is, as its title indicates, a database of short clips of filmed images of moving objects, chosen for their potential to support the teaching and learning of physics. Images of events such as crashing vehicles, sports activities, simple laboratory events and motion in the microgravity environment of the space shuttle, recorded on 16mm film using high-speed cameras, have been transferred to the videodisc. Novel software has been developed to enable the computer to control the disc and carry out high-quality motion analysis. The result is a unique laboratory resource to support the teaching and learning of motion analysis. Because the range of subject matter is wide, there is likely to be something that interests everyone. Furthermore, since the choice of subject is individual the system is ideally suited to individual work. And because the same phenomena may be analysed at many different levels, the visual database is relevant to the study of physics at other stages of education as well as the undergraduate context discussed here.

Given such a system, our approach to the study of motion can be radically different from that adopted in a traditional physics course. Faced with a desire to comprehend a particular action, we can first of all examine it in a qualitative way by simply running through the film. More detail can be observed if the action is viewed in slow motion or even by stepping through the action frame by frame. This level of analysis, although revealing, is essentially qualitative and precedes the real business of quantifying our observation. Quantifying motion immediately requires that we define our terminology. At this stage tutorials are needed to support further study. These could be independent computer-based packages run on the same PC as that controlling the system, but this is not yet a feature of *Motion*.

To move on from qualitative to quantitative analysis, the student first uses the motion analysis software to calibrate the screen, so that accurate measurements of image points can be made. Next the student steps through the chosen film clip and marks the position of the object being analysed on the screen frame by frame. The mouse is used to position the cursor over the object in each frame: clicking once on the mouse button leaves a small cross on the screen, tracing the object's motion, and also adds the co-ordinates of that location to the set of data which the software is collecting. Once sufficient data has been acquired it is stored in memory or on disk. The data can be processed in a number of different ways to enable conclusions to be reached. This procedure differs from the traditional approach in as much as key concepts and procedures need only be introduced as they become necessary in order to proceed to the next stage of analysis. This is not, in itself, a radically new philosophy, and several initiatives in science education have used it.

The pedagogical objectives addressed by *Motion* are that students should:

- become acquainted with the concepts used to describe motion, such as displacement, velocity and acceleration
- gain some appreciation of the scale of these quantities
- understand the concepts of momentum, force, work, energy and power, and their interrelationships in interacting systems
- learn a number of laboratory skills associated with the acquisition and processing of data, including calibration procedures, the use of tables and the production and interpretation of distance/time, velocity/time, acceleration/time and other graphs
- develop an awareness of random and systematic error of measurement, procedures used to reduce or eliminate the effect of such errors, and the limitations these errors impose on the conclusions which may be reached from experimental work.

If all of these objectives could be achieved by directed self-study using interactive video, it would have achieved more than any other single laboratory system. There are a number of reasons why the ideal is rarely if ever achieved, and some of these are discussed later. Although the starry-eyed ideal may not be realized, the system does have a lot going for it, not least because it allows students to address real problems, not just contrived laboratory events.

Consider the following example of how an analysis might proceed. The example selected is a popular one and the data quoted has been obtained independently by countless students. The event is a tennis volley: we see the ball enter the screen from the right, and see the player strike it.

Having decided to examine the action the student first uses the computer to find the first frame of the action. The action was originally filmed using a high-speed camera running at 500 frames per second (fps). Playing it back at the standard 25 frames per second on the video results in a slow-motion effect, but one in which detail can be seen. Stopping the action at the point of impact between the ball and the racquet, then stepping forwards and backwards a few frames, reveals that the ball is substantially flattened by the impact, and that it is in contact with the racquet for only one frame. This gives the first quantitative information – the duration of the impact was less than two frames, or less than four-thousandths of a second.

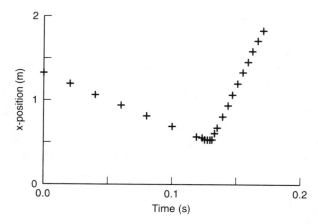

Figure 9.1   *Sample distance/time graph*

The screen is then calibrated for distance and time measurement using the fact that the action was filmed immediately in front of a half-metre grid, and the given frame rate of 500 fps. Once the screen is calibrated, the position of the ball is measured on a selection of frames both before and after the impact. At each measurement, three bits of information are recorded, namely the x- and y-position of the ball and the time which has elapsed from the first measured frame.

Using these data, the student then plots a simple graph of the x-position of the ball against time on the computer screen. This graph is reproduced as Figure 9.1.

The graph clearly reveals two sections, before and after the impact. If necessary a little tutorial assistance may be needed to interpret this graph. Straight lines on distance/time graphs indicate constant velocity, and the slope of the line gives the actual velocity, so from this graph the student can conclude that the ball was moving from right to left at a speed of about 7m s^{-1} before the impact, and from left to right at a speed of about 35m s^{-1} after the impact.

If the student is already familiar with the methods of measuring speed from a distance/time graph, he or she may choose to have the computer process the data and plot the graph of velocity in the x-direction against time directly. After all, data-processing is one of the major functions of computers, so once we know what is going on it is a job best done by the machine. The velocity/time graph is given in Figure 9.2.

This confirms the initial calculations of speed, but in passing we can note that there is a bit of 'scatter' in the plotted data. This is caused by the initial random error in the positional data being exaggerated by the processing method used. The extent of the scatter depends strongly on the sampling rate involved, and on the care with which measurement is made; it is usually improved by practice and the lessons learned are important.

From either graph we can deduce that the velocity has changed from 7m s^{-1} in one direction to 35m s^{-1} in the opposite direction, a change of velocity of over 40m s^{-1}. The duration of the change was less than 4/1000 second. Further tutorial assistance may now be needed to introduce the concepts of acceleration and force, and the acceleration of the ball during the impact can be determined. It turns out to be over 10,000m s^{-2}. This is already an interesting result, and probably news to any student (and most teachers of

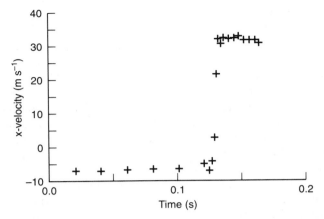

Figure 9.2 *Sample velocity/time graph*

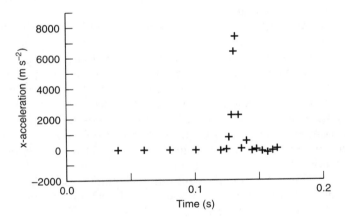

Figure 9.3 *Sample acceleration/time graph*

the subject). It is interesting because it is over one thousand times the acceleration of free fall due to gravity. Put in terms of dynamics rather than kinematics it implies that the force on the ball during the impact is over 1000 times the weight of the ball. Curiously enough, the weight of the tennis player is just a bit more than one thousand times the weight of the ball; is this what is meant by putting one's weight behind a shot?

Sceptics may doubt the figures, and point out that weight acts downwards not sideways, so why should there be any connection? Corroboration comes from the observation that the ball is flattened by the impact, and standing on a tennis ball achieves a similar effect.

The data can be further processed by the computer to obtain acceleration directly, and more advanced students could have elected to plot the acceleration/time graph immediately. This graph appears as Figure 9.3.

Some unexpected benefits

Notice that Figure 9.3 shows a single very large peak corresponding to the acceleration during impact. Careful examination of this shows that even though it is very large, the peak value is somewhat lower than the earlier calculated value. Either the previous hand-calculated value or this computed value must be wrong, or at least have a substantial systematic error. One of the problems of using computers to process experimental data is that the precise details of the way the data are processed may not be revealed to the user, who must assume that it is going to perform the task correctly.

This result provides an object lesson. In this case, for very good reasons not worth elaborating on here, the computer calculates velocity by using a weighted average from three positional data points, and calculates acceleration from three velocity points. As a result it actually uses five positional data points to calculate one acceleration point. But we know, from direct observation of the impact, that the ball was in contact with the racquet for less than two frames, so the computer has 'extended' the duration of the impact. The effect is that the acceleration peak has been broadened and lowered. (The really bright student might consider whether or not the area under the graph was altered by this process, and if not, whether a more accurate result might be obtained by some further number crunching).

The important message here is that computer-processed data can give misleading, even wrong, results. All students of science who ever need computers to process data should be aware of this problem, and exercise due caution.

In examining this single event, a very simple dynamic collision, students must come to terms with the concepts of displacement, velocity and acceleration, and be able to construct and interpret distance/time, velocity/time and acceleration/time graphs. In addition they have been made aware of some aspects of experimental error, and the limitations of computers in processing original data. They have been able to appreciate the magnitude of the forces involved in the impact. That is an impressive range of pedagogical pluses, but it is not by any means all.

Astute observers will question the calibration technique used: the grid used for scale is obviously further away from the camera than the action is. This means that there could be a significant systematic error.

Newton's third law of motion states that 'To every action there is an equal and opposite reaction'. The reaction to the force on the ball is the force of the ball on the racquet. We have already shown that the force is equivalent to the weight of the player, but if the racquet was fixed and the player hung from it, the racquet would undoubtedly break. So why does it not do so when this force is experienced many thousands of times during its lifetime? There is a good engineering response to the question, but we would be happy if the question was asked.

Comparison with other collisions

The event just examined is a member of a class of events, collisions, which is studied in considerable depth by physicists and engineers and at scales ranging from that of sub-atomic particles to galaxies. Engineers study collisions for a variety of reasons, but often to learn how to design packaging to protect fragile contents such as eggs or people. They also use collision tests to trial the designs they produce.

One such spectacular and well-publicized trial was a train crash arranged to demonstrate the integrity of a flask used to transport nuclear fuel. This event has been the subject of much discussion and criticism, but most of the criticism has been made without reference to any quantitative analysis of the crash. Using essentially the same procedure as already outlined, students can measure the acceleration sustained by the flask in this dramatic event. The result is very revealing: the acceleration was about $200m\ s^{-2}$, or about twenty times the acceleration due to gravity. This is similar to the acceleration experienced by a dummy in a modern car hitting a wall at 30 mph.

This acceleration is very modest, largely as a consequence of the collapse of the locomotive structure. It is substantially less than would have been experienced in the standard drop test to which these flasks are routinely subjected. In some respects it was not a severe test of the flask, but it is comforting that this trial demonstrated that standard engineering tests are often far more demanding than any realistic event is likely to be.

Comparing the tennis volley with the train crash, it seems that tennis balls can survive many thousands of collisions, each of which is something like fifty times more severe than that of the train crash, without ever fracturing. Perhaps the student might speculate on the nature of packaging for nuclear fuel transport!

OBSERVED STUDENT WORK

This, then, details how we might hope that a serious, dedicated and determined independent student would proceed through this one analysis and what he or she might expect to gain from it. So how does this scenario compare with our observation of real-life students, new to the subject of physics?

For a very small minority of them, the picture is not far from the truth. Motivated by a realistic event they persevere, learn the necessary concepts, and in the end produce some high-quality analyses.

For an equally small minority, the system has little more value than that of a casually watched video. Some features are recalled, but they are the oddities, such as a banana spinning in the space shuttle, or the unexpected method of drinking coffee in the same vehicle. These are non-science observations, unless time is taken to discuss the oddity involved and, importantly, to record the observation and pertinent points of the discussion. Simple entertainment can initiate an active interest but sometimes it is quickly forgotten.

For the bulk of students exposed to the new medium, not surprisingly, it is a curate's egg. Certainly motivation is increased in almost every case. Until the introduction of the IV system, they had been restricted to the analysis of contrived laboratory motion. Such motion is often pedagogically important, but dull. Furthermore, important experiments such as the study of free fall take only a second or two to perform, followed by extensive analysis and processing of the data acquired. The analysis took up most of the time. Now students can work independently, examining any activity which takes their fancy. The same event is often studied repeatedly, but the strategy of analysis is varied until a confident conclusion is reached. Because the chore of data-processing is taken over by the computer, more time is spent examining the action, and important but incidental detail is noticed.

For reasons which are not immediately obvious, students will spend long periods of time in front of the screen, looking at images, making measurements and plotting graphs from data obtained.

Paradoxically the power of the system both to acquire and to process data has actually led to the biggest problem encountered when using IV in this way. It is very easy to make measurements and quickly acquire a great volume of data. Data acquisition is unfortunately not by any means the only activity involved in motion analysis. In practice, many students appear to be overwhelmed by data, and are then at a loss to see how to use them. The exercise is incomplete without substantial parallel study of the important concepts and principles. It is unreasonable to expect any student to work out, from a few simple experiments, the profound laws of dynamics which evaded the best minds of the ancient world and were not finally formalized until Newton's time. Students must be prepared to support their study with substantial reading; perhaps it would be more correct to say that the use of the IV supports the independent reading.

The negative observation then is that many students appear to enjoy the activity of motion analysis using IV, but do not appear to be prepared to undertake the somewhat arduous parallel reading and learning of the very concepts necessary to complete the analysis. As a result they seem to be content with the collection of data, and the processing of these to create a number of graphs. In the absence of comprehension, any graph will do, since little or no interpretation is offered.

In some senses this means that the system has failed: students have not come to terms with the concepts involved, and have not understood the processing which they have undertaken. But, it must be emphasized, even this low level of outcome is not as low as would have been achieved by the same students using the traditional methods. Such students are unlikely to have the qualities demanded from creative research scientists, but they are very likely to become successful technicians capable of high-quality routine laboratory work, and this early exposure to computer-operated systems will serve them well.

CONCLUSION

Motion: A Visual Database is a unique application of IV designed to support the teaching and learning of the study of motion. Although initially designed to address the needs of teachers and students of introductory physics, it is remarkably well suited to independent study by *ab initio* students of the subject at any age. It is not complete, in the sense that it does require the student to carry out independent reading and understand key concepts, but it provides a set of stimulating images and powerful software tools to allow both qualitative observation and serious quantitative analysis to be carried out. Students who have used the system enjoy the experience, and in every case gain something from the enriched laboratory experience.

The application of interactive video in education is characterized by rapid development. Since this chapter was written, the pedagogy of *Motion: A Visual Database* has been transferred to a CD-ROM entitled Multimedia *Motion*, produced and marketed by Cambridge Science Media, 354 Mill Road, Cambridge CB1 3NN.

BIBLIOGRAPHY

Latchem, Colin, Williamson, John, and Henderson-Lancet, Lexie (1993) (eds) *Interactive Multimedia: Practice and Promise*. London: Kogan Page.

Louvre: vidéodisque (1989) Videodisc and catalogue. Paris: Musée de Louvre.

Motion: A Visual Database (1987) Videodisc, user guide and software. Cambridge: Anglia Polytechnic University.

Orsay: vidéodisque (1989) Videodisc and catalogue. Paris: Musée d'Orsay.

Chapter 10

Using Audio and Community Radio

Virtue Jones

INTRODUCTION

This chapter describes an 18-month project in which a number of Sunderland institutions combined to explore the viability of using community radio as an open learning (OL) medium. The project should be seen against a background of major institutional change during the period February 1991 to July 1992. During this time the Polytechnic became a corporate institution, underwent fundamental departmental reorganization, achieved University status and saw a rapid increase in student numbers. The city's two further education (FE) colleges were also working towards corporate status. The Borough of Sunderland was granted City status, but at the same time suffered the severe cuts affecting all local government, and Community Radio made its debut in the north-east in the shape of the newly licensed Wear FM.

To avoid confusion this chapter will refer to the 'university' and the 'city' throughout, except where the old names are necessary to understand programme titles.

The opening of the community radio station Wear FM in November 1990, on campus at the University of Sunderland, provided a set of conditions ripe for the development and exploitation of flexible learning using audio and radio. Overnight, almost, it became possible to reach an audience well beyond the campus and, significantly, to be able to speak directly to the very target groups among whom the university was trying to widen access – mature students, women returners and local people in an area where the take up of post-16 education was traditionally low.

Wear FM was one of the second batch of small community stations licensed under the Independent Broadcasting Authority (IBA) incremental licence scheme. Under this scheme contracts were offered only in existing IBA-regulated local radio engineering areas, and Sunderland's was the only contract offered in the north-east. The three-year licence permitted the contract holder, Sunderland Community Radio Association, to transmit to Wearside, reaching a potential of over a quarter of a million listeners.

It was no accident that the new radio station should be housed on campus and particularly in the School of Humanities, which had had a long association with local radio in the north-east. Previously, undergraduates on BA Communications courses had used the BBC's Sunderland studio and received training from the BBC's district producer (the prospectus even carried a photograph of students using this facility). Staff, particularly in social sciences, humanities and pharmacy, enriched BBC Radio Newcastle's education slot with a regular contribution of programme series, and there was a fortnightly input into the station's *Poly News* from across the polytechnic. One member of staff, Andrew Crisell, completed a 12-month secondment to BBC Radio Newcastle following production training at the BBC's training unit in London. Back in the university, he was able to use this experience to strengthen the teaching of radio, while in the wider community he was able to add his weight to Sunderland Community Radio Association's bid for the incremental licence.

By the time the licence was granted and Wear FM was on air, the vacuum left by BBC local radio's withdrawal of educational programming in the north-east placed an even greater importance on Wear FM's contractual 'promise of performance' to broadcast education programmes. This situation was further strengthened by the appointment as Wear FM's first manager, of Pieta O'Shaughnessy, an Australian broadcaster who arrived with a wealth of experience in campus and public service broadcasting, coupled with the energy and charisma to lead an unwieldy mixture of a small team of professionals and an army of volunteers. Their success was rewarded with the prestigious Sony Gold Award for Best Radio Station an the end of their first year on air.

So, with a number of experienced broadcasters among university staff and a reservoir of goodwill and enthusiasm in both the university and the community, conditions were ready to exploit broadcasting opportunities at precisely the time when new approaches towards flexible learning were being sought in a combined effort by the university and local colleges.

A Distance Learning Unit was set up, funded jointly by the university and Monk-wearmouth and Wearside Colleges. The unit was managed by a four-member team who represented those institutions and were actively involved in broadcasting on Wear FM to the extent of presenting their own weekly programmes. A radio producer was contracted to identify suitable material for broadcast and work with academic staff to develop programme material.

The unit's initial objective was to use Wear FM broadcasts to widen access to further and higher education (FE and HE), particularly from the local community. To this two further objectives were soon added, namely:

- to produce quality audio materials in keeping with the university's learning resources strategy
- to produce audio materials for external markets, for example the Open Learning Foundation and the university's franchise partners.

This meant that the unit would be working in two distinct media – radio and audio; but, while the finished products were different and would be used in very different ways, many of the production skills are the same and the same production facilities could be used in both cases. Later this was to have implications for the cost effectiveness of the whole project.

The first objective, to widen access from the local community, recognized the problems identified in Sunderland's successful bid for government funding for urban renewal in the 1992 City Challenge:

- low uptake of education by post-16-year-olds in Sunderland
- low attainment level
- high unemployment
- poor study skills
- consequent lack of confidence in returning to study.

The priorities, therefore, were to use radio to:

- raise aspirations
- raise awareness
- widen access by providing stepping-off points into education and training at many different levels
- facilitate a flexible learning approach, where appropriate, via both radio and audio materials.

The unique facility of Wear FM with its target audience of 25–40-year-olds in the C1–D social groups, coupled with the station's policy of day-part scheduling (whereby specific interest groups are targeted in specifically dedicated programmes) rather than the sequence programming now favoured by BBC and independent local radio, which aims to hold most of its audience most of the time, made it possible to target specific groups at specific times. This meant that Wear FM could target mothers in the, afternoon before children need to be collected from school, and 15–16- year-olds listening to the chart programme between 6 and 8 p.m.

Experience during the first months on air demonstrated that it was possible to broadcast prerecorded, structured programmes in such widely differing disciplines as chemistry, child psychology, quality assurance, and English as a second language and achieve good listener response with requests for programme notes, cassette copies of programmes, and enrolment on FE courses. Admittedly, actual numbers of identifiable responses were not large: but as a direct result of broadcasts two new child-care courses were set up, 17 students enrolled on the Science and Engineering Access course, 50 English-language tapes were collected by members of the city's small Bangladeshi community, and some close personal contacts were made with Bangladeshi women. This in itself was a significant step for all concerned in view of the sheltered domestic environment in which the women live. So although the immediate response may have seemed quite small, it was recognized that a new station takes time to establish itself, that many more people would have heard broadcasts without taking any immediate action, and that at the very least those listeners would have become better informed about some locally available educational possibilities.

Broadcasting also proved to be a flexible and effective tool for promoting courses, both in the station's regular output and in themed specials such as Further and Higher Education Week, which stimulated local initiatives to tie in with nationally organized promotions.

There were two main approaches to increasing awareness. One was simple-to-provide course information – what it is, where it is, who it is for and how to find out more about it. Course information in this form is easily slotted into the general output in much the same way as commercials. The consequent 'drip-feed' of information was supplemented by more in-depth interviews in programmes specifically scheduled to promote the university and local colleges.

The other approach, which was employed simultaneously, involved the broadcast of actual course content to act either as 'tasters' for prospective students or as a revision aid for existing students. Again, this was aimed at specific targets at specific times. This approach required a clear understanding of objectives and a high degree of co-operation between providers, producers and broadcasters.

Two examples illustrate how these approaches were applied, initially simply to raise awareness and increase enrolment. In fact, by translating teaching material into a different medium, radio projects resulted in the production of new teaching materials which are currently used in a multiplicity of flexible and OL approaches in the university and local colleges.

REACHING WOMEN RETURNERS

The first example involved the production of six 12-minute programmes on child psychology, and required the collaboration of three distinct agencies, as follows:

- The series was written and presented by Ann Kernohan, a lecturer in psychology employed with the Open Learning Van (an outreach facility run by the City's Leisure Services Department).
- It was produced by the university's Distance Learning Unit.
- It was broadcast by the community radio station, Wear FM.

The objective was to use radio to widen the audience for Open Learning Van outreach work in the City of Sunderland.

The programmes were targeted at women returners, particularly mothers with no formal education beyond 16, who could use their experience of child care as a 'stepping-off' point. The aims were as follows:

- to provide an introduction to child psychology based on a child-care course already being piloted by the Open Learning Van on one of the City's housing estates at the premises of yet another community initiative, Women on the Move
- to use women's own experience of motherhood to illustrate teaching points raised in the course (an early suggestion that illustrations should take the form of role play was rejected in favour of using the special ability of radio to allow real people to talk about their real experiences)
- to allow women in the target audience to have an input into the series
- to demonstrate the value of the target group's experiential learning
- to provide a starting point for further study.

Originally the child-care course had a greater emphasis on the practical aspects of child care and concentrated on physical needs. However, at the pilot stage, it was found that because the women on the course already had considerable experience and knowledge in this area, the course had little new to offer them in this respect. Consequently the course was modified to meet the students' requirements, and the emphasis moved away from child care and on to child psychology.

It soon became clear that women who have raised families know much more about psychology than they may realize, even though they may have had no formal education in the subject, their understanding may be unstructured and they may lack the terminology to express the concepts involved. By providing an introduction to psychology based on the target audience's experience of motherhood, the intention was to:

- introduce some psychological concepts
- enable the target audience to formalize their previously unarticulated understanding of child psychology
- provide a starting point for further study.

It was felt that community radio was an excellent way of reaching the target audience which had already been identified by the Leisure Services team with the Open Learning Van. During the 10-week pilot course at Women on the Move, the women were asked by the distance learning project whether they would be willing to be interviewed for a radio series on some of the areas covered by the course. After some initial reluctance to take part, it was agreed that the producer should meet the group to explain the aims and format of the series. Subsequently, four two-hour interview sessions were recorded at Women on the Move, following a brief outlined by the course tutor. The edited interviews were used to illustrate the teaching points made in the series and constitute approximately 60 per cent of the finished programmes.

Wear FM allocated 15 minutes to each broadcast, which included a 30-second cue and a 12-minute pre-recorded structured programme, and allowed 2½ minutes for Open Learning Van course information. This was updated each week to give precise information on the whereabouts of the Van, which provided a mobile drop-in centre throughout the city. Programmes were scheduled for transmission at 2.45 p.m. on Tuesdays, to allow mothers time to hear programmes before collecting children from school.

Apart from the acquisition of new skills (such as writing for radio and radio presentation), the experience of preparing the programmes gave a sharper focus to the content of the course, which as a result became more structured and more relevant to the needs of the target group. This was achieved without losing the informality necessary for outreach work. The experience of involving Women on the Move in the making of the programmes, together with the 10-week pilot course, made it possible to identify a clearly defined target group. This particular group was not being served by the existing OL audio materials that were available to the course at that time. For example:

- The target group found it difficult to relate to interviewees from different class and regional backgrounds. Not only were these differences immediately apparent in the spoken word, but the interviewees' cultural and social terms of reference were also perceived as alien to the target audience's personal experience. To a lesser extent this alienation is also experienced when using written materials.
- Moreover, existing materials were found to be inappropriate for mature women students who already had considerable experience in the physical aspects of child care, but who wanted to study child psychology.

Following the pilot courses, and as a result of publicity through the radio series, similar short courses were organized across the city.

Students who completed these courses received a Certificate in Child Care and Effective Parenting from Monkwearmouth College and were encouraged to use the course as a stepping-off point into FE. Of the original eight students on the Women on the Move pilot course, two enrolled for GCSE Psychology and two enrolled for Access courses at Monkwearmouth College. The remaining four, who felt they were not yet ready to attend college, asked for another 10-week course to be organized by the Leisure Services Open Learning Van.

The radio series established a model for co-operation between the providers (in this case the Borough of Sunderland Leisure Services and Monkwearmouth College), the production unit in the university and the community radio station. Most importantly, students within the target group were involved in developing the course to suit their own needs and, through the production of the radio series, not only publicized the course, which resulted in similar courses being run, but also provided appropriate audio materials for use on those courses.

In consultation with Monkwearmouth College, OL uses for the audio materials were identified in the Certificate in Child Care and Effective Parenting, Nursery Nursing and Health Education. These uses, however, depended upon the conversion of the pre-recorded radio programmes, which were originally produced just to whet the appetite for introductory outreach courses, into audio tapes forming part of specially written OL packs. The development is still some way off.

KILCOYNE'S CHEMISTRY

The second example, *Kilcoyne's Chemistry*, also grew out of a simple idea for a radio series, but has progressed through the conversion process to emerge as flexible OL materials now used on a range of courses from pre-Access to Level 1.

Once again, production was based on co-operation between a number of agencies. A radio series of eight programmes scheduled for transmission just before GCSE exams was planned as a revision aid. This had to be produced very quickly as the production unit had only recently been set up. The series was to be written and presented by the university's head of chemistry, Dr John Kilcoyne, and based on the chemistry core module of Monkwearmouth College's Access course. Dr Kilcoyne had already become a regular contributor on *Polyfilla*, Wear FM's weekly programme devoted to the then polytechnic, where his lively and often irreverent explanations of chemical theory had attracted very positive audience reaction.

This time, the objective was to use radio to present chemistry as an understandable and enjoyable subject to a wider audience. Specifically it was designed to provide a revision aid for GCSE and to increase enrolment on the college's science and engineering Access course.

The series was based on the premise that all science is founded on experiment and observation; that all theories, hypotheses and ideas must be tested by experiment; and that experiment can be carried out with modest, cheap equipment. The last was important bearing in mind that the target audience of students revising for GCSE would not have access to laboratory facilities at home. This was later to be of particular significance when the time came to develop the original content of the radio series into a truly flexible OL package.

The eight-part series was broadcast on Wear FM over a four-week period on Tuesday and Thursday evenings prior to GCSE exams. In order to reach the target group, the series was scheduled into *Wear Classy*, a two-hour chart-based schools programme.

Wear Classy owes as much of its success to its teenage presenters as to some smart programme scheduling to coincide with the great TV switch-off at the end of *Neighbours*. Speech items in the show are kept more or less to the duration of a disc: beyond that listeners simply desert the programme. (Educational broadcasting is littered with worthy programmes with no listeners.) This caused some initial worries – how could the material be covered in such small chunks? Clearly it had to be made to fit the programme policy if it was to reach the target audience. Put another way – the audience exercised the ultimate sanction over delivery of the material. Unlike the child psychology series, which had its own dedicated 15-minute slot, *Kilcoyne's Chemistry* would be only a small part of an existing programme. Moreover, that programme was based on music, not speech.

So, whereas the format had to be in keeping with the overall style and sound of the programme in order to reach the target audience, the content had to provide an effective revision aid to fulfil the aims of the project. Following consultation between the various agencies involved – that is the writer, producer, the broadcaster (Wear FM) and the user (Access course leader) – the agreed solution was to cover the content in eight broadcasts as planned, but to split each broadcast into two four-minute segments, separated by the 7 p.m. news headlines and a disc. For this to work, the segments had to be fast moving, entertaining and memorable; and, as possibly seven minutes would elapse between segments, the first segment had to leave listeners in anticipation of more to follow. Because of the transitory nature of radio, which gives listeners only one chance to get the message, a decision was made to offer support notes and cassette copies of the whole series. Although it was not envisaged at the time, these notes and cassettes ultimately sparked the idea of developing the materials into an OL package.

The series itself included four experiments that could be carried out by listeners at home using readily available kitchen equipment and ingredients and, to illustrate the point, the broadcasts included recordings of Dr Kilcoyne in his own kitchen showing co-presenter Andrew Crisell how to use a washing-up-liquid bottle and a length of plastic tubing to measure the rate of reaction of vinegar on bicarbonate of soda and, equally important, how to record the results. The series, then, was as much concerned with scientific method as chemistry theory, but the underlying message was that chemistry can be fun.

Several things happened as a result of the broadcasts:

- There was a good response to the offer of notes and cassettes.
- The series was rescheduled into *Polyfilla* and repeated, together with course information, just before enrolment for the next Science and Engineering Access course.
- Access enrolment increased by 65 per cent over the previous year.
- Cassette copies of programmes and notes were used in their 'raw' form as teaching materials during the early stages of the course to assist students with a weakness in basic chemistry.
- Colleagues teaching courses such as BSc Environmental Studies or BSc Health Studies began offering the tapes and notes to students who were struggling to reach basic chemistry requirements for those courses.
- Both FE and HE students found the tapes to be entertaining, confidence building and a very real help in understanding scientific facts and experimental method.

Responding to a questionnaire, several students noted that concepts that had proved baffling for years were suddenly explained in ways that even a non-scientist could understand.

Old barriers to learning chemistry were being removed, but still the tapes and cassettes did not go far enough. The broadcasts which had been produced very rapidly to coincide with GCSE revision had served the original objective of using radio to present chemistry as an understandable and enjoyable subject to a wider audience. Now a new objective emerged: to convert the recordings into an accredited OL module for use at Level 0 on courses where a basic understanding of chemistry is required. This was to be a much larger project. The emphasis was to shift from providing information to producing a flexible OL package.

Choosing the medium

The principal medium for the broadcast series was obviously radio, supported to a much lesser degree by written materials and audio cassettes. This had proved to be an effective means of reaching the target audience and achieving the original objective.

The strength of radio lay in its ability to speak directly to the target audience, and the success of the series lay in Dr Kilcoyne's ability to make an apparently difficult subject accessible and enjoyable to both the target audience and the 'eavesdropping' audience who inevitably heard the radio broadcasts. But producing OL materials for use on a range of FE and HE courses was another matter, and was going to demand some fundamental rethinking. Most importantly, it demanded the recognition that radio and audio are two distinct media. Switch on a radio and one expects to listen – to music or to someone talking; but a mere copy of a radio broadcast, particularly one intended for a clearly identified target audience, as in the case of the chemistry series broadcast in *Wear Classy*, will not serve the same function as an audiotape. An audiotape must be presented within the context of written materials. Give a cassette and a sheaf of notes to a student and the student invariably looks at the notes first for guidance and direction.

This presented two major problems for the production unit. First, as discussed, the appeal of the radio broadcasts lay in Dr Kilcoyne's style and delivery. When questioned about their reaction to the cassette copies, students invariably attributed their enjoyment and consequent understanding of the content to having heard Dr Kilcoyne's presentation. The materials made available after the broadcasts were inevitably audio-led, being mere copies of the broadcasts: consequently the cassette tapes had far more appeal in terms of content and presentation than the support notes, which were of only secondary importance in terms of the original objective. But herein lay an obvious weakness in their suitability as OL material. Clearly, with the cassettes in their present form and without active encouragement from lecturers, students were unlikely to be stimulated to listen to the cassettes, and so the whole value of the audiotapes would be lost.

The second problem for the production unit sprang directly out of the first. The Distance Learning Unit had been set up to produce radio; now that the emphasis was moving to include audio it was becoming apparent that to produce successful audio it was necessary to produce written materials also. This demanded new skills in an area in which there was little experience in the university at that time. Fortunately the strong links between the colleges and the university which had led to the setting up of the unit in the first instance meant that it was possible to draw on a very considerable FE experience of producing OL materials.

Building a production team

The principal tasks for the production team were:

- to write an OL course book
- to seek accreditation for the module
- to re-edit and where necessary to re-record the original tapes
- to package materials so that they could be used without tutor support
- to investigate marketing possibilities.

Piloting and evaluation were recognized by the team as being of crucial importance, but were outside the scope of the production unit, which closed in July 1992.

To accomplish these tasks the team needed a range of skills. Audio production skills were provided by the Distance Learning Unit's contracted radio producer (the author) who was simultaneously employed on several other audio projects in the university. This maximized the cost effectiveness of having to buy in production skills and the use of limited audio production facilities. The producer had the additional roles of co-ordinating academic input from the institutions involved and overall responsibility for production of the combined print/audio package.

Academic input, concerned principally with the content and writing of the module, came from Dr Kilcoyne and from John Nicholson, franchising co-ordinator and team leader for Monkwearmouth College's Science and Engineering Access course. This ensured close collaboration between the two main users, that is the university and franchise partners. To formalize this partnership, John Nicholson was seconded to the university for two days a week over a six-week period.

Product development and market research were handled by Nicola Jackson, a student employed on full-time placement from the university's Business School. This placement provided some extremely useful insights into what students expected from an OL package, and played a key role in determining the format of the finished product.

Using the materials

From the outset the package was intended for use in both FE and HE. In both sectors it was possible to identify students who needed extra help to reach basic requirements in chemistry. This need posed two main problems for the institutions. On the one hand, running a special 'remedial' course was very costly in terms of staffing. OL was an obvious solution, but existing OL materials required laboratory time (already at a premium) and therefore supervision, and that again raised the question of cost. What was needed was a package that would allow students to work without tutor support and without the use of laboratory facilities.

In a climate where colleges are being forced to look at the unit of resource and see that the greatest cost is staff, the question being asked is 'How can I get through the same amount of work in less time?' But the package has got to do at least as good a job as the teacher in the classroom. As John Nicholson says 'I want an open learning package which will support what I do in the classroom. I don't want one that I've got to work all the way through beforehand. I expect it to reinforce the basics I've taught.'

But the OL package has got to be sufficiently 'user friendly' for the student to take it off the shelf in the first place. John Nicholson describes the students who benefit most from foundation courses as those who were quite probably thrown out of class at school, who possibly got a few CSEs at grade 4 or 5. 'These people', he says, 'have ability but lack confidence. The wrong open learning materials, full of jargon and solid blocks of text, undermine that confidence even further. I want to build up that confidence, not shatter it.'

Since introducing *Kilcoyne's Chemistry* into all three of its flexible learning centres, Monkwearmouth College has found it is no longer necessary to run an expensive laboratory-based remedial course for weak students. Now students can take the package home and carry out the experiments in their own kitchens. *Kilcoyne's Chemistry* can be used as part of a formal course of study, with a recommendation that it should be worth 10 credit accumulation and transfer scheme (CATS) credits at Level 0 and be equivalent to 30 hours' learning support time or 40 hours if tutor-supported. Provision for the formal assessment of the package includes a practical exercise, similar to those in the package, the preparation of a simple report and a one-hour written examination.

The two examples described in this chapter of using community radio as an OL medium were piloted over an 18-month period alongside several other radio and audio projects. These included:

- *Electoral Politics*, a four-part audio and print package based on interviews recorded with candidates and their agents during the run-up to the 1992 general election. Produced initially as an audio and print OL package targeted at students on four separate degree courses, it was also adapted as a four-part radio series to encourage enrolment.

- *Psychology and Health*, an audio and print OL package produced to deliver the Psychology and Health module for BSc Podiatric Medicine. Units from this package have proved useful as support material for BA Communications, and with adaptation would be appropriate for other degree courses. An entire print-based package, *Microbiology for Dispensing Chemists*, was converted into audio materials, the object being to speak more directly to students whose only real access to teaching staff and laboratories is during a week's summer school. For these students the opportunity to hear difficult specific names and terms correctly pronounced and used in context was in itself an advantage, with the additional bonus of being able to replay the tapes as often as necessary. Once again, several additional uses were identified for modified versions of the audio material, with wide application on several degree courses.

- *Cancer and Anti-cancer Drugs*, a pharmacology audio package, produced, at students' request, as an audio conversion from existing written materials. Although in this case intended for postgraduates, it had much the same objectives as *Microbiology for Dispensing Chemists*, and parts of it have an equally wide relevance to other degree courses. Moreover, this material, like most of that produced during the project, was much more than an audio version of a written text. The tapes were produced to take full advantage of the strengths of the medium by presenting the opinions and experiences of people not normally available to the student in the classroom. In this case tapes included interviews not only with physicians involved in the treatment of leukaemia and in national clinical trials, but also with patients and their families, who described the effects of the disease and its treatment.

CONCLUSION

Much of the material produced during the project was never intended for broadcast, but the existence of community radio in Sunderland and its close association with the university was the catalyst which led to the formation of the Distance Learning Unit, with its dual purpose of using radio to disseminate course information to a locally identified target audience of potential students, and producing audio materials to facilitate the development of an OL approach on a wide range of FE and HE courses. A number of practical considerations emerged during the course of the project, which may be worth the attention of anyone undertaking a similar venture.

Large institutions often experience difficulty in transferring budgets between departments. This creates problems in developing projects beyond the specific objective of the pilot stage. This is a pity, because production costs are always heaviest at the development stage, whereas modifications for use on other courses can be achieved with very little additional cost to the institution as a whole.

Even where secondary uses are identified in original funding submissions (a feature normally viewed favourably in support of bids), there is a tendency, when it comes to the actual practicalities of production, to restrict project development to a narrowly defined objective exclusively serving the needs of the principal user. By and large it is easier to find new money for new projects than to develop an existing project beyond the pilot stage. Where secondary development is to take place, it is better to have interdepartmental agreement and funding from the outset so that materials intended to serve several degrees are produced simultaneously rather than in sequence. The overall cost effectiveness of production is adversely affected when the production process is fragmented.

In radio broadcasting the role of the producer is to provide the ideas and to ensure that those ideas are translated into programmes that achieve agreed objectives and reach desired target audiences. An audio producer has a similar role in the production of OL packages. Clearly, the basic technical skills of audio production are essential to produce good tapes which are well recorded, scripted and presented. Interviewing and editing too are skills which can make or break an audio production. These are the craft skills that an institution buys when it employs an audio producer, but the producer's role goes far beyond that by providing an understanding of the particular strengths of the medium. It is as important to know *what* should go on the tape (what the tape will add to the understanding of the subject, how that understanding will be achieved, whether it will be used with other materials and how it will be used) as it is to know *how* to get a decent recording. The producer is concerned with content, form and method: recording skills are a means of packaging the product which is developed in collaboration with academic staff. It is desirable, therefore, that the producer should be centrally involved in the development and production of the materials from the outset if the package is to form a cohesive whole. Otherwise the audiotapes may be no more than an add-on extra, an afterthought to include another medium, having little regard as to whether it will enrich the learning experience.

Audio and print materials make a low-tech contribution to OL that is cheap, easy to use and non-threatening. The human voice is still the most effective means of communication and, as many a stand-up comic will testify, it is often not the story but the way that you tell it that counts.

Chapter 11

Interactive Transmission by Satellite

Ray Winders

SATELLITE SYSTEMS

The European Space Agency (ESA) stimulated the use of satellites for education and training by launching the Olympus satellite in 1989. European institutions were given free satellite time for both technical and educational experiments and developments. ESA also provided transmission stations at the University of Plymouth and for a time at the University of London. There were transmitters in Italy and Belgium, too, which led to the formation of a pan-European consortium named EUROSTEP.

Satellites used for education and training are geostationary – that is, they remain in the same position in relation to a point on the earth's surface. In order to do this they must be above the equator and at a height of 36,000 km. This elevation is known as the 'Clarke Belt', since it was forecast in a science fiction article by Arthur C. Clarke in 1942. Each satellite has a given longitude and is separated from nearby satellites by distance and transmission frequency under international legislation. In order to receive a programme from a satellite, the dish must be pointing at the correct longitude – for example, Olympus was 19.5°W – and the receiver must be tuned to the specified frequency. The area covered by transmissions from a satellite is known as the footprint. Signals are strongest in the centre of the footprint, and as its edge is approached a larger dish size is required. The Eutelsat satellite being used for current education and training transmissions covers western Europe, and for most countries a dish of 0.9m is adequate. In the UK a dish of 1m or more requires specific planning permission. Currently a dish and receiver cost about £300 including installation, and feed into a standard television or videorecorder. There is a wide range of educational programmes available free of charge.

Satellite transmission is tightly regulated. Earth stations (uplinks) are individually licensed after site inspection, or companies are licensed to provide transmissions for a few hours from a mobile transmitter such as is used for sports. Transmitters for data are smaller and are known as V-SATs (very small aperture terminals). These are often used in a network to provide both transmission and reception. The ESA transmission station at the University of Plymouth, which has a 3.5m dish, is currently transmitting twenty hours of education and training programmes each week to a commercial Eutelsat satellite transponder being rented by the ESA. Figure 11.1 illustrates the transmission and learning process.

The University of Plymouth has created and transmitted over 650 hours of live programmes from its television studio. Most programmes have two or three experts in the studio and include specially created video and graphics. Because the programmes are live they are relatively cheap to produce. The control of the programme is with the lecturer rather than with a director following a carefully prepared and timed script. There is no post-production editing, voiceovers or music and, since they are scheduled, they go out on time. Some programmes, particularly to eastern Europe, are low-cost lectures. The lecturer delivers to camera a session similar to a normal lecture and uses a camera pointing vertically downwards at an A4 sheet in exactly the same way as an overhead projector. Most programmes include interaction by telephone, with viewers calling the studio with questions and comments during the programme. The Plymouth studio is linked to the transmitter, which is about 1 km away, by a BT cable which also gives access to the national television cable links used for programming by the BBC and ITV. This system is currently being used for programmes from Bangor, from London University and from Newcastle, all of which are cabled from local studios to Plymouth for transmissions. As well as transmission of recorded programmes and repeats, a Parallel ESA transmitter in Belgium also transmits 20 hours per week, giving a total of 40 hours between 8 a.m. and 4 p.m. on weekdays.

Satellites have an advantage in the transmission of data, particularly when the same information is required at several sites. Data only require a narrow channel and can be sent at the same time as a television programme without interference. The University of Plymouth has developed a datacard which fits an expansion slot on a standard personal computer (PC), linked to the satellite receiver. Data can be transmitted at a page of A4 per second and can include full-colour pictures. The data are received on the PC disk under a Windows environment and do not affect the use of the PC. Once the data are received they can be printed just as though they had been entered from the keyboard. Each datacard has its own identity similar to a PIN number, which means that data can therefore be sent to selected users who are either authorized or paying to receive the information. Transmission of training support materials by satellite ensures delivery and provides a means of charging the user.

INTERACTION

The triangular relationship between the expert, the learner, and the information or concept to be delivered is fundamental. Traditionally the trainer or lecturer has analysed and synthesized information for delivery in the lecture room. In theory the students present in the room then ask questions for clarification or extension. The students themselves can continue their study through individual or group research and discussion.

In most technology-based training there is a change from the interpersonal system to an industrial system. The material for presentation is prepared in advance and delivered as required to the student. Increasingly sophisticated systems of computer-

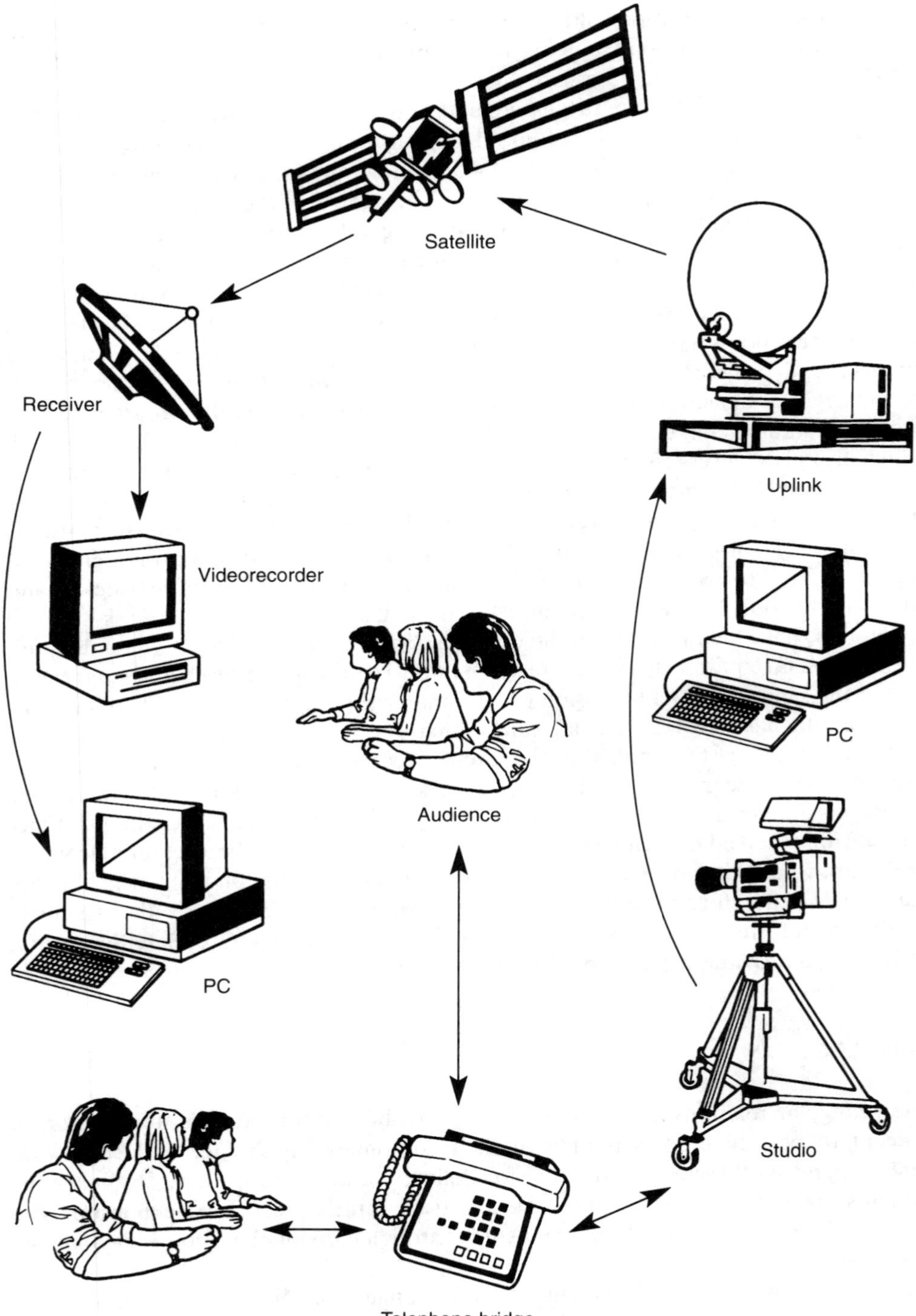

Figure 11.1 *Learning transmission system*

based training have enabled authors to present material in carefully structured and, indeed, variably structured forms. Interactive video (IV) has facilitated realistic illustration and simulation. There are, however, three inherent problems in the industrial mode of delivery:

- In order to cater for varying learner experience, speed and style, alternative pathways are necessary. Predicting and creating these is time-consuming and expensive.
- In areas where there is rapid change or where the learner population is small, a complex system may not be cost effective.
- Where correct solutions are not predetermined, a more interactive and creative style may be required.

The use of live teleconferencing techniques adds an extra dimension. The expert can be put back in the triangle and distant learners can form a learning community.

Various forms of interaction are possible using satellite or telephone conferencing, including:

- live questions to studio
- questions and comments which are asynchronous
- activities during or between programmes.

Live questions to a studio

The students at a distance view the programme and ask questions via a telephone line back to the studio. For group work a loudspeaking telephone device is used. Most of these consist of a loudspeaker and a number of 'press to speak' microphones, but there are problems associated with these, particularly 'howlround', which occurs when a student is speaking to the studio with the television sound in the room at high volume. The student's voice is then picked up by the microphone from the television at the same time as the direct speech. This causes a screeching noise. Several loudspeaking telephone conferencing systems have a device which turns off the received sound while the student is speaking.

It is useful to have an assistant or facilitator with a group of students if no lecturer is present. The facilitator prepares the room and checks the system, but also has the important function of encouraging the students to ask questions. Experienced pre-senters ask simple questions or ask for comments early in the programme to encourage later interaction. The presenter or lecturer in studio can either use a telephone to receive questions or have the incoming voice broadcast. Our experience has shown that some groups prefer the presenter to use a phone to create a feeling of equality and to reduce the feeling of personal exposure in calling the presenter publicly, but groups in industry tend to prefer the presenter to hear via the loudspeaker. Where preparation time allows, a photograph of the site or a map can be transmitted while the question is being asked. The possibility of computer videoconferencing for questions is described below.

Asynchronous questions and comments

A satellite-delivered lecture should be a stimulus for other activities in class or in groups. If the programme is in a series, questions can be answered at the beginning of the next programme. This proved quite successful with transmissions to eastern Europe, which suffered from the unavailability and unreliability of local telephone systems. It was, however, possible to receive questions by E-mail or by fax, in time for the next programme. Electronic mail has also been used during programmes. By having a screen on the studio floor, the presenter or an assistant can view questions on the screen and either answer them directly or, if more appropriate, ask the viewer to develop the question live by telephone.

Activities

If a programme is for an hour or longer, then a break for activity, such as asking each group to prepare questions or answers, may be appropriate. This is a useful technique when students are wary of using the equipment to answer. In a series for the British Library, the viewers were given searches to undertake on their library terminals to practise the technique which had been demonstrated. The programme then continued with the results of the search after a break of 15 minutes.

The value of interaction

Research on STARNET, a project funded by the Department of Employment,[1] showed that viewers valued the interaction highly even though an individual might be reluctant to participate. The questions gave a feeling of ownership to the group and went some way towards equalizing the power balance between the lecturer in studio and the viewers. In recorded programmes being transmitted as repeats, the questions from students are seen as being valuable even though the viewer is unable to ask a direct question. For the lecturer or presenter in studio, interaction provides immediate feedback, varying from checking on understanding to, in more advanced programmes, receiving valuable contributions from the experiences of viewers. Experiences formed a valuable part of the STARNET *It's Your Business* series described below.

PROJECTS

STARNET

The aim of STARNET was to demonstrate and evaluate the use of satellites for training. The project ran over two years with four full-time staff working with the then Polytechnic South West (University of Plymouth) studio and transmission teams. It was agreed that the unique selling points of satellite transmission for training are that it is:

- live and topical
- interactive
- designed to enable widespread delivery.

Three series were designed, each of which emphasized one particular advantage.

The first series, *A Competitive Edge*, was selected for topicality and rapid change. It dealt with aspects of advanced manufacturing technology which are changing daily. It was presented by Michael Rodd and featured experts from companies which were developing and experiencing the technologies in question. *Just in Time*, *Total Quality Management* and *Set-up Time Reduction* dealt with topics new to many in industry and of particular value to students in further and higher education (FE and HE) whose lecturers clearly needed authoritative and up-to-date support. The programmes were illustrated by video shot on company premises. Normally a representative of that company was in the studio to amplify the video content and to answer questions. In order to involve the audience, tasks were set during the programme. Students were asked, for instance, to write down the precise sequence of activities in a video of glass blowing. This illustrated the need for careful analysis before computerization or the introduction of robots. The programmes were supported by notes which gave more details on the content and set tasks related to the live programme. At the end of each set of notes was a preview of the next programme, including some questions for consideration by the watching groups before they were posed again during the following live programme. The series was transmitted, evaluated by an independent team, and improved before being transmitted in its final form.

It's Your Business was a series chosen to promote interaction. Whereas in *A Competitive Edge* the information was new to the audience and therefore most questions were of clarification, *It's Your Business* was aimed at individuals and small groups who had just started or were about to start a new business. Though the live format meant that new information, for example on Business Start-up grants, could be given, the main aim was to draw on the experiences of the audience. Several owners of small businesses came to the studio, with Khalid Aziz as the presenter. Two men who had opened up a business selling belts for trousers and skirts described their search for premises, which grew from a market stall to a town centre shop. At each stage a video was shown with a town map and the audience was given a choice of premises available. Following the telephone discussion the owners showed a video of their choice and discussed its advantages. The programme on raising finance gave more opportunity for participation. One of the studio experts was a small business manager from a national bank, who was intensively questioned by viewers who had not been able to obtain the loans they deserved! The medium provided a useful forum for the exchange of experiences from the wide range of businesses represented in the studio and at a distance. There was also an audience of FE and HE students, who obtained valuable first-hand information and opinion for their small business options.

The idea for the third series was to reach those for whom access to updating training is difficult because of distance or specialization. For example, in a previous audio-conferencing project, an FE college had been able to offer a Diploma in Acoustics, which is a required qualification for local authority officials, but is never viable outside London. Another ideal target group was pharmacists, who are required to be on their premises but also require update. Unfortunately the availability of receivers was not sufficient to make this option viable. Some programmes were designed for important minority interests, such as *Green Consumerism* and *Antarctic Pollution*. Others dealt with one-off special topics of wide interest, such as *Computer Viruses* and *Dyslexia*. A programme which stimulated a good response was *Telecommuting*, which explored the possibilities of working from home and later led to special programmes on telecottages.

All the programmes were evaluated by a team led by Diana Laurilland of the Open University. Their report is available from the Department of Employment.[2] They found that interactive satellite television appears to operate successfully where:

- programmes are relevant to students' and trainees' needs
- participants receive briefing and debriefing, and integrated study materials follow up the issues raised in the programmes
- participants are able to attend all group viewings of the programmes at the transmitted times
- a local facilitator is available to supervise technical set-up and to provide control and encouragement of the use of the audio bridge
- the local institutions value and give support to the medium
- an understanding of the subject is enhanced by detailed and anecdotal discussion and argument, or the subject matter is topical and requires immediate delivery, to ensure that benefits are maximized
- participants are likely to value each other's questions and viewpoints, to ensure that benefits are maximized
- participants are located near to a satellite receiving station, to reduce their time costs
- delivery costs can be shared with other projects also requiring satellite reception
- programme production costs are commensurate with audience size.

Thus the models most likely to offer the best chances of viability are corporate training, professional updating and international conferencing.

SOLSTICE

Following on this evaluation, a training programme by satellite for college and university librarians, SOLSTICE, was transmitted.[3] Librarians are required to carry out searches of electronic databases such as the British Library's BLAISELINE, for which training is normally provided as a three-day residential course at the British Library headquarters in Boston Spa, Yorkshire. Including travel, this means a trained librarian is absent for a week. In colleges often there is only one trained librarian, and even in universities there will be only one specialist trained librarian for a faculty or a group of faculties.

The British Library funded a course paralleling the residential course, using the same two tutors but delivered by satellite. Extra cabling and interfaces were installed in the studio so that the actual computer screen could be transmitted directly. The audience was able to see the movement of the cursor and the consequent screen changes, and was also able to receive real-time data over the system. Each group of librarians in 12 participating sites was also on-line to BLAISE in order to carry out activities. There were four programmes, in each of which a particular search strategy was demonstrated. During each programme questions were invited from each site, and the expert often used the system to illustrate the answer, following this up with a task requiring the search technique to be used. There was a short interlude in transmission but the telephone lines were open for questions. At the end of the break the group presented their findings, which were then confirmed by screens transmitted from studio.

Evaluation showed that participants rated the learning experience as highly as face-to-face tuition. Disruption to normal routine was minimal. An unexpected bonus was that the groups of librarians working together at each site were able to help each other and add considerably to the learning of the group, as well as giving support back on the job. A frequently mentioned advantage was that training was given on the librarians' own equipment in the situation in which it was actually used. Previous experience of travel to courses delivered in a special training facility had shown that in some instances operations which appeared clear during the course were difficult to apply when back at work.

VEHICLE TECHNICIANS OF EUROPE

The first award-bearing course in the UK to be transmitted by satellite was *Vehicle Technicians of Europe*. This is a registered BTEC course offered by Preston College in Lancashire. It consists of detailed workbooks to support the programmes together with an electronic mail enquiry service.

Preston College worked closely with both motor manufacturers and local industry, and indeed, some of the video used was supplied by the manufacturers. The programmes were presented from the Plymouth television studio by staff from Preston College. In each programme, experts in vehicle technology appeared in the studio to give authentic comment and advice. Sections of engines, carburettors, catalytic converters, etc., were brought to the studio to give a close-up camera view to the audience. The programme notes closely followed the content and were updated by electronic mail 48 hours before the actual broadcast.

All programmes were live and interactive. Though most of the 29 viewing sites were in the UK, there were some groups in mainland Europe who also telephoned in. Telephone conferencing was used throughout, but there was also extensive use of electronic mail for questions during the programme, where an E-mail screen in studio enabled the presenter to select questions or group them together. E-mail was widely used throughout the course, for example for sending and returning assignments.

Trainees worked at their own pace and were able to apply for assessment when they felt ready. In most colleges receiving the programme there was a local tutor to give on-the-spot advice. These programmes drew on the STARNET evaluation and incorporated most of the recommendations in a very successful series.

AREA TRAINING

This section considers some of the projects to which the University of Plymouth has contributed, which are indicative of the kinds of opportunity currently being opened up to bring often rapidly changing information to increasingly widely dispersed groups. One emerging benefit is the capability for creating learning communities for people who were previously isolated, either geographically or because of constraints on their time or simply because of the specialist nature of their interest, whether we are talking about potential A-level students in north Wales or research scientists throughout Europe and beyond.

Most colleges of FE are now linked to their local university in a local network, and there are numerous examples of FE and HE institutions sharing the delivery of courses. Often university staff visit students based in FE colleges to give key sessions and tutorials. This is expensive in both travel and opportunity costs, particularly if the session is repeated in several colleges. This is a particular problem in south-west England, where the area covered by the University of Plymouth extends from the Isles of Scilly to Bridgwater, a distance equal to that between London and Sheffield, and is served very poorly by roads. Jersey College in the Channel Islands has recently joined the consortium. Plymouth, in common with most universities, has campuses at a distance of forty miles from the main campus. The use of satellites to deliver courses to university campuses, and particularly to the wider campus incorporating local FE colleges, is now beginning.

Information technology training

A course on information technology (IT) featuring software in use was recently transmitted. The word-processing programme *Ami-Pro* and the spreadsheet programme *Excel* were introduced and illustrated. These packages were being made the standard in the university at the time. The computer screen was transmitted directly so that the audience could see each command in operation. A staff member who was unfamiliar with the packages sat beside the expert presenter and questioned each step, and there were also phone-in periods throughout the programme. As well as programmes on software there were others on computer viruses, and there was a very popular session on the new European Union regulations on working with VDUs. An interesting finding of the evaluation was the mix of viewers: secretaries 27 per cent, computing staff 24 per cent, other administrative 21 per cent, technicians 10 per cent, visitors 10 per cent and lecturers 8 per cent. The series was described and illustrated in a live transmission to the ESA conference in Seville, and a detailed report of the proceedings is available.[4]

Study skills

Courses to help students work more effectively have also been transmitted for the area. The programmes feature students as experts talking about their own study and presentation procedures. The programmes included *Essay Writing*, *Presentation Skills*,

Revision and *Exam Techniques*. The *Essay Writing* programme featured a mature student, who had won a national prize, describing step by step how she prepares for and writes an essay. In *Presentation Skills* a group of younger students described the process and problems of group work and group assessment of their presentation.

Supporting telecottaging

An extension of the existing network of established colleges and training centres is now developing as part of the telecottage movement. Telecottages are centres in rural areas providing support for small business in the form of photocopying and fax services, sometimes with secretarial services on a drop-in basis. There is growing demand for these also to act as local training centres. Satellite delivery is by definition an excellent medium for reaching remote areas, which will be the last to be served by fibre-optic or Integrated Services Digital Network (ISDN) systems. Some demonstration trans-missions have already taken place, and proposals have been made for both UK and European Union regional funding to launch an extended trial and demonstration.

WELSH CHANNEL

Wales has particular problems of geography, with the major areas of population in the north and south coastal areas. The Welsh Office has provided the first regional reception structure in the UK. Every community large enough to have a secondary school has been provided with reception equipment for community use. This is particularly important in the rural areas for two reasons: the decline in farming means there is a need for employment training, and the overall low student numbers mean that schools and colleges in these areas can offer only a restricted curriculum choice. One initiative has been to broadcast an A-level course in sociology from Gwynedd in north Wales to supplement class teaching and thus enable a subject not usually available because of low numbers to run. The system has also been used to teach basic Japanese to students in areas where Japanese companies have become established.

UNIVERSITY OF WESTMINSTER

Whereas in Wales the channel is linking regional groups, the University of Westminster is linking European groups at the forefront of electronic research. A series of specialist sessions on digital signal processing has been transmitted to fifteen institutions in eight countries, including Poland and Slovenia. The 'tele-seminars' reported the latest research. Most of the transmissions were direct from the University of Westminster and included direct viewing of real-time, computer-based demonstrations. A new feature of the programmes was remote presentation, in which a researcher in Portugal and one in Warsaw spoke on a normal telephone line to the studio. All the visuals were then transmitted by the studio on the commands of the researcher. This is a very low-cost method of bringing together on average eighty leading-edge researchers through-out Europe.

NEW DEVELOPMENTS

Eastern Europe

For the foreseeable future the greatest opportunity for development in which UK universities can participate is in eastern Europe, and there is also considerable demand for current and relevant training in Africa and South America.

As well as the fact that satellite transmission can cover a large area, it also has the advantage of not being dependent on the telecommunications infrastructure, which, in eastern Europe, is often unreliable. There is, however, a rapidly growing satellite entertainment industry, and dishes and receivers are readily available in most towns and cities. This means that live programmes using UK experts can be transmitted direct to local colleges in eastern Europe and received on low-cost equipment.

Currently there is a drive to deliver training to eastern Europe, funded by the European Union and the World Bank. The European PHARE (Commission of the European Communities' Programme of Assistance for Economic Restructuring in the Countries of Central and Eastern Europe) project will deliver training in multidisciplinary studies, the promotion of curriculum and course development, links with industry and the development of new modular course structures. Eleven countries are eligible for funding, with countries of the former USSR also being funded by the Technical Assistance to the Commonwealth of Independent States (TACIS) programmes. Funding totals more than one billion pounds. Some training needs are common to all countries and the cost of flying out teams of experts on a regular basis would be prohibitive: delivery of learning using new technologies is therefore very relevant.

In this context, the University of Plymouth has already begun transmissions. With the help of the British National Space Centre and the ESA, a V-SAT receive-and-transmit station was supplied to the Institute of Radioelectronics at Kharkov in the Ukraine. The V-SAT received full video and could transmit voice and data in return, thus by-passing the unreliable telephone system. Series on computing and business were successfully transmitted, with questions being asked live over the satellite link. The data transmit/receive facility enabled the Institute to link in to the university databases in the UK and to participate in group software for electronic design – the ultimate wide area network!

A regular series of programmes has also been transmitted to Sofia, in Bulgaria. A new curriculum centre is proposed for the Balkans, which will use the satellite delivery to support local groups and to provide specialist support to visiting tutors. Data will be transmitted and linked to the new countrywide broadband network linking all Bulgarian universities.

Technical advances

There is a convergence of video and computer technologies. As more information can be carried on a given band width, there are two advantages for satellite transmissions. Full motion video transmissions from studios are using 27 MHz of band width. The development of compression techniques already makes video at 8 Mbit/s possible, and for limited movement, such as in a lecture, 2 Mbit/s or even less are acceptable.

The cost of video CODECS (enCOder-DECoders) is high at present, but it is expected that the receive decoders will be available for under £200 in 1995, which makes equipment for educational centres viable. If transmission at, say, 6 Mbit/s is viable, up to four programmes could be carried simultaneously on one satellite transponder, thus reducing costs from perhaps £600 to £150 per hour.

Video compression is already making limited videoconferencing possible using desk-top computer/camera units. Using ISDN2 at 128 kbit/s, the small camera on top of the computer sends a picture of the operator together with voice and data. The picture is acceptable for a still 'head-and-shoulders' portrait of the speaker, but movement is blurred. The new SUPERJANET data links to all UK universities include videoconfer-encing at ISDN6 – 384 kbit/s. At this speed, limited movement is possible. Though most of these systems are currently point to point, linking experts and questioners by ISDN to studio for satellite transmission to a Europe-wide audience shows enormous potential. Experts in Aberdeen, London and Paris could in turn contribute to a programme. The head-and-shoulders picture could be 'windowed', just as reporters are shown on TV news programmes, or could take up the corner of a screen while a full data screen is directly transmitted. The system would also enable questioners to appear on screen or to clarify their questions with data transmission. This concept brings the low-cost global village much nearer.

Links between satellite and cable are also developing. EUROSTEP programmes are already received by ANTWERP cable and distributed to homes. Blackburn cable in Lancashire is supplementing its cable education and training series with satellite delivery. It seems sensible that, as cable develops, urban areas can be served direct to home by cable while more remote areas are served direct by satellite.

CONCLUSION

The first stage of transmitting live interactive programmes supported by data has proved successful, and it has been demonstrated that satellite transmission is particu-larly cost effective when:

- there are large numbers of participants
- expertise is scarce
- rapid update of knowledge is needed.

But there is still a long way to go before the use of live interactive programmes comes to be recognized as 'normal'.

In the USA, the National Technological University is already transmitting cost effective courses. Reception is free of charge but students must register and pay for course notes, examination and certification. In the UK there has been little tradition of delivery of distance education using live media. However, the modularization and franchising of courses, together with National Vocational Qualifications (NVQs) and other national standards, have created a new climate of mutual recognition, and a willingness to look at new learning strategies. Delivery to homes or local centres throughout Europe may not be far away.

NOTES

1. Armstrong, B. (1991) *STARNET – Interactive Training by Satellite*. Sheffield: Department of Employment.
2. Laurilland, D. (1991) *STARNET Evaluation Project Final Report*. Sheffield: Department of Employment.
3. Millard, P. (1992) *The SOLSTICE Project*. Department Report 6072. London: British Library Research and Development.
4. European Space Agency (1993) Proceedings of the Olympus Utilization Conference, Seville. Noordwijk: European Space Agency.

Chapter 12

Action Learning as a Means of Helping Professionals into a New Management Role

John Bothams

INTRODUCTION

This chapter describes how action learning was used in the development of consultant medical practitioners in their new role as medical directors of Scottish National Health Service Trusts. The programme provided an opportunity to explore the potential and the limitations of action learning as a way of understanding management action, diagnosing management needs and establishing ways of meeting these needs more effectively. The main thrust of this chapter is to examine the processes of interactive learning and to explore the dynamics of the learning relationship. The outcomes of this particular action learning programme are considered from the perspective of the participants and the facilitators.

More specifically, this chapter sets out to:

- explore the background to the programme and identify the issues and values which influenced how the action learning programme was set up and facilitated
- comment on some of the practical techniques we used to support the interactive learning *process*, including taperecording discussions for later reference and analysis, and cognitive mapping
- illustrate how the opportunity was taken to use the action learning sets themselves as the basis for collaborative research. As well as casting some light on the learning processes which take place in action learning, this provided further insight for participants into how they think and operate as managers, and strongly reinforced the learning partnership between the university and the clients, at corporate and individual level.

'Closer involvement of doctors is so critical to effective management', said Griffiths of the Health Service in 1983.[1] Ten years on from then I found myself involved in what must be the biggest expansion of involvement of doctors in managing the Health Service. To be precise, I was involved in providing a development programme devised by Strathclyde Graduate Business School (SGBS) in conjunction with and at the request of the Management Development Group (MDG) of the NHS in Scotland.

While the trust approach had taken off quickly south of the border, only two trusts were approved and operational in Scotland by April 1993. The programme was devised for the potential medical directors of the trusts becoming operational in 1993 and beyond. It is unlikely that there will be more than 48 such trusts operating in Scotland even when all the possible units take on trust status. The Health Service in Scotland has many differences from the set-up south of the border. There is a strong Scottish identity, probably encouraged by the fact that funding is 26 per cent higher per head of population. This higher funding arises from a response to the much poorer health statistics of the people (for example, Scotland's death rates from conditions of heart, stroke and other circulatory diseases and cancer are the worst in the Western world), the higher costs of a geographically spread community, and an attempt over many years to respond to the greater health needs. It was clear from the *Final Report of the National Evaluation of the First Wave Management Development for Hospital Consultants*, carried out by Lancaster University in June 1992,[2] that previous attempts at developing consultant medical practitioners had not been entirely successful. Many of the doctors reported lack of relevance in the inputs and negative reactions to being mixed with managers from profit-oriented organizations. We took note of the recommendations, which included tailoring a course with emphasis on personal development and including an action learning element. It was agreed generally by the joint developers that there was a high potential for building a supportive network of medical directors in Scotland due to existing professional communication patterns. Indeed the participants on this programme have gone on to found the Scottish Association of Medical Directors of Trusts.

The programme consisted of two main elements: a series of seven residential workshops, varying in length from an initial week to a more normal two days; and the action learning element. However, it should be emphasized that the first week was devised to be a platform from which the action learning element evolved as naturally as possible. The programme, which was fully funded by MDG, had 12 participants from future trusts of widely different geographical locations, types and sizes of units. The course commenced some six weeks before trust status was assumed. In many cases this was before official appointment to the post of medical director had been made, and in most cases long before a contract had been drawn up and signed by the course participants. Indeed, not everyone was destined to take up the role, some continuing in the role of clinical director. There was a considerable degree of role ambiguity for the participants in virtually every way: personal, organizational and managerial.

BACKGROUND: UNDERLYING VIEWS AND VALUES AND THEIR RELATION TO THE OPERATION OF THE ACTION LEARNING SETS

There are some strong views and values underlying the arrangements and process of the action learning sets:

- I take the view that the programme can only be a success if the overall rate of learning by participants on a programme is greater by an order or orders of magnitude than if the individuals were learning on their own.

- Learning, in particular management learning, takes place at a deeper level (that is, becomes part of an individual's understanding and behaviour) when the learners interact with each other. This occurs when individuals expose their thoughts or thought processes and then modify these as a result of that exposure. If the individuals interacting feel unhindered in the exposure of their thoughts, it helps not only the individual expressing them but those around them. Each individual in an interacting group can help or hinder the learning of the others by the way in which he or she intervenes or is perceived to intervene. The effect of interventions on individuals is likely to be stronger when the intervener is in some ways different from the individual; for example, someone who is an activist is more likely to have an effect on a reflective person than on a fellow activist.

- The process of action learning is a way of legitimizing and structuring reflection on practice, and as such can form an important vehicle to progress round the Kolb learning cycle of action, reflection, forming concepts and experimentation.[3] This means there is nothing extraordinary about action learning as a way of learning, except that it takes as its focus real or potential action on concerns that the learner has to do something about and has subsequently to live with the consequences of. This would suggest, from the work of, for example, Janis and Mann,[4] that the type of thinking and therefore perhaps learning may be different from that on imagined or 'textbook' issues.

- I hold the view that action learning is a useful way of learning, but is only one way and not *the* way of management learning. I would also contend that our understanding of learning has advanced considerably since Reg Revans[5] ran the first programmes in the Health Service some forty years ago, but the process within action learning has not benefited much in its practice from that understanding. This is not in any way arguing against its use. Action learning has at its heart learning principles which fit our understanding of how learning is enhanced: ownership of the learning by the participants, focus on learning and interaction of ideas rather than teaching. This means, if practised with sincerity, that action learning has much to offer. It is likely that a rigorous investigation may enhance our understanding of the process. This would mean that the benefits could accrue for all members of an action learning set rather than some members, as seems to be the case at present, according to published accounts.

Some important design issues arise out of these convictions, which I will put in general rather than particular terms. The successful outcome of the learning set will be determined by:

- how individuals are assigned to or become members of an action learning set
- the skills or otherwise of the set facilitator
- the congruence of the facilitators' theory in use and their espoused theory
- the perceived threat(s) of one set member to another
- the perceived worth or esteem in which members and facilitator hold each other

- the differences and similarities between set members (for example, age, gender, experience, professional discipline, organization – size, resources, culture, location – learning style preference,[3] team role preferences,[6] etc.)
- the nature and confidentiality of the real issues to be tackled
- the other learning opportunities including the rest of the programme.

A short contemplation of this list leads one rapidly to the conclusion that even if one could sort out the sets in some way which meant everyone was in a set in which there was mutual respect, it is unlikely that this would necessarily maximize any useful differences between the learners. There is also likely to be a suspicion of facilitator manipulation, which would perhaps destroy trust. There are quite marked differences between physicians and surgeons and there are many other issues of hierarchical or professional pecking order within the NHS, and so the groups people find themselves in are of real consequence to the way they interact and develop trust. What is being argued here is that a random group is more likely to be of benefit than one created along preconceived ideas of best membership of that group. There is the proviso that the people should have opportunities to work with all people on the programme in some other way.

I have faced this issue over many years, and it was some time ago that Brian Day[7] and I developed a workable solution. What is needed is a mechanism free from manipulation and yet which mixes participants. If 12 people are to be mixed there are nearly a thousand ways that they can sit in a row (horseshoe etc.: $12 \times 12 + 12 \times 11 + 12 \times 10$ . . .). Normally, if people are broken up into small groups, it is very easy for them to avoid being in a group with people they wish to avoid, particularly when one considers how frequently people will continue to sit in the same seats for every session. The issues that underlie feelings of being grouped (or being left out of a group) are extremely powerful. I believe that they are a legitimate and very important issue, which a professional with responsibilities for others' learning should understand. However, I now take the view that it is best to tackle the problem by removing it while attempting to maximize the advantages of the differences between learners in most other courses and programmes.

When we researched the literature on the mathematics of combinations we could find no solution to mixing people in such a way that every person was combined next to every other number in a set in the minimum number of remixings. Brian Day produced the algorithm and a computer program in Basic to solve this. Use of his algorithm and mixing participants accordingly has been highly beneficial in a large number of courses, because it ensures everyone meets everyone else in the minimum number of sessions and there is no bias or manipulation by tutor or participants in the subdivision of groups. It takes six sessions to sit everyone in a group of 12 next to everyone else.

During the first day of the first workshop after giving feedback on learning style and Belbin[6] questionnaires, the idea of mixing the participants by changing the seating order was introduced and discussed in terms of the advantages that it might bring. The group accepted the advantages and the seating plans were drawn up for each session in the week. It was agreed that the action learning sets would be based on the seating plan for the day on which the action learning session took place. The sets were three groups of four people split between the fourth and fifth and eighth and ninth person on the seating plan. There was a proviso that if there was a reason for anyone not being in the particular group of four then he or she had a right to raise it and arrange a swap. One rearrangement occurred because of a potential competitive problem: two hospitals were likely to combine at some time in the future and there was rivalry over which hospital would survive.

This issue has proved far more difficult to deal with in a second programme run for trusts becoming operational in April 1994. Many more of the participants said they felt competitive issues might compromise the openness within an action learning set. The solution the second time was to look for a plan within the set which provided the minimum of such conflicts. This had the merits of being open and preventing other issues influencing the arrangements.

There were three facilitators: one woman (Chris) and two men (George and I), all with markedly different styles. The styles used by the facilitators have been commented on by the participants, and the comments fit the espoused styles. Chris has stated she has a non-directive style and operates in the main by asking clarifying questions – the set she facilitated described her as non-interventionist and wished at times she would have told them if they were 'doing OK at action learning'. I have a strongly activist style and had some problems remaining sufficiently quiet – the set commented on this and on the additional material and reading provided by me. George is non-interventionist but structured the set by starting each session with a summary of each participant's last contribution, revealing the feelings picked up as well as the issues.

The facilitators were allocated randomly. It was noted that Chris had two of the participants with the most difficulties in working with women, but also two of the most able at working with women (from pre-course evaluation and observation during the running of the first week). I had the least confident (but not necessarily the least able) medical director designate together with the most confident and also very supportive two people, so an activist style was appropriate. The third group had the people most likely to appreciate, at least intellectually, the confrontative summaries.

HOW THE SESSIONS WERE RUN

Sessions were run at the start or end of each residential workshop, and these were spaced approximately a month apart. The action learning sets normally started about two hours before dinner, with a break of an hour and a half when all twelve participants ate together with the facilitators, and finished later when the group/facilitator felt appropriate. Each participant in a set had a period of time to describe and discuss his or her issues.

Facilitators varied as to whether they started or concluded each session with a summary of all the issues raised or dealt with people individually, summarizing all of the issues or just dealing with one person at a time. A taperecorder was available to record each individual's session, and he or she could take away the tape if wished.

One of the three groups had no travel problems and met in between sessions. The others had some formalized telephone contact procedures, but these were not strictly adhered to.

From the outset it had been stated that there would be a final session where the three groups would share with each other what they found useful. The participants were strongly resistant to any outsiders, such as a chief executive, attending this session, and in the event only the manager of the programme from MDG and the facilitators were present.

WHAT THE PARTICIPANTS GAINED

The majority of this section consists of verbatim comments made by the participants during a final session specifically designed to reveal and share the benefits between them. First is one of their accounts of what action learning is supposed to be, and a reaction to it which was shared by most participants:

'From what we have been told, action learning is becoming widely accepted as a method for the development of managers and improving managerial competence. In simplest terms, it is a form of management education in which learning is based on actions rather than built upon theory. That is, real and active problems are talked through with a group of what has been called "colleagues in adversity" and this experience modifies behaviour. This is fundamentally different from the more traditional approach, when faced with a problem, of falling back on the underlying theories of management and the literature on how to deal with the situation and then building a management solution upon this. I suppose equally it could be regarded as a systematized form of learning on the job, the so-called university of life, a method which is undeniably effective in finding particular solutions to particular problems but which may not result in the definition of paradigms of management behaviour which can be applied to situations not previously met.

Others have tried to describe what action learning is and McLaughlin and Thorpe[8] in a paper in the *British Journal of Management* in 1993 gave three descriptions and three perspectives. The descriptions were of previous writers in the subject and are as follows (all were written in 1982):

Lessem – "Action learning at its simplest is an approach to management education. At its most profound it is a form of personal therapy, a means of social and economic transformation and even a way of life."

Newbold – "In action learning real managers share ideas and tackle real problems with their counterparts, which affect change in the real world by helping each other."

Revans – "It is a development of the self by the mutual support of equals; even if we cannot describe it as a communion of saints, it is at least a conspiracy of innocents."

These descriptions, although clarifying some of the factors that are regarded as important in action learning, are not really adequate as descriptions of something new. They range from regarding action learning as a very functional toolbox to regarding it as a faith or religion: regard it as simply and no more than a technique for exploring and examining problems in an open and non-threatening environment with mutual support from people who have or could have similar problems and who have perhaps viewed them from different perspectives and experience. At best it is nonsense, and at worst positively dangerous, to begin to think of action learning as a form of therapy, far less a philosophy or way to view the world. To my mind it is no more nor less than the formalization of a process which is commonplace in the professions if not in management circles. *That is, a group of colleagues getting together in a convivial and mutually supportive atmosphere to discuss their work problems openly and help each other towards understanding and the finding of a way forward.* For this it is a functional and effective process.'

'It is difficult for me to put into words what I feel about the action learning concept and particularly what I have gained from the exercise. I applied to attend the course to learn about the NHS and how it was run and also to find out about the methods of management which I would have to become familiar with to be effective as a medical director of a trust. The concept of action learning was completely new to me and I approached the suggested programme within our overall training programme with more than a little scepticism, as I think many of us did.

As the group met I discovered that whereas the main course provided me with a lot of information and trained me in techniques on management, it was in our group discussions, sometimes going on until well after midnight, that I learned the practicalities and the difficulties of the director post. The ability to discuss, freely, openly and in complete confidentiality, worries and problems was almost cathartic and as the monthly meetings went on I found it very reassuring to find that I could pick the brains of my three colleagues, all of whom were much more experienced within the NHS structure than I was. Problems with sick doctors loomed large on my agenda and, in fact, are still on-going in that I have a colleague who has a chronic illness which he controls himself with recurrent difficulty. To be able to discuss this openly and freely and to get advice on how to handle such problems was more than a little useful. I have two colleagues who literally cannot work agreeably together. Again the advice and suggestions gleaned from our action learning discussions helped me to stabilize an extremely difficult situation.

As my workload increased I found myself drowning in a mass of paper and problems. The course had taught me a little about time management but it was largely the comments of my friends at our meetings between 7 o'clock and midnight about what a pillock I was to allow myself to have so much heaped on my plate by the chief executive that encouraged me to have some serious discussion with him regarding the workload.

Problems of laboratory management and equipment replacement were also clarified by discussion and the path to solutions made more obvious.

Many other difficulties including the management of junior doctors' hours of work, the possibility of merger and problematic management activities by our parent Health Board are just a few of the other subjects which open, frank and free discussion at our action learning group meetings helped me to cope with.

The complete course has been very worthwhile, but I found as the months went by that for me the evening sessions became more enjoyable. I became more relaxed and I am in no doubt now that because of them I am much better able to cope with my directorship.'

'My problem was a continuing clinical input – but it's not such a great problem. It has been an advantage to be able to be half time on paediatrics and three-quarters time medical director. It makes one a little more acceptable to clinical colleagues. I enjoy the paediatric part of my job. Problems of bundles of unread journals I am still strongly concerned about. It is easy to lose one's skills in parts of one's clinical roles.

For the first time in my life I feel professionally isolated at times. It is not that anyone is particularly unpleasant to me but I feel that I have problems that I can only talk to people like you [group of fellow medics and facilitators] about. I cannot talk to colleagues in the hospital with whom I have been friendly for years and years.'

'The professional isolation – I raised this at the interview and I was told not to worry about it, I'd soon find new friends. I had a problem with a colleague who had allegations of sexual impropriety made against him. The action learning group was the only place where I could discuss this problem openly. I was able to handle it much better as a result. I found great solace in the group discussing the medical/legal problems. There is expertise in the groups.'

'The role of medical director is completely different from the administrative role I had been carrying out before. It would have been impossible to carry out the two roles – especially the job of strategic management.'

'The thing I've gained from action learning is learning about others, what they were doing – what they could afford to get rid of – what they had not taken on board because it was not seen as their responsibility. I learnt a lot because all of us had completely and totally different ways of relating to the board and the clinical directors. I learnt a lot about how I was going to shape up with the clinical directors, just listening to what was expected.'

'It helps in two ways, one you share the angst and two you learn from another's experiences.'

'Basically it's realizing you are not alone in this job and that other people have the same problems and are benefiting from one another. That is the usefulness of it.'

A COMPARISON

Work was carried out with action learning sets of newly appointed medical consultants in the Yorkshire region in 1986 by Tony Winkless.[9] He described four areas of concern the medical consultants expressed at the end of their programme, which seem very similar to those described above by the medical directors and, according to the facilitators, were certainly strong themes in all three sets:

- *self-management/development* – coping with feelings of being threatened/isolated, building self-confidence in dealing with management colleagues
- *colleague relationships* – introducing change in the face of opposition, separating friendships from professional relationships
- *management relationships* – clarifying the roles of doctors *vis-à-vis* managers
- *'small m' management* – balancing work priorities.

It is perhaps not surprising that impressions we have gained from the learning sets are that while most of these issues are still of concern, the broader role required of the medical director of a trust widens the concerns. In particular, the relationships with many individuals both within and outside the trust appear to have gained considerable attention during discussions. This would seem to fit the time-use observations of Mintzberg[10] and Kotter,[11] and the differences between effective and successful managers described by Luthans.[12] This last research was presented as part of the first week's input to the programme – with concentration on how successful *and* effective managers as opposed to *only* successful or *only* effective managers use their time. This offered guidelines and specified a goal for using their time to best advantage. As medical director appointees they filled the 'successful' criteria automatically, since they had already climbed the hierarchy!

THE FACILITATORS' PERSPECTIVES

There was a considerable degree of concern among the facilitators about how they would manage to facilitate these particular clients. The concern arose out of the very considerable professional ability that had been shown by all the participants in their careers. Every one of them seemed to have an extremely strong self-image and thus an air of confidence.

By the end of the first week, including a short action learning session, it was clear that the sets were going to work. The real problem became one of giving sufficient structure to avoid the quieter members' being drowned out. Indeed, one group abandoned use of the tapes because the large amount of talking over each other made them difficult to understand.

The problems and issues raised were of considerable complexity and delicacy and stretched all three facilitators' technical and process skills. The progress being made on solving problems was obvious from session to session and provided intrinsic reward for the facilitators. Perhaps more importantly, it quickly became apparent there was an opportunity here for collaborative research with the participants (described later). This sharpened the degree of attention paid to what was being said by participants and encouraged an analytical response by two of the facilitators in particular. I suspect that the opportunity for research may also have increased the interest shown by participants, as they were keen to be involved in moving the research to publication.

The facilitators noticed considerable changes on two fronts: a shift in the content of the issues raised from detail to strategic perspective, and the managerial development of participants. The first was general to all sets and the second more marked with some individuals than others, but all demonstrated an ability to describe problems in a managerial way with clarity and, perhaps most strikingly, all were able to ask clearer questions about the problems colleagues were struggling with.

TAPERECORDING ACTION LEARNING

Each participant had a period of time for discussing his or her own issues and problems during learning set meetings. Taperecordings were made during the discussion of an individual's problem and the tape then offered as an additional resource that the participant could use or not. The tape was confidential to the individual.

The practical problems can make this process fall into disrepute very easily. It is essential to have not only a reliable recorder but a suitable microphone able to pick up the five or so set members as they move about the room, for example to draw on a flipchart. Our early efforts nearly ended in catastrophe from the use of inadequate microphones alone. There is also the necessary discipline in taperecorder management. The taperecorder needs to be as unobtrusive as possible, which means, for instance, that there must be no difficulties with trailing leads and it must be easy to swap or reverse tapes or pause at extremely confidential moments. In general it must work without being noticed.

The advantages of the tapes were quite significant for some individuals. They could be listened to while driving; taped summaries provided a useful to-do list; and the tape was more confidential than notes. By listening to the tape of discussion of their own issue, participants were encouraged to reflect further on what they said and how other people interpreted it. During a highly active discussion it is easy to miss, mishear or wrongly interpret what has been said by others. Recognition of such misperceptions has apparently been the major benefit to those taking up use of the tape. It was also recommended as reinforcing the will power to make a change, as the enthusiasm and support of the other set members came through so clearly on the tape. Once the research potential of the sets had been discussed, one group allowed a duplicate tape to be kept, which has proved invaluable for research purposes.

RESEARCH POSSIBILITIES

The whole programme was designed to develop the medical directors' understanding of both strategy and decision-making. They therefore acquired a common language of concepts shared with the facilitators, through which they communicated about the issues facing them in their new managerial role. The effects of their power and influence in this new situation was and is likely to be considerable. During the discussions in the action learning sets there was considerable potential for exposing the particular strategic, operational and personal issues in the language of managerial concepts.

This seemed a unique opportunity for research which would capture data unavailable by any other method. There were several individuals in similar but distinctive situations all trying to carry out the same role. If common themes were to emerge over time it might be possible to begin to generate more widely applicable theory. This would be action research which met most of the criteria suggested by Eden and Huxham,[13] and had the potential to involve the participants as researchers.

There were two different research aims on which it seemed worth focusing:

- the role of medical director, the development and development needs of people taking up this role
- the use of new tools to enhance the action learning process.

In terms of the first aim, it is clear that results could contribute to the understanding of any professional or technical person entering a management role because what was being researched were situations in which action had had to be taken. However, there would also be the richness of specific data from which there could be an incremental development of theory. For medical directors the output would be a catalyst for increasing understanding of the role.

In terms of the second aim, a paper was presented to the World Congress on Action Learning, Action Research and Process Management in 1994 describing an analysis of the participants' involvement in the sets and demonstrating the usefulness of certain patterns of intervention among participants.[14]

RESEARCH APPROACH

A rigorous and orderly method of recording and reflecting upon the data was required, together with an understanding of the effects of the research(ers) on the process.[15] The method chosen to record data was that of cognitive mapping (CM).[16]

Cognitive maps can be built to represent the views, knowledge and perceptions of an individual by capturing 'concepts' and relating them to other people's ideas and 'concepts' by means of a map. A map consists of a network of linked ideas and is built up from the concepts discussed in the action learning set. One of the facilitators is a skilled proponent of CM and, using software developed in the Department of Management Science of the University of Strathclyde, was able to map during the action learning sets. An example map, drawing on a few of the 500 and more concepts identified in discussion and numbered, is shown in Figure 12.1. The mapping technique was used during the sessions and as part of the analysis of the tapes. This meant that the maps could be used both as a means of focusing discussion during sessions and to explore the issues beyond those which the CM method was originally framed to record. This provided a further tool for action learning, whose use could be researched.

While it is not possible to give findings here, it was possible to present a preliminary set of them to all the course participants. The results described were found to be useful

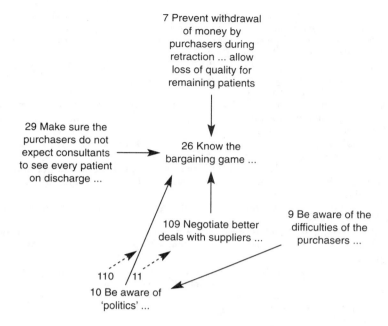

Figure 12.1   *Extract from a cognitive map*

and all agreed we should try and publish them quickly. One group – those who had cognitive maps developed live in each session – is keen to develop the maps and the research further.

CONCLUSION

It is clear from the medical directors' comments that the action learning process is useful in supporting people entering new roles but is not seen as anything like a new paradigm of learning. However, without research and development its full potential as an aid to managerial learning is unlikely to be realized. It is equally evident that action learning sets provide an as yet untapped setting for action research. Research within this setting may provide valuable insights which are not obtainable in any other way into how managers react and cope as they face real issues, and into how action learning itself works.

NOTES

1. Griffiths, R. (1983) NHS Management Enquiry. Letter to Secretary for Social Services (October). London: DHSS.
2. Lorbiecki, A., Snell, R. and Burgoyne, J. (1992) *Final Report of the National Evaluation of the First Wave Management Development for Hospital Consultants*. Lancaster University Department of Management Learning.
3. Kolb, D. (1984) *Experiential Learning*. Englewood Clliffs, N.J.: Prentice Hall.

4. Janis, I.L. and Mann, L. (1977) *Decision Making: A Psychological Analysis of Conflict, Choice, and Commitment*. New York: Free Press.
5. Revans, R. (1982) Action learning takes on health care. In *The Origins and Growth of Action Learning*. Bickley: Chartwell Bratt.
6. Belbin, M. (1981) *Management Teams: Why They Succeed Or Fail*. London: Heinemann.
7. Day, B. (1986) Maximising mixing during training courses. *Industrial and Commercial Training* (January–February), 19–22.
8. McLaughlin, H. and Thorpe, R. (1993) Action learning – a paradigm in emergence: the problems facing challenge to traditional management education and development. *British Journal of Management*, **4**, 19–27.
9. Winkler, A. (1991) Doctors as managers. In Pedler, M. (ed.) *Action Learning in Practice*. 2nd edn. Aldershot: Gower.
10. Mintzberg, H. (1973) *The Nature of Managerial Work*. New York: Harper and Row.
11. Kotter, J. (1982) What effective general managers really do. *Harvard Business Review*, **60** (November–December), 156–66.
12. Luthans, F., Hodgetts, R.M. and Rosenkrantz, S.A. (1988) *Real Managers*. Cambridge, MA: Ballinger Publishing.
13. Eden, C. and Huxham, C. (1993) Action research for the study of organizations. Paper presented to the British Academy of Management Conference, Milton Keynes (September).
14. Bothams, J. (1994) Action learning sets for medical directors as a setting for action research on action learning facilitation. Papers presented at World Congress 3 – Action Learning, Action Research in Process Management. University of Bath.
15. Bothams, J. (1986) Throwing light on evaluation? *Management Education and Development*, **17** (1), 65–73.
16. Eden, C., Jones, S. and Sims, D. (1983) *Messing About in Problems*. Oxford: Pergamon Press.

Chapter 13

Learning Contracts in Management Development Programmes

George Boak

INTRODUCTION

This chapter sets out to explain some of the key features of the use of management learning contracts (MLCs) as part of management courses. It is based on the experiences of the author and his colleagues at the Northern Regional Management Centre (NRMC) over the past ten years. The chapter identifies the reasons for the use of MLCs, defines their essential characteristics, and explains the four main stages in using them.

PRACTICAL SOLUTIONS TO A PRACTICAL PROBLEM

The motives of those who attend programmes for management education, development and training are many and various, but a strong driving force is often the search for pragmatic solutions to practical problems. Unfortunately, this search is often in vain, partly because most courses and programmes are group-based, and embrace managers with different job roles, different backgrounds and different learning needs. On most college programmes, the participants will come from different organizations – with diverse cultural and situational factors, too. The different practical problems faced by each participant are therefore likely to require different pragmatic solutions.

Depending on their level of understanding or experience, the members of the group may benefit from a foundation of basic theories and techniques. The same fundamental tools, after all, can be used to tackle problems that are on the face of it quite diverse. Real progress, however, usually requires a focus on the specific problem area, which entails more individualized learning, directly applied to the workplace.

Effective, individualized, work-based learning requires a structure that enables the learner to make choices and to shape the learning experience to his or her particular needs, but at the same time provides the support necessary for success. MLCs provide such a structure.

MANAGEMENT LEARNING CONTRACTS

Consultants from NRMC first used MLCs in working with unemployed managers in 1983/84. They were later used on a variety of short management development programmes, and from 1985 on a longer programme leading to the Certificate in Management Studies qualification.[1] From 1989, MLCs have been used at NRMC as part of a programme leading to the award of a Master's degree in business administration. They have been equally effective at this higher academic level.

Some benefits of MLCs were obvious from an early stage. More responsibility for learning was passed over to the individual, and this increased the relevance of what was learned and also the level of personal motivation. People became very enthusiastic over what they were learning. This was quite natural – they had chosen their own learning area, it had very practical consequences for their daily lives, and they were able to see improvements in short periods of time. What people chose to learn covered a wide range of areas, including improving their time management, becoming a better delegator, acquiring financial analysis skills, getting to grips with information technology (IT), and a variety of interpersonal skills such as team-leading, persuasion, presentations, interviewing and networking. It was apparent that MLCs could work in all of these areas.

The terms 'learning contracts' and even 'management learning contracts' have become common over the past ten years. This is a welcome development, beginning from a positive recognition of the need to address diversity and the benefits of harnessing the motivational power of individual choice, but it means that the labels are now applied to a multitude of slightly different methods. To clarify terms, for the purposes of this chapter, an MLC is a formal agreement between a manager and a tutor about what the manager will learn and how the learning will be demonstrated. The agreement also specifies an action plan and the resources that will be needed. The agreement is formal in that the terms are set down in writing and the document is signed. The learning is assessed in some way at the end of the contract.

Essential features

Where they have been used most successfully, MLCs have the following features:

- They are about learning, not short-term task achievement (see Box 13.1). The explicit focus is on the development of the individual's skills and knowledge, and not on any changes the individual may seek to bring about in the organization in the short term.
- They allow scope for individual choice on the part of the learner, and negotiation with a tutor, or line manager, or both, about the objectives of the MLC, how they are to be achieved, and the measures of performance.

In terms of enhanced motivation and improvement in skills, the wider the range of choice for the individual, the better. In order to fit MLCs into an organized programme, or a course leading to a qualification, however, some restrictions may be necessary (see below):

- They are written agreements. The terms of the contract are set out in writing and agreed by all relevant parties. Ideally this agreement is evidenced by signatures.

Box 13.1 Learning objectives and task objectives

- Have a clear understanding of the oral communication skills I need to work with branch managers and staff in my current job.
- Improve my ability to ask open questions when reviewing staff performance.
- Become better at using flipcharts as visual aids in presentations.
- Improve my ability to be more patient in helping a member of staff to change.
- Understand the principles of assertiveness.

These are all examples of learning objectives from MLCs used at Certificate level. Typically, each contract has between two and four objectives. Objectives which focus on knowledge and understanding, such as the first and last of the examples above, usually form the basis for skill development.

The following objectives are all about achieving task results. They are industrial project objectives, rather than learning objectives.

- Improve merchandising within the branch.
- Improve the way in which [a member of staff] performs her job.
- Design a training package for new entrants to the office.

In the course of meeting these task objectives, the individual may do some learning, and even develop a new skill, but the learning is not explicit in the objective.

Setting the terms in writing leads to them being more precise. The targets of the MLC are thus clearer and – all things being equal – should be more achievable.
- They are assessed at some point. There are performance measures and a deadline for completion, and the learner reports back on progress to someone – an individual or a group. The detailed form of assessment will depend on the programme – but without assessment in some form, a key part of the power of an MLC is missing.

At this point it may be worth taking a brief survey of some of the other methods that are related to MLCs, or purport to be.

Relatives and impostors

MLCs grew out of *learning contracts*, thoroughly described by Knowles.[2] Learning contracts have been used as part of academic courses to allow individual student choice; for example, as Chapter 2 illustrates, there has been extensive use at Empire State College, part of the State University of New York.[3] At Empire State, students work with faculty members to define target areas of learning and then proceed to research the area and demonstrate – through papers and dissertations – that they have achieved their target.

These learning contracts are fairly close relatives of *academic projects*, a long-time component of management education programmes. Typically, academic projects in the management field set out to analyse potential changes to organizational systems or procedures, and provide a vehicle for the demonstration of analytical skills and the application of relevant management or organizational theory. Learning contracts in the Empire State model are more thoroughly defined in advance than the terms of reference for most academic projects.

Both of these learning methods are generally centred on analysis, intellect and knowledge, and explore what lies outside the learner – a subject area or an organizational problem. MLCs are generally geared towards skill development and explicitly focus on the individual's own learning.

Another forebear of MLCs is *action learning*, championed by Revans.[4] Principally geared towards learning through action in the workplace, the MLC approach is a type of action learning, but MLCs establish the individual's targets very clearly and unambiguously, whereas not all action learning approaches do this.

Linked to action learning by the common thread of learning-by-doing are what we might call *industrial projects* – to distinguish them from their more purely analytical academic cousins. Industrial projects involve an individual manager bringing about change in his or her organization – often by being given a secondment or a special task. They are often used as development activities by companies and company trainers.

Industrial projects are often confused with MLCs. They may overlap and co-exist with MLCs, but they differ in that their explicit focus is on changing the organization, and individual learning objectives are usually implicit or vague, whereas MLCs focus on changing the individual learner, and the learning objectives should be explicit and precise.

The increasing popularity of the term 'learning contract' has led to it being applied to methods that would have been called something else until recently. This change of name appears to be particularly inappropriate when the older descriptions of 'assignment' or 'action plan' more accurately capture the essence of the method. These cases of mistaken identity are often deficient in one or more essential aspects of a learning contract: for example, they provide no choice for the learners, or there is no agreement of the contract's terms between the learner and another person, or the agreement is vague and unwritten, or there is no assessment or follow-up.

Free choice

For those who encounter an MLC for the first time, one of the most difficult things to grasp is the freedom of choice of the individual learner. This is a powerful component of the MLC: the individual takes a large hand in creating the contract, and therefore feels ownership for it and is motivated to achieve its objectives. In any programme or learning system, however, it is likely to be desirable to provide some structure to support this freedom of choice and to apply some restrictions.

Some of the structural aspects are mundane but necessary. They include deadlines: a particular set time by which the MLC must be agreed, a date and time at which it will be assessed. There should be a given format for the written MLC, so the learner knows they must propose, for example, goal, learning objectives, action plan, required resources and assessment points. The roles of the parties should be made clear: for example, clarity is needed about whose role it is to take the initiative in proposing the first draft of the MLC (it is best if it is the learner). Free choice for the learner is supported by firm decisions taken in each of these areas.

Some restrictions may appear necessary or desirable because of the context of the MLC, particularly those concerning the subject of the contract. For example, the Certificate in Management Studies programme provided by NRMC since 1985 requires the following:

- The MLCs must be about some aspect of management. This is a broad field, but it prevents professionals learning more about their area of professional expertise. (The qualification is, after all, in management.)
- At least one MLC (out of three) must be about some aspect of interpersonal skills. Again, this is very broad, with great scope for choice. The results have been valuable.
- The MLCs should relate to skill development. Although MLCs which are purely about the acquisition of knowledge are not forbidden, they are discouraged.

These restrictions have enhanced the power of the MLCs used on the programme. It is worth noting, however, that in addition to these MLCs, managers on the programme also complete a number of assignments, which ensure some coverage of syllabus areas in general management, people management, finance and information management. These assignments thus satisfy the core content requirements of the validating body, and the MLCs are similar to options. Indeed, the precedent of an academic project as part of the accepted structure of a programme, allowing individual choice of subject matter, may facilitate the introduction of an MLC. In other circumstances it may be feasible to require participants on a programme to tackle an MLC in broad subject areas such as finance, supervision or IT, which would allow some choice and also some systematic coverage of syllabus areas.

MLCs have also been used at NRMC in conjunction with a competence model on a programme leading to an MBA. Here choice is restricted to a greater extent, as contract objectives must be based on sections of the competence model, and assessment operates within tight university restrictions. These contracts take longer to prepare and establish. The participants need more time to learn the rules – to become familiar with the competence statements and with the assessment regime. Because of these factors there is very often less perceived personal ownership of the MLC than in the simpler, Certificate-level system, although the participants can still benefit.

MAKING IT WORK

We can split the process of using MLCs on a programme into four parts: briefing the participants, negotiating the contract, supporting the contract and assessing results. I propose to look briefly at each stage in turn.

Box 13.2 Diagnosis

One approach to diagnosis – or training needs analysis – is to ask the participant to:

- identify three things he or she does particularly well in his or her job
- identify three areas where he or she would like to improve
- discuss this analysis with his or her line manager (or mentor, or colleague).

A more structured approach can be used where a company has a competence or skills model and/or an appraisal system. Participants are asked to assess themselves against the model and to discuss this assessment with their line manager (or mentor, or colleague) or take into account recent appraisals.

Where participants are introduced to a competence model as part of the programme, time must be allowed for them to understand it before they can use it as a framework for assessment.

Briefing the participants

This is a very important part of the process. At NRMC we have come to see that it comprises two components: explaining how the MLC will work and what the participant is required to do – which we call *priming*; and helping the participant decide what to choose as a contract area – which we have called *diagnosis*.

Priming covers the basic logistics (when the MLC will be agreed, how long it will last, how much time must be spent on it, what it can cover, who agrees it, who assesses it, how it will be assessed, what happens if it is not completed by the deadline, etc.) and also basic philosophy (why we are using MLCs, what the benefits are). Priming is part of the necessary structure that supports MLCs, and it repays careful planning. Printed briefing material as well as face-to-face explanation is advisable. Face-to-face explanation can be carried out cost effectively as a group activity. Depending on the programme, the priming process can include negotiating and carrying out practice MLCs: one in-house management development programme, for example, includes a number of short (three-week) MLCs between workshops, prior to a longer (nine-week) contract that is the culmination of the programme.

Diagnosis is the process of the individual establishing what he or she wants to learn. Initially we had used complex self-analysis questionnaires for this stage, but they often produced prescriptions that the individual did not own or accept. A preferred method is to require the individual to undertake some less mechanistic process of self-analysis; ideally this includes some discussion with a line manager or a mentor about what would be suitable areas for development. This can be supplemented by a focus on models of good practice, from which the individual can benchmark his or her own standard of performance (see Box 13.2).

This approach does not guarantee that individuals will choose a skill to develop that is seen by others (such as their line manager or their tutor) as a priority area for development. For many reasons, particularly a blindness to their weaknesses or a fear of failure in attempting to remedy them, learners may skirt around what appear to others to be high-priority needs. These situations should be handled with care. In our experience, people will only make a genuine effort to tackle a learning need if:

1. they accept they have a problem
2. they believe they can do something about it
3. they think that doing something about it is a priority.

Diagnostic, or self-analytical, systems can be simple or complex, quick or time-consuming, depending on the programme. The best diagnostic systems provide accurate feedback to the individual learner, and then allow sufficient time and support for this feedback to be accepted, and to be used as the basis for an MLC. Richard Boyatzis[5] and I[6] have explained this in relation to MBA courses elsewhere.

Negotiation

The role of the tutor in negotiation is first of all to agree an MLC that fulfils the requirements of the programme. Typically this will entail ensuring that the negotiation produces an MLC – and not an outline for an industrial project, or a piece of analysis that might fit the requirements of an academic project. This means focusing the learners on what they intend to learn, what skill they intend to improve, what they expect to be able to do better at the end of the contract.

Secondly, the aim of the tutor is to achieve a contract that is:

- realistic
- clear and precise
- owned by the learner.

In pursuing the first two objectives, the tutor must be careful not to sacrifice altogether the third, and vice versa. An approach that questions, suggests and amends is preferable to one that decides and directs. The first two objectives should not be abandoned, however, and the role of the tutor is sometimes to challenge and to doubt the learner's proposal.

Lack of realism in a contract often originates with learners, who can make unfounded assumptions about the degree of co-operation they will get from others, or about the time they will have available to complete the contract, or about the resources that they will be able to access. The tutor should question these assumptions.

In order to be realistic, the original objectives of an MLC may need to be scaled down. It is useful for this purpose to represent development as a series of stepped improvements (Figure 13.1), and to discuss with the learners how many steps they will, realistically, be able to climb in the time allowed for the contract. This can also help when it comes to negotiating stretching of the targets of those learners who appear to be setting themselves objectives that are too easily within their reach.

Realism implies some degree of expertise in the area of the contract. A good qualification for tutors who are to negotiate MLCs is a broad background in management development work, particularly in the personal development areas. Beyond a certain academic level it is essential for subject experts to negotiate the MLC. This can

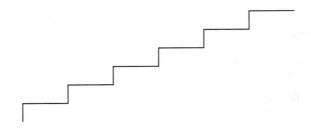

Figure 13.1 *Stepped improvement*

give rise to logistical problems; in the course of discussion, a contract area that seemed at first sight to be about, say, effective oral presentations and self-confidence can turn into a contract about understanding and explaining discounted cashflows (or vice versa), and the subject experts originally delegated to negotiate the MLC quickly find themselves out of their depth. Expertise of other sorts may be necessary to negotiate (and to assess) the contract – particularly expert knowledge of the learner's organization or industry – and the learner and tutor may need to enlist the help of someone within the company, whether a specialist (for example in finance or personnel) or simply a more senior manager.

Clarity and precision are particularly important when it comes to defining assessment measures and action plans (see Box 13.3). The tutor's questions can help to define the particular target step of improvement the contract is designed to achieve, and can ensure that the learner and the tutor both interpret the action plan in the same way – and that it is realistic.

Throughout the negotiation it is important to obtain agreement from the learners. The more the learners own the MLC, the more they will be committed to it. This can give rise to difficulties when a learner presents a contract proposal that is unrealistic, or is vague and imprecise. Many changes may be necessary. The tutor should be careful to help the learner to contribute to these changes, and should ensure that the final form of the contract is understood and accepted by the learner. There is often a genuine case, however, for trading off the technical merits of a contract – the clarity, precision and realism – against the need to let ownership rest with the learner, and it may be better for the tutor to agree to MLCs which are less clear and precise than is desirable, and which may contain some areas where the tutor has doubts about the realism of the plan, in order to proceed with a contract that has been initiated by the learner.

The time it will take to negotiate an acceptable and successful MLC depends on many factors. The learners must have been primed and given a chance to think about what they want to learn. With the relatively small contracts at Certificate in Management Studies (CMS) level, the learners are thoroughly primed and then an hour is scheduled for individual discussion of each contract proposal. Depending on the level of preparation the learner has done beforehand, and to some extent the simplicity of the skill area, the discussion may need less time than this or, exceptionally, more time may be required. With the much more complex contracts at MBA level, several drafts of the proposal are often needed, and face-to-face meetings may be supplemented by telephone conversations.

Box 13.3 Lack of clarity

Examples of broad and vague terms in contract proposals include the following:

Objective: Improve interpersonal skills
The manager actually wanted to improve his ability to carry out informal counselling interviews with his staff – a much narrower definition of the skill area, but still one that is more of an overall goal than an objective.

Action Plan Item: Interview members of my team
How long will the interviews be? How many people in the team? The proposed action may be very time-consuming (and perhaps unrealistic on this count) or so slight as to be insignificant.

Resources: Books, videos, CBT
It is worth checking whether the manager knows that there are relevant learning resources, and that he or she will be able to access them.

Assessment Measure: Produce a report
This is probably the most frequently suggested assessment measure! It is useful to agree what the report will cover – that is, to specify the section headings – and to specify its approximate length.

Achieving greater clarity in each of these cases of vague proposals helps the learner to think more clearly about what he or she is going to do, and come to a better decision about the realism and the value of the proposal.

Support

Support for someone undertaking an MLC can take the following three forms:

1. *Practical advice and information* – the tutor may be a source of this at the outset of the contract, directly providing advice, providing handouts, or recommending books which the learner will find helpful. Exposing learners to new information, new ideas and techniques can be a very valuable part of the MLC.
2. *Access to other resources* – in this context the opportunity to take action can be an important resource; for example, the opportunity to chair a meeting, present a proposal for expenditure, etc. IT contracts create an immediate need for resources. In this context the tutor needs to have a clear idea of what he or she can provide, and ensure that the MLC is within the realms of the possible. If the tutor or the college is unable to provide access to IT equipment, then either the learner must find this resource elsewhere or he or she must choose another area for his or

her contract. Similarly, if there is no opportunity to chair a meeting it will be difficult for the learner to improve skills in this area.

3.   *The psychological support of someone to talk to* – even though the talk may not yield advice, information or other resources, talking through one's ideas can help to clarify them, and the fact that someone else takes an interest can have a positive effect.

While a tutor can provide support of all three types at the beginning of a contract, there is sometimes a question about ongoing support, as the learner works towards the contract objectives. Using MLCs can be a lonely experience.

Obviously, different individuals (and different contracts) have need of different levels of support. Some generalizations are possible, however.

The length of a contract is one important factor. As a rough rule of thumb, where contracts are scheduled to run over more than two months, it is very desirable to organize some structured interim support. Where contracts are complex and contain key contingencies which make their outcome risky, it is desirable to state at the time they are agreed that the learner will check back with the tutor at specified points.

The degree of ongoing support – of the advice and information, and the psychological kinds – that the tutor can provide is limited chiefly by time and costs. In designing the programme, it can be tempting to look to two other sources of ongoing support – the group of learners, and a representative of the learner's employer.

The group of learners at first sight seems a good source of support. They should all be tackling contracts at the same time. They should have sympathy, and ideas to share. In practice, we found limitations on the support the group actually provides. There are generally a limited number of common issues where people have tackled very different contract areas. Members may have a limited interest in other people's contracts. Scheduling large blocks of time to review progress is not always productive. However, we have now structured group sessions to focus attention on what all members do have in common – that is, they are learning a new skill, learning alone, working with a learning contract – and work in this direction may be fruitful.

On the positive side, some partnerships between group members have proved productive, as individual learners have been able to offer information, advice and other resources to each other. With longer contracts, therefore, there is a case for providing a forum for group discussion, but structuring it so that each individual communicates, quickly and clearly, progress and any questions he or she has for the group; follow-up may be in individual meetings rather than in the setting of the whole group.

Employers' representatives can provide significant ongoing support in the workplace. They can provide all three types of support noted above, and can play a valuable part in helping the learner to think about his or her learning needs before undertaking a contract. NRMC has worked successfully with employers' representatives at Certificate and at MBA level.

The success with which employers' representatives play their role depends on a number of factors, including their relationship with the learner, their predisposition to assist in developing others, the pressure of other commitments, their degree of expertise in the specific contract area and, finally, their understanding of their part in the MLC. The programme design, and the actions of the tutor, can help in some of these areas – by providing a clear briefing to the employer's representative and by assisting the learner in choosing a suitable mentor from within the organization – but problems may remain in a number of individual cases.[7] The best policy appears to be to build a role for the employers' representatives such that they can contribute to the success and value of the contract, but to ensure that the MLC system does not depend on this role to the extent that it will fail without it, a strategy which David Thompson and I explored elsewhere.[8]

Assessment

Some aspects of assessment may be dictated by the regulations of the awarding body. Others can be established by the course team. This includes the form of assessment – how do the learners show they have achieved the contract's objectives? Methods of assessment may include some or all of:

- direct demonstration
- oral explanation
- written report
- samples of work
- feedback from others.

Before we look briefly at each of these, it is worth noting that we should be careful not to assess a contract in terms of end results – although this may often be proposed by the learner. For example, one learner wishing to improve her sales technique proposed that her development could be shown by increased sales in the later weeks of the contract. A number of factors influence the level of sales, however, and there was a danger that sales might increase without any improvement on her part, or might remain the same or even decrease despite her improved skills. Other learners have drawn direct causal links between their ability to motivate their team and the team's productivity. End results of this sort should not be used in isolation as a means of assessing an MLC.

The identity of the assessor will depend also on regulations established by the awarding body or the course team. There are advantages and disadvantages in having assessment carried out by a tutor other than the one who negotiated the contract, or in having assessment carried out by a panel of assessors. On the NRMC Certificate programme, assessment is carried out by three parties who negotiated the contract (learner, tutor and employer's representative), and any one of these has a power of veto. For the rest of this section, for the sake of simplicity, we will assume that contracts are assessed by a tutor.

Direct demonstration

The learner demonstrates the enhanced skill directly to the tutor. This is suitable for IT skills or analytical skills where the tutor can ask the learner to perform certain actions or analyses and test the learner on the spot. It is difficult to assess interpersonal skills in this way, although as part of an interview the tutor may ask the learner to role play what he or she said – or would have said – in a certain situation.

Learners have sometimes offered audio- or videotaped examples of their performance in interpersonal skills, particularly in set pieces such as interviews, and particularly where their employing organization is able to set up simulations in the training suite. These tapes nearly always require some commentary from the learners: are they pleased with the way in which they asked their first question or do they see it as the weak point of the interview? How do they evaluate their performance overall? With this commentary, recordings of performance can be quite valuable, but they are likely to be a time-consuming method of assessment.

Oral explanation

In an interview and/or an oral presentation, the learners explain what they did and what they learned. The interview in particular can be a very effective form of assessment, enabling the tutor to sample and probe behaviour, and to hear detailed accounts of the learner's actions.

Written report

This can form a good basis for assessment. The terms of reference should be established very clearly in the MLC agreement. It may be used to provide:

- an account of what the learners have done
- an evaluation of what they believe they have learned or developed
- an action plan covering any further learning they deem necessary
- a summary of any key points of theory they have used or researched.

The report may include records of activity the learners use to analyse their behaviour, such as time logs or diary entries.

The prominence of the written report will depend to some extent on the programme. On the Certificate programme, learners are usually asked to provide short written reports specifically covering key points. These have the benefit of concentrating the mind. On the MBA programme, where university regulations require the written report to be the main form of assessment, the reports are detailed and extensive.

Samples of work

This is a suitable way of assessing planning and analysis skills, or written communication skills (and can include the provision of the visual aids used in a presentation). There will often be a need for the learner to explain why these represent good or improved practice – and there may be a need for confirmation of this fact from someone within the organization.

Feedback from others

This can be useful where a line manager or a company expert can corroborate the learner's account of what has happened. Learners can also usefully seek feedback from others in a structured way, asking for ratings against categories of behaviour. In some

Box 13.4 Assessment

Examples of evidence specified for assessment for Certificate-level MLCs include:

An MLC on presentation skills
1.   Written reflection on my presentations:
- what I did
- what I did well
- one thing I could do better
for each presentation.
2.   Presentation notes.
3.   Feedback from [line manager and colleagues] on feedback sheets.
4.   Oral discussion of above.

An MLC on assertiveness
1.   A brief report outlining the main principles of assertiveness, covering rights, scripts and inner dialogues (two pages).
2.   A log of 12 situations where I was or should have been assertive, describing what I did and a review of how well I did it.
3.   A written summary of what I learned over the period of the contract, noting any areas for further development (one page).
4.   Discussion of the above in an interview.

cases where MLCs have overlapped with other projects or courses, learners have produced authoritative statements from others, for example certificates showing that they have passed a test in the theory of counselling, or of quality assurance, which can contribute to their case for having completed the MLC.

The appropriate use and mix of methods of assessment will depend on the contract area and on the suggestions made by the learner (see Box 13.4).

BEGINNING TO USE MLCs

The advantages of MLCs are usually clear to see. They can provide an effective structure for helping people to learn skills that are relevant to their needs. They can motivate learners by giving them much of the responsibility for their own learning, and more control over what and how they learn. They provide a means for supporting flexible learning in the workplace.

Finally, I should like to consider a number of practical issues facing any course leader or course team wishing to incorporate MLCs into his or her programme.

Where can we fit MLCs into the programme?

If in an existing qualification programme, MLCs may replace a project or projects, or they could be the way in which options are assessed.

Generally, they appear to work best if learners are forewarned, so they can think about what they want to do. Thought needs to be given to the timing of the first priming sessions, and what diagnostic aids or procedures will be used.

For purely logistical reasons, there are benefits in assigning MLCs a start date (to apply to the whole group) and an end date at an early stage in the programme.

How will they be assessed and what is the value of the assessment?

The choices about how they are assessed are outlined above: there must be a clear policy on this which is communicated to the learners. On value: if they are part of a qualification course, assessment of the MLCs must count towards the qualification, otherwise they will be assigned a low priority.

What areas can they cover?

Again, this is a policy choice for the course team and/or the awarding body. The very broad choices afforded on the NRMC Certificate programme ensure that the contracts are flexible and are owned by the learners. Restriction of choice, by placing contracts in subject areas (finance, IT, etc.) or by linking contracts to competence models, means that more work must usually be done with the learners in advance of their agreeing the contract, if the full benefits are to be experienced.

Resources – including the opportunity to take action – will also influence what can be undertaken successfully.

Negotiation: who and where?

Depending on the level at which contracts are being used, tutors need either to have a broad understanding of a range of relevant skill areas, or be subject specialists. Tutors new to MLCs will need to learn how to negotiate them – often this is a matter of learning to be less directive, but tutors will also need to identify what resources they will use, in terms of handout material, recommended reading, available videotapes, software packages, etc.

It can be very beneficial to involve an employer's representative in the negotiation and assessment of an MLC. Ideally, negotiation is carried out in a three-way meeting, but the logistics of this are often difficult to arrange. It may be easier if the tutor travels to the company premises. Alternatively, the learner may undertake a series of one-to-one meetings with the tutor and the employer's representative.

Of course, if employers' representatives are involved, they need to be briefed in sufficient time for them to think about their role.

How much?

One of the problems of individualized learning is the extra time and cost it demands. Regular individual tutorials with a capable tutor will provide excellent support to an interested learner, but at a high price. MLCs are a way of establishing objectives, action plans and targets in such a way as to provide individual support at a reasonable cost. As the programme is being designed, and decisions about methods of negotiating, supporting and assessing contracts are being contemplated, it is important to calculate the expected costs and to be able to translate these into a price to the customer.

It is equally important to monitor the time and cost of using MLCs – remembering the effects of the learning curve – to make sure that early practices, or the original estimates (and prices) are adjusted in the light of experience.

MLCs can be heavily supported and heavily resourced by a programme provider. The approach can also work very effectively with fewer resources, intelligently used, and the commitment of the learner. Above all, MLCs are designed to provide a practical solution to a very practical problem.

Which is where we came in.

NOTES

1. Boak, George (1991) *Developing Managerial Competences: The Management Learning Contract Approach*. London: Pitman.
2. Knowles, Malcolm (1975) *Self-directed Learning*. New York: Follett.
3. Hall, James and Kevles, Barbara L. (1982) *In Opposition to Core Curriculum*. Westport, CT: Greenwood Press.
4. Revans, R.W. (1980) *Action Learning*. London: Blond and Briggs.
5. Boyatzis, Richard (1991) Developing the whole student: an MBA course called Managerial Assessment and Development. Paper presented to the Academy of Management Annual Conference, Miami, 12 August. Bradford: MCB Press.
6. Boak, George (1991) Three dimensions of personal development. *Industrial and Commercial Training*, **23** (5).
7. Boak (1991) ch. 8.
8. Boak, George and Thompson, David (1991) The third partner. In Reid, Peter (ed.) *Conflict and Synergy: Individual and Organisation Development*. Berkhamsted: Ashridge and AMED.

Chapter 14

Mixed-mode Delivery: The Best of Both Worlds?

Andrena Telford

INTRODUCTION

It is clear to interested observers that over the past decade an increasing number of people who want to work towards a higher education (HE) qualification, finding themselves unable to attend part-time, never mind full-time, courses have been turning to open learning (OL) as the answer to their problem. While the various forms of self-directed or distance study may offer them the flexibility they need, it must be recognized that there are certain disadvantages for the student in this approach. In particular, many people find individual study a rather lonely business and have difficulty in maintaining their motivation without the support of a group of fellow students. Moreover, while most OL programmes offer some kind of tutorial support, students often feel the lack of regular, direct contact and discussion with a tutor whom they know personally and with whom they can maintain a relationship throughout their period of study.

This chapter examines one institution's attempt to find a solution to this dilemma. Over the past four years, Newcastle Business School at the University of Northumbria has been developing the concept of 'mixed-mode' delivery, which offers students a half-way house between part-time, taught courses and what might be called 'pure' OL. In this chapter, I look at what is meant by 'mixed-mode', what the rationale for it is, and, at more length, how it has operated in one particular case. I examine what has been learned from the process, and the ways in which this particular course has been modified and adapted to respond to the needs of the students and the capabilities of the institution. I consider a number of new factors and their potential effect on the programme which has emerged, and finally I suggest some guidelines for other HE institutions which may be considering the introduction of mixed-mode delivery as an alternative or adjunct to their present provision.

DEFINITIONS

It might be as well to begin with some definitions, since this area of education is notorious for its inability to pin down the particularities of open/flexible/self-directed/student-centred/resource-based and assorted other less traditional forms of learning. Many reams of paper and many hours of time have vanished in the attempt to impose some order upon this unruly flotilla, so perhaps I may be forgiven if, for the purposes of this chapter, I somewhat arbitrarily assign to each of these my own particular distinguishing tags.

'*OL*' I use as a cover-all term for any type of provision in which the student is studying prescribed materials on his or her own for a substantial part of the learning programme. '*Distance learning*' indicates geographical distance and therefore implies that communication between student and tutor is largely, though not exclusively, by mail, telephone or some form of electronic medium (I would consider both the old-fashioned correspondence course and, in earlier days, the sophisticated, large-scale courses/organization of the Open University as coming into this category, though the OU has long had study centres, tutorial groups and summer schools built into its support structure).

'*Flexible learning*' I would describe as another cover-all term, inclusive of all forms of learning which, though institution-based, do not follow a laid-down pattern but are adaptable (in terms of time, place, method, etc.) to individuals or particular groups. '*Self-directed learning*' I see as the type of study programme which is principally initiated and managed by the student, and which may be quite informal in nature (for example, learning a language on one's own, with whatever resources are available). '*Student-centred*' is a descriptive term which may be applied even to rather formal courses, provided the major emphasis is on learning through the student's own activities rather than by passive listening. Finally, '*resource-based learning*' depends upon the existence of a bank of materials which are available to the student and form the main vehicle for his or her programme of study, either within the framework of a tutor's direction or as a pool into which he or she may dip as the learning process directs.[1]

In all of these, it must be emphasized, there is a large degree of overlap. Resource-based learning must by its nature be student-centred. OL is inevitably flexible; it may or may not be distance learning. And so it goes on. Perhaps rather than trying to achieve definitive descriptions of these types of learning, it would be more appropriate to construct a matrix which would reflect the positions of various types of provision on a series of scales indicating degrees of self-direction, use of resources, tutor involvement, interaction with peers, prescription of materials, flexibility of time and place, formality/informality, purpose (leisure/professional) and so forth. I leave it to the enthusiast to carry this forward.

So where does 'mixed-mode' fit into this welter of definitions? As the term itself indicates, it denotes a hybrid, combining two or more different approaches in the implementation of one programme of study. In theory, it could be applied to many existing courses which, for example, follow a period of classroom-based teaching with a large-scale project or dissertation completed by each student on an individual basis. Where the University of Northumbria is concerned, however, the label is used to designate a course which is principally by OL but incorporates regular, though less frequent, group sessions or workshops with a tutor/lecturer, and through which the student proceeds with a cohort of fellow students. This is, of course, to simplify the format, which generally includes various other elements, but it defines the core of this type of course.

WHY MIXED-MODE?

The rationale for mixed-mode provision has already been touched upon in the introduction to this chapter. In the main, it centres upon the need for tutorial and peer support, which is so often the weak point where providers of OL are concerned and the principal lack felt by open learners themselves. By 'mixing in' to what is basically an OL programme a judiciously spaced number of tutor-led group sessions, and by supplying the occasion for students to form supportive relationships among themselves, it is hoped to compensate for the isolation of the OL experience. At the same time, the learning itself is enhanced by the variety which this introduces into the course methods and by the opportunity for joint learning (for instance, through small-group projects or learning sets). There are other advantages in this for students. For example, it is not uncommon for this regular get-together of course members to result in further informal group meetings organized by the students themselves, in which they can compare notes and provide further tutorial support to each other. From another point of view, the regularity of the group sessions provides a kind of time framework for the course and encourages the members to plan their time accordingly (a very necessary – and frequently difficult – discipline for open learners).

From the point of view of the tutor, the workshop sessions allow for the application (through exercises, simulations and discussion/sharing of experiences) of the more theoretical aspects of the study programme, and provide dedicated time for students to consult tutors and for tutors to monitor learners' progress. The workshop activities can provide additional opportunities for assessment other than by assignment, examination or paper presentation, and can be used to supplement the course content where the OL materials may be limited or lacking. Perhaps most attractive to the beleaguered lecturer, the inevitable additional coaching, clarification, problem solving, etc., is much more economical of his or her time when conducted with a group rather than in repeated one-to-one tutorials, no matter how brief.

CASE STUDY: THE CERTIFICATE IN MANAGEMENT STUDIES (CMS)

Background

When this type of programme was first envisaged in 1989, Newcastle Business School, one of four faculties within what was then Newcastle Polytechnic, already offered the BTEC Certificate in Management Studies on a part-time basis. However, there was a greater demand for places than could be accommodated, in spite of the fact that there was actually a decrease in the number of traditional day-release students, particularly from manufacturing industry. Some means to accommodate larger numbers was clearly required. Coincidentally, the Business School had recently set up an Open Learning

Unit to encourage the development of more flexible approaches to teaching and learning within both its undergraduate and postgraduate/post-experience provision, and to increase access for non-traditional students. The mixed-mode solution was the brainchild of the then head of the unit, Diana Thomas, who worked with the course tutors on the existing part-time CMS to develop an alternative based upon study of OL materials but still incorporating most of the features which had made the original course so successful.

In the process of constructing the programme, each element of the part-time course – lectures, assignments, residential weekend, tutorial support, group activities – was considered and adapted in such a way as to ensure that an equivalent learning experience for each was provided by the new format. The content of the lectures was to be covered by the OL workbooks; assignments were still required but would be sent in to the Business School by the student for marking by the appropriate lecturer; and the residential would be translated into two one-day workshops, allowing for group activities and covering topics relating to personal development which could not easily be conveyed through the OL method. The applied, job-related emphasis of the course would be retained by the requirement that each student negotiate (with his or her tutor and an appropriate senior manager at work) two learning contracts. These were envisaged as larger-scale pieces of work, related to the student's present job, which would develop some area of the individual's management skills within the context of an actual situation at work.[2] There remained the element of additional teaching and tutorial support, and it was determined that this should be met by evening sessions at monthly intervals.

Where the OL materials were concerned, it was fortunate for the fledgling programme that a series of management-education workbooks were readily available from the locally based Northern Regional Management Centre (NRMC). Even more fortuitously, much of the actual content of the Choice II management series[3] had actually been written by lecturers from Newcastle Business School, and so fitted with exceptional closeness the content of the existing CMS.

Beyond the actual content and organization, the administration of the course required adaptation. While the course leaders and the lecturers (who were to mark assignments and tutor in the monthly sessions and one-day workshops) remained largely unchanged from the part-time course, additional administrative processes would be required, particularly in the handling of assignments. It was agreed that the Open Learning Unit would be responsible for all CMS mixed-mode students and their work, as well as providing clerical back-up to the course leaders. A record-keeping system was set up and procedures worked out for the reception, marking and return of assignments and learning contracts (with a two-week turnaround requested). The unit would also be the principal point of contact for students, dealing with general enquiries, relaying messages to tutors, and (not least in importance) ensuring a friendly, known voice at the end of the telephone.

Where the timetable of the programme was concerned, it was agreed that, initially at least, enrolments would take place annually in the regular September slot. All tutorial/group sessions would be fitted in to the academic year, but the date for completion was to be left open-ended, to allow students the maximum flexibility in achieving the qualification.[4] In other respects, the mixed-mode courses would tie in with an overall CMS pattern; as with the part-time equivalent, regular course-team meetings would take place throughout the year and students who successfully completed the work of the course would be submitted, along with part-time candidates, to a single CMS examination board (which still meets twice yearly, usually in July and January).

When the programme was first advertised in 1989, the hope was that not only would the mixed-mode addition to the CMS stable cope with the increased number of prospective students applying for the course, but it would also attract the people for whom some form of OL was the only possible route to the qualification.

Developments

The first mixed-mode CMS course began in the autumn of 1989, when 17 students enrolled. Numbers on this programme have remained steady, with between 17 and 21 students in each cohort. Students are mainly in the 25–45 age range, with a sprinkling of course members either older or younger. All have been in employment, the applied nature of the course making it difficult for anyone not in work to complete it successfully.[5] The types of employment represented have varied widely and have included manufacturing industry, local government, the Health Service and the university itself, which each year enrols a number of library and administrative staff members on the course.

There have been two main developments over the first four years of the programme. In the first place, there has been the introduction of an additional course specifically for women managers. This resulted largely from a particular interest on the part of one of the course leaders in the role and style of women in management, and a feeling that a good number of women, particularly those who had barely begun to ascend the management ladder or who were recent returners, might flourish better in an all-female group. The tutor, herself the mother of a small son, felt too that the timing of the mixed-mode sessions – between 5 p.m. and 8 p.m. – was particularly inappropriate for women to attend. After taking thorough soundings, she proposed that the Women Managers' course meet for a shorter period every three, rather than four, weeks and that the session should take place on a Friday over an extended (two-hour) lunch break. This last had the added advantage that any of the participants who worked on a flexi-time basis could actually integrate the sessions into their working week without disruption and even without having to seek permission from the boss.

The first cohort of Women Managers enrolled for the 1990/1 academic year, and the idea proved to be a valuable extension of the programme. The content of the course mirrored that of the mixed-mode General CMS, but included additional material on and discussions of women's management styles and of the particular problems likely to be encountered by women in management. The individual success stories emerging from the Women Managers groups have been particularly striking.[6] Numbers, however, have always been lower with this group, ranging from 9 to 15, and unfortunately a reduction in CMS enrolments overall in the current academic year has led to a merging of the two groups, so the Women Managers' course is in what we hope is temporary abeyance. Investigations indicate that the cause is principally financial, with fewer employers or individuals willing or able to cover the fees at the present moment in this area.

A second major development was the franchising of the course to two colleges of further education, in Consett, County Durham, and in Carlisle. In each case the programme is run by the college, but is monitored by the Open Learning Unit, together with the Business School's course leader and other staff, and successful candidates are awarded their certificate by the University of Northumbria. Initially assignments were double-marked by Business School staff, but now that college tutors are familiar with the standards this no longer applies. Close contact is maintained, however, among staff from the three institutions, with regular discussions and staff training sessions, as well as twice-yearly Joint Academic Consultative Committee meetings of a more formal nature. Students and tutors from the franchised courses are invited to join the Newcastle-based one-day workshops, and many have in fact done so.

The Consett course, based at Derwentside College, has had to struggle to establish itself, not unexpectedly in an area still attempting to recover from the devastation of British Steel's departure and where employment is more than ever dependent on small companies. Nevertheless it has managed to survive and is beginning to pick up. The Carlisle College course has been in operation for one year (its initiation owed more than a little to the establishment of the University of Northumbria's new campus in Carlisle), and has got off to an excellent start. The great advantage of these franchised courses is that they open access to the first rung of management training to people in areas where no post-experience management courses are available locally. At the same time it allows the university to extend greatly the service it provides within its own backyard, without having to find all the usual resources for staffing and running yet more courses.

Over the four-year period, certain changes have taken place within the mixed-mode CMS, including the introduction of new, updated materials.[7] This necessitated the writing of new assignments, which in turn resulted in the tasks being more closely work-based. Alterations have also been made in the course timetable, with a change to fortnightly sessions for both the General and the Women Managers' groups, a closer tying in of one monthly session to each workbook topic, and, significantly, the decision to set an 18-month deadline for completion of the course. This last was felt to be of help to students by bringing in some pressure for completion, tutors having discovered that the longer the student continued, the less likely he or she was to complete.

A number of these changes have resulted from student feedback, largely from discussions between tutors and students, but confirmed by a survey (carried out in June 1993 by the Open Learning Unit) of mixed-mode students' attitudes towards, in particular, the support element of the programme. One strong theme to emerge from the survey was the pressure for more than monthly contact. This led to the introduction of fortnightly class meetings already referred to, but although the course leader's offer of additional drop-in consultations was also received with enthusiasm, in fact few students turned up, which probably indicates that the limit to these students' capacity for attendance had already been reached (despite their best intentions).

Certain early ambitions for the programme have not been fulfilled; for example, roll-on/roll-off enrolment, which would have allowed individual students to begin their programme at any time of the year. The timing of tutorial sessions and workshops during the academic year, combined with the aim of providing a fairly constant group of fellow students for course members, have deterred attempts to meet this particular goal. However, non-September start dates for groups of students have been introduced by both of the colleges which run franchised courses, and the overlapping of two groups within one academic year has proved to be feasible within existing academic structures.

The future of the mixed-mode CMS

The programme which has resulted from the process described above has by no means settled into a fixed pattern; it continues to alter and grow as it encounters new situations. A number of developments have recently come to the fore and are impelling new thinking about the course.

The impact of National Vocational Qualifications (NVQs)

At the time of writing, three modes of the Certificate are operating within Newcastle Business School: part-time and mixed-mode CMS and the competence-based BTEC Certificate in Management. This last was introduced in 1992 and is run by the Accreditation and Training Centre of the Business School's Centre for Enterprise and Management Development. There is no question that ever-increasing interest, particularly among employers, in NVQs and the Management Charter Initiative's framework for management training is impinging upon courses such as the CMS, which operates at NVQ Level 4, but is not necessarily set up to accommodate the complex process of NVQ accreditation.

An attempt is presently being made to bridge the gap between the current mainstream (part-time and mixed-mode) CMS and the wish on the part of a number of students to obtain the appropriate NVQ. An information session for all interested course participants on NVQs, portfolio building and NVQ assessment has been introduced, and candidates have been supplied with additional material for action planning and for recording activities demonstrating competence (together with the underpinning knowledge and understanding) in line with the appropriate NVQ units and elements of competence. This is still in the development stage and other alternatives have been mooted; for example, the provision of an add-on 'conversion' module to permit students to gain the parallel NVQ award.

Modularization

The arrival of unitization within the HE sector has had its effect on the CMS as upon all other courses within the University of Northumbria. As a broad-based, first-level management course, sections of its content meld well with that of many other courses within the university, from Health Studies to Arts Management, and make it potentially a very useful component in a unitized academic structure. In addition to lateral combining with other units both within and outside the Business School, the CMS has an important function as an entry route to higher management qualifications, in particular the Diploma in Management (DMS). A significant number of 'graduands' from the CMS have gone on to the DMS and in a few cases thereafter to the MBA degree. Students who have come through the mixed-mode route for their Certificate have a natural inclination to continue by this method when tackling further study, and thus the CMS has a key role in vertical progression within a suite of unitized, mixed-mode courses covering all levels of management education.

However, discussions with course members past, present and potential have indicated that there is some demand for even further modular breakdown. Part of this is financial in origin – the Certificate, in line with many other postgraduate/post-experience qualifications, carries a not insubstantial price-tag, and self-financing students in particular may be discouraged from undertaking the course by the lack of some form of instalment payment. There is also an argument in terms of time commitment for a breakdown of the course into smaller segments which could be tackled over a longer period, as the student's work and domestic commitments permit. As it happens, a natural set of subdivisions arises from the particular OL materials currently in use. At present, students use six workbooks in the *Competent Manager* series, each covering a major aspect of management,[8] and one tutor-led session per month focuses upon each of these topic areas. It would, therefore, be possible to break the course down into six free-standing modules,[9] thus increasing the flexibility and accessibility of the programme for the future, but without the complications of staffing which would arise with a full-time or part-time course.

Customization

A further area for potential development lies in the customization of the CMS programme to fit the requirements of particular organizations or of certain sectors of the economy (such as the retail trade, travel and tourism, care organizations, local government and education, to name but a few). As universities seek to increase their commercial potential, and become increasingly involved in certain kinds of provision to employers (and management training features prominently here), there is likely to be a growing requirement overall that programmes be individually tailored to meet more precisely the requirements of one particular company or industry. At the first level of management, the CMS in its mixed-mode version would appear to be the most appropriate vehicle for this type of adaptation. Its OL component offers the flexibility which the employer requires, while its support and accreditation systems supply the elements which the employer is least likely to be able to provide in-house.[10]

Developments such as these seem bound to ensure that the mixed-mode CMS does not become set in concrete, but continues to expand its boundaries and its capabilities for some time to come.

Lessons from the CMS

Experience with the mixed-mode CMS over the past four years has proved to be a learning experience for all who have taken part – for course leaders, for tutors and (not least) for the Business School, all of whom have had to adapt to a different way of doing things and to contend with a certain amount of uncertainty and frustration in the process. Probably the greatest burden has fallen on the course leaders, who are responsible for the organization of the course and who have found it to be a considerably more complex and time-consuming task than organizing the more traditional type of provision. A course which meets infrequently, whose lecturers are involved more episodically, and whose students are less accessible is bound to cause problems, and the majority of these fall upon the hapless but heroic individual who has undertaken to run the thing.

These same factors constitute a challenge to the institution's own imagination and elasticity in creating a space for and an adequate back-up to non-standard provision. Timetabling which takes account of a lecturer's occasional commitments to mixed-mode courses, a room-booking system which can find adequate, consistently available accommodation for groups meeting fortnightly or monthly: these are the kind of requirements which constrain a department or faculty to rethink its organizational systems (and one should not underestimate the headaches caused). For tutors, there can be difficulty in seeing their participation in mixed-mode courses as more than a very peripheral part of their teaching. Since most of the subject-specialist lecturers involved take part in perhaps no more than a single session and may find themselves marking assignments from students whom they have never encountered, this is hardly surprising, but does not benefit either the students or themselves. There is the danger too, particularly where the CMS is concerned, of seeing the work as being of a lower level and thus of low status and importance within the Business School's overall provision – a demotivating factor for lecturers embroiled willy-nilly in the highly competitive race for promotion.[11]

Perhaps the greatest adjustment, however, can be for the students on a mixed-mode course. A number may have had some previous acquaintance with OL, but the majority usually have not, and so may have their expectations of the educational process severely shaken. Most enter the programme very uncertain of what may be required of them and of what standards they must meet. During their time as students on the course, they must develop effective study skills, learn the discipline of solitary study (often under less than adequate conditions), and develop the motivation to pursue their goal over an extended period of time, the latter part of that, after the end of the teaching year, without the support of their fellow participants.

It has to be said that the OL approach, even within a mixed-mode context, is not suitable for all students and the rate of non-completion is slightly higher than in the part-time course, though still comparing favourably with OL courses in general.[12] It may be of interest to note that the course leaders have had some success in predicting who can or cannot cope with mixed-mode by using Honey and Mumford's Learning Styles Inventory.[13] Although not intended as a piece of research, their use of the Inventory for diagnostic purposes has led to the observation (perhaps not unexpected) that students who lean towards the Reflector and Theorist styles in their learning preferences are more likely to be successful in this kind of course. Whatever their starting point, however, it must be emphasized that the need of mixed-mode students for an adequate system of human support, particularly in the early stages, is as great as that of students on any other type of course.

SETTING UP A MIXED-MODE PROGRAMME: SOME GUIDELINES

From our experience with Newcastle Business School's mixed-mode CMS, we can draw some conclusions about the requirements for a successful mixed-mode programme. There are, in particular, three main elements which must be in place:

- good materials
- effective student support
- an efficient administrative system.

Of course, it could be argued that these are essentials in all good educational practice. What we have discovered is that in other types of provision, the presence of two (or even one) of these can often carry the course and make up for its other inadequacies. Where mixed-mode programmes are concerned, all three *must* be present, at least to an adequate extent, to counteract the fragmenting tendencies of OL.

Encouragingly, there is an increasing pool of OL materials available for HE, though the distribution of these among the various disciplines is patchy to say the least.[14] There is, in addition, a growing cadre of academics experienced in the production of OL materials and certainly no shortage of individuals prepared to offer advice, in person and on paper.[15] Where the selection of suitable open learning materials is concerned, I cannot do better than refer the reader to the comprehensive and down-to-earth checklist in Race (1989),[16] which provides a sensible and very useful set of criteria to apply.

The outline of what constitutes an effective student support system will inevitably vary from one institution to another, depending upon its own structures and facilities. These can, however, be summarized as including:

- a reliable contact point for students
- an identifiable peer group of fellow students
- visible and contactable tutors
- detailed preliminary information about the course
- assistance with the development of good study skills
- a clear programme of sessions/events, however infrequent
- guidelines on course requirements, in particular on standards
- a consistent and well-publicized route for transmission of information to and from students
- adequate and reasonably speedy feedback to students on their performance.

Finally, of great importance is a reliable system of record-keeping, assignment handling and overall administration. Lost assignments, learning contracts not logged in, unanswered phone calls, information not passed on and other demotivating omissions can sink a student (or a course!) if care is not taken. Where there are no casual encounters between tutor and student in the corridor to compensate for human fallibility, a consistent pattern must be established and maintained. Well-kept records allow tutors (and in particular the course leader) to keep tabs on student progress – and also allow the administrator to keep an eye on dilatory assignment markers! In our experience a good administrator, particularly if he or she is also the primary contact person for students, can be the glue that holds a course together.

Beyond these three blanket requirements, any institution introducing a mixed-mode programme must find out for itself what is the right 'mix' for its courses and its students. What has been so successful within Newcastle Business School may not, in its details, be the right format for a different educational setting. What we *have* concluded, however, is that this 'half-way house' can be of enormous benefit to any student whose main resort must be to OL but who will find the addition of the human contact element a boost to enjoyment, a prop to maintaining motivation and an incentive to completion.

CONCLUSION: THE BEST OF BOTH WORLDS?

It must by now be clear that our experience at the University of Northumbria has reinforced our initial assumption that mixed-mode delivery would indeed ensure a more effective service to OL students. However, there are also some outside indicators of the success of this particular approach, not least in the positive responses from graduands of the flagship CMS course and their subsequent promotions within their own organizations,[17] and in the fact that certain local employers send a cohort of their management staff on the course each year. This particular programme has featured in the press,[18] and a former course tutor, Patricia Bryans, was winner in 1992 of the Woolwich Building Society prize for OL,[19] in part for her work on this course. While great satisfaction can be taken by staff and students alike in these attestations of quality, what is of greatest importance is the confirmation of the usefulness of the *concept* of mixed-mode courses. In the rapidly changing world of HE, where accessibility, flexibility and student self-direction are ever more insistent watchwords, the mixed-mode programme provides an effective option, offering truly 'the best of both worlds'.

NOTES

1. One other point concerning clarification of terms: throughout this chapter I have used 'tutor' and 'lecturer' more or less interchangeably. As in most HE institutions, staff members in fact fulfil the stricter definition of each role as circumstances (and students) require.
2. Although intended to make a contribution to the individual's work, and to the organization, the learner's development had to be paramount, and it was this alone which was to be assessed.
3. *Choice II* (1985). Washington: NRMC.
4. In fact, an effective time-limit operated from the start because of a three-year BTEC registration.
5. Placements might allow an unemployed individual to complete assignments, learning contract, etc., but in fact the question has not arisen, which makes one wonder about the screening effect of one's course promotion!
6. See Griffiths, S. (1992) Half our future: maximising the potential of women in the workforce. *PICKUP in Progress*, no. 26 (Spring) London: DES. This features the Women Managers' CMS and some of our students.
7. Students now use *The Competent Manager* workbooks. Washington, DC: NRMC (1992).
8. *Management Foundation*; *Managing Finance*; *Managing Information*; *Managing Operations*; *Managing People* and *Management in Context*.
9. In fact, this process is likely to take place shortly within the context of another project being undertaken by the author.
10. A project conducted by Newcastle Business School Open Learning Unit for Tyneside Training and Education Council (TEC) and presently nearing completion is piloting this kind of joint venture. A report is in preparation.
11. It should be said that this is not a problem with the franchised courses in the colleges, where the CMS is recognized as being a valuable addition to their menu of courses.
12. In 1989/90, 11 out of 17 students completed; in 1990/91, 24 out of 28; in 1991/92, 22 out of 32. Figures are not yet available for the last two intakes, since students from these groups are still in the process of completing.

13. Honey and Mumford (1982).
14. Here the Open Learning Foundation, formerly the Open Polytechnic, must surely be given both credit and support for its efforts to extend the pool of materials at this level.
15. A particularly useful handbook for new writers of open learning materials is Rowntree (1990).
16. Race (1989), ch. 13.
17. Out of one cohort of Women Managers, 80 per cent of the participants were given promotion while still on the programme!
18. See, for example, Griffiths, op. cit. (note 6 above).
19. Awarded under the Partnership Trust Scheme for Commending Innovation in Teaching and Learning in Higher Education.

BIBLIOGRAPHY

Honey, P. and Mumford, A. (1982) *The Manual of Learning Styles*. Maidenhead: P. Honey.
Honey, P. and Mumford, A. (1986) *Using Your Learning Styles*. 2nd edn. Maidenhead: P. Honey.
Race, Phil (1989) *The Open Learning Handbook*. London: Kogan Page.
Rowntree, Derek (1990) *Teaching Through Self-Instruction: How to Develop Open Learning Materials*. Rev. edn. London: Kogan Page.

Chapter 15

Supporting, Assessing and Accrediting Workplace Learning

Pauline Thorne

INTRODUCTION

While there is no single definition of the purpose of higher education (HE), few could doubt its role in preparing people for work in general and the professions in particular. This is reflected in the mission statements of many institutions of HE. Sheffield Hallam University, for example, has clearly positioned itself as a national 'professional university'. As such, one of its primary concerns must be those educational processes by which an individual becomes a professional.

The definition of a professional has to be interpreted broadly; it cannot be restricted to those occupations requiring a licence to practise, or even those where chartered status is desirable if not essential. However, it should carry with it some implications about a person's competence in a work role, particularly his or her ability to carry out certain higher-level functions involving both specialist knowledge and judgement. In many vocational academic courses, the role of the workplace in developing such knowledge and skills is implicit; in others it is explicitly recognized and the process supported and assessed.

This chapter looks at a number of examples where academic credit has been awarded on the basis of what has been learned at work by employees essentially performing their everyday duties. It draws on examples from areas where workplace learning has not been traditionally recognized as an essential part of the academic educational process.

Clearly people can, and do, learn at work. This may be as the result of planned training and instruction or, more haphazardly, as the result of experience. Many older lecturers in HE have received no formal training in how to teach. A degree in mathematics was considered a sufficient qualification to enable you to teach someone else that subject, even though the knowledge and skills necessary to be a good mathematician may not be those required of a teacher. If you were lucky, as a new lecturer, you might have had the support of colleagues, but otherwise it was very much learning from experience.

Unfortunately, history is full of examples that experience is not in itself a guarantor of learning. Kolb (1984) argues that if we are truly to learn we have to go through a number of stages (a learning cycle). We need to reflect on experience and to relate it to general principles, which in turn help us plan future actions. Many people need help to go through this process. In particular, they may lack the theories and concepts that would enable them to relate their own experience to a broader body of knowledge. What is learned is assessed (if at all) entirely by the individual's performance in the work role as part of existing appraisal systems. Learners may never be required to articulate, or question, the principles that lie behind their actions.

Enlightened employers have always supported learning at work. People who went through a good apprenticeship scheme were not just sent to college once a week to gain an understanding of theory but were often given many additional hours of coaching by their workplace supervisor. However, while the world of education was willing to accept the learning that took place in its classroom, it often ignored or treated as incidental the learning that was taking place during the rest of the week. It is not difficult to see why workplace learning might be ignored. Traditionally, courses in HE have been evaluated as much by their inputs as by their outputs. Content, subject development, entry requirements, learning and teaching methods and assessment procedures are regularly reviewed both internally and externally (for example, by professional bodies). In contrast, workplace-based learning is variable in terms of the range and quality of experiences offered to the learner. It is only relatively recently, with the development of the credit accumulation and transfer scheme (CATS), that HE has become willing to define the educated person in terms of demonstrated knowledge rather than the time spent in a classroom. However, it is not sufficient to acknowledge that learning takes place outside the classroom; we need to develop a methodology to help us put a value on what has been learned.

The difficulties academics find in writing learning outcomes for traditional degree courses are well documented (for instance, Otter, 1992). The process is even more complex for work-based learning because the ways in which knowledge is acquired, transferred and used are less explicit. Eraut (1988), for instance, in his work on management knowledge, identified six types of knowledge which he believed could also be found in other occupations. These were situational knowledge, knowledge of people, knowledge of practice, conceptual knowledge, process knowledge and control knowledge. They are briefly summarized below:

- *situational knowledge* – the way people conceptualize situations and adjust to them
- *knowledge of people* – the basis on which people learn about and make judgements about others
- *knowledge of practice* – simple factual information and knowledge of courses of action that might be appropriate
- *conceptual knowledge* – formal and informal theories that guide behaviour and may be used to improve it
- *process knowledge* – how to do things or get them done
- *control knowledge* – self-management, self-awareness and sensitivity, self-knowledge and self-assessment, representing the interface between doing, thinking and communication.

This is a very different picture of knowledge from one that might be used to describe the outcomes of a traditional taught course. This might include some knowledge of practice and processes, formal conceptual knowledge and, increasingly, control knowledge, but the emphasis would be different. One reason for this difference is how such knowledge is used.

Eraut argues that it is important to recognize that knowledge is transformed by the process of being used. Further, much of the learning of new knowledge takes place while it is first being used, not when it was originally introduced. If we take the example of a student being told a theory in a lecture, he or she may be required merely to recall it and repeat it without any real thought in an examination. On the other hand, he or she may be asked to apply it to a particular situation, or use it, along with other theories and concepts, to interpret a particular situation. The student could be said to be demonstrating learning in any of these situations, but the knowledge he or she is displaying is different even though the original information was the same.

Clearly, this is already recognized to some extent and is reflected in changing methods of assessment in HE. However, the emphasis is still on transforming knowledge through application. It is less easy to see how to transform knowledge acquired through experience into a form that can be assessed. An important element in experiential learning is association – the transfer of the principles of one situation to another. Association is largely intuitive and people may experience great difficulty in articulating the concepts and theories that they have used to arrive at a particular decision. Highly proficient performers are often unable to describe what they do, although, if pressed, they may provide some retrospective justification. This clearly creates a dilemma for those seeking to award academic credit for learning in areas that have not traditionally awarded credit for performance.

This separation (and subsequent devaluing) of critical forms of knowledge is encouraged by a 'technocratic' model that divides professional education into three main elements. The student acquires a knowledge base, usually through the study of academic disciplines; this knowledge base is placed within a professional context, and the student is encouraged to apply it to practice in classroom problem-solving exercises; and finally there is an element of supervised practice. Bines (1992) argues that even where the rhetoric suggests that the supervised practice is a major element of the course, in reality it is marginalized or afforded low status. There is a sharp division of labour between specialists in the academic disciplines and the practice tutor, who is likely to be afforded a lower status.

Bines's arguments can be extended beyond that narrow range of professions that involve practice placements. There has been a great deal of rhetoric about the benefits of sandwich education. Much work remains to be done, however, on identifying the learning outcomes of periods of supervised work experience, and even more on their assessment and accreditation. Political pressures mean that supervised work experience is unlikely to remain as a relatively unmediated and unstructured experience if it is a funded part of an academic course. Unfortunately, this increased demand for improvements in the organization and curricula of placements is taking place at a time when resource constraints make it difficult to implement any necessary changes.

Although many organizations that employ sandwich students do demonstrate a high level of interest in the development and supervision of such students on their period of supervised work experience, it would be unreasonable to expect them to have the same level of commitment to them as they have to their own staff. It is hardly surprising therefore that much of the real progress in supporting, assessing and accrediting work-based learning has occurred with people who are full-time employees and only part-time students.

The next few sections of this chapter concentrate on a number of actual examples. They look at how various course planners set about identifying the learning that was, or could be, acquired in the workplace, and the relationship of that learning to what we normally expect at different stages of a student's academic development; how that learning could be supported; and, finally, how it could be assessed.

IDENTIFICATION OF LEARNING

The experience of many academics of the course design process in the not so recent past would have left them with the impression that it was about deciding what the content should be and how it should be delivered. Such decisions were often dictated by tradition, the requirements of a professional body, and the particular, and possibly idiosyncratic, interests of the staff involved. The aims of the unit and how it should be assessed were often an afterthought. Clearly, such an approach is not appropriate when designing learning that is to take place in the workplace and outside the direct control of the academic community. How then do academics set about designing workplace-based units?

One approach is to modify existing classroom-based units. This essentially was the approach taken by the course team on a part-time Housing degree where work-based units were devised without consulting employers or students. An analysis of the learning outcomes showed the typical academic bias towards propositional knowledge (knowing that) rather than process knowledge (knowing how). More importantly, the relevance of some of that knowledge to students' current or potential work roles was unclear. The workplace was used as a learning resource, in the sense of being a source of information, but there was little effort to understand what students did as part of their normal duties or what facilities were available in the workplace.

When it was clear that such an approach would not work, the course team revised their approach. They developed a framework within which the students could reflect on what they were doing in the workplace, analysing and evaluating their own practice. The students were given responsibility for identifying their own learning, although the decision as to whether that learning was at the appropriate level remained the responsibility of the tutor. This approach encourages the student to present all six categories of knowledge described by Eraut (1988).

The approach adopted by the second course team was to take as their starting point the test of competence set by their professional body. This team was attempting to reduce the amount of time it takes someone already working in a biomedical laboratory to get a degree. It is essential that such laboratory workers understand, and are able to carry out, standard procedures safely and effectively. Although much of the theoretical knowledge underpinning these procedures can be and is acquired through formal teaching, laboratories are still required to test the competence of trainees in the workplace.

After extensive discussions with staff in laboratories, the course team developed a series of units based on those activities which a trainee would have to do to satisfy his or her supervisor that he or she was competent. The Level One units that emerged were very much concerned with knowledge: knowledge of terminology, conventions, methodology, procedures, etc. In fact they greatly complemented what was happening in the classroom. By Level Two, it was clear that both the academics and the supervisors were expecting progression in the way students handled intellectual material, the complexity of the tasks undertaken, and the amount of supervision required. Because these units were described in terms of behaviour, they did not resemble a traditional syllabus. However, the academics had no doubt that they covered material that was at the appropriate level and developed the skills and qualities demanded of undergraduates at this stage in their educational development.

In the previous example, the basis for workplace-based learning was an existing set of occupational standards. This situation is likely to be more common with the growth of National Vocational Qualifications (NVQs). The next case study looks at a situation where standards did not exist at the time the planning process began and had to be developed by the course team.

The university had undertaken a training audit of the estates branch of a government department responsible for the management of a large number of properties throughout the country. As is typical in the Civil Service, most people had served in a number of different departments before finding themselves in the estates branch. Many had joined the Civil Service as school leavers and nobody in the department was professionally qualified. Despite this, the level of technical knowledge and the quality of the work done by the staff was very high.

Changes in government policy had meant that the estates branch was taking on a greater responsibility for property management, and senior staff in the department were concerned that their apparently unqualified staff were at a disadvantage when dealing with other professionals. They approached the university about accrediting training courses. In the light of the audit, the university decided that, if it took the narrow view and just looked at formal training sessions, it would seriously undervalue the learning of staff. Instead it looked at the functions actually performed by staff and designed a number of units around the competences it identified. The end result was a Certificate in Estates and Property Management.

In designing the Certificate, the course team made it quite explicit that the programme must exploit the whole range of opportunities for employees to improve their knowledge, skills and performance. This ranged from unplanned learning in their current job, through planned directed learning from line managers and colleagues, to short courses and open learning (OL) material provided in the workplace. To get the Certificate programme validated, however, the course team had to address two important issues: how that learning was being supported and how it was assessed.

SUPPORTING LEARNERS IN THE WORKPLACE

One of the chief concerns when learning is shifted from the classroom to a place of work is that the learners will have no one to support them in the process. While it is possible to build in tutorial support into a part-time programme, gaining the co-operation of the employing organization has clear advantages. It is easier to gain this co-operation when employers (and, in particular, the line manager) can see some personal advantages in assisting the learner.

Clearly, it is easier to persuade line managers that they should be helping subordinates learn when that learning is directly related to their performance in their work role. In the case of the original Housing units, which had been developed without consultation, line managers viewed college work as something that should be done at college or in the employee's own time. They objected to their staff researching topics that took them away from their desks and which did not seem relevant to the successful operation of their department.

The approach taken by and to biomedical laboratory supervisors was completely different. As the units were designed around learning that the employee had to achieve in order effectively (and legally) to operate in a laboratory, supporting the learner did not impose an additional burden. Furthermore, the course team saw its obligations as going beyond supporting the learner; it offered support to the supervisors too. It was stressed that supporting learning at work was a natural management role and should be seen as part of the staff development of laboratory supervisors. As the course team were essentially looking for people with the skills necessary to help people in their working roles, it was decided to use the term 'coach' rather than 'mentor'. Those responsible for coaching students were able to attend a short course at the university as part of their continuous professional development. These courses covered understanding how and why people learn, promoting a learning environment, preparing learning plans and ensuring that learning has taken place. They were also provided with a practical handbook on coaching skills.

The emphasis in supporting the workplace-based learning on biomedical units was not on supplying academic and technical material. This was available to them at the university as part-time students. Instead, it was on providing the right environment, in which learning would be encouraged and valued as a natural and essential activity in the workplace. The situation was more complex for those on the Certificate in Estates and Property Management, as learning was primarily managed in the workplace with no requirement to attend university classes. Central to the philosophy of that programme was the explicit recognition of both the learning cycle and different learning styles.

Unlike much traditional academic study, which tends to start with concepts but may not provide sufficient opportunities to apply them in practical situations, learning, particularly unstructured learning, in the workplace may well begin with practical experience. Such an approach may leave the learner with inadequate opportunities for reflection and reduce the opportunities properly to conceptualize and develop knowledge at a deeper level. The Certificate programme was designed to ensure that, whether the learner started with the theory or with the practice, all participants would go through all stages of the cycle. It did this through offering an extensive range of learning opportunities and by the use of learning plans.

All participants on the programme began with an analysis of their learning styles. From this they were encouraged to recognize their strengths and weaknesses as learners, and shown how to exploit learning opportunities as they arose. Each participant was actively involved in the planning of his or her individual training needs, and was given a trained coach who was responsible for encouraging and enabling the individual to exploit learning opportunities.

Recognizing that people learn in different ways, opportunities included short courses, OL material available in every location (textbooks, manuals, videos, etc.), and special practical assignments to cover areas of the syllabus that did not form part of that individual's regular duties. Managers were encouraged to give study groups access to meeting rooms and time to study. Senior management recognized that the best way of encouraging staff to take advantage of these opportunities was to show they were valued. This was done in a number of ways. Firstly, there was a regular newsletter to staff that pointed out the advantages of the programme and publicized learning opportunities. Secondly, senior managers went through the programme themselves and led by example. At the time of writing, ways of linking the programme to the staff appraisal system were being explored.

People at work are already being assessed on what they have learned, either informally through day-to-day feedback from their line managers or, more formally, through appraisal and promotions. How do these processes relate to what is meant by assessment in academic institutions? The next section looks at some of the issues that arise when we seek to assess workplace-based learning for academic purposes.

ASSESSMENT AND ACCREDITATION OF WORKPLACE-BASED LEARNING

In looking at how we can and should assess learning in the workplace, there are a number of factors that must be taken into account. These can be put under three broad headings: relevance, credibility and feasibility.

Relevance is concerned with the extent to which the assessment process fulfils the identified purposes of assessment. Assessment can be used to achieve a variety of aims, some of which may be categorized as administrative, while others are more directly concerned with encouraging or enabling learning. The relative importance of these different purposes of assessment is going to vary, for the learner, the teacher and other interested partners (such as the employer or professional body). The different purposes of assessment may be complementary or they may be conflicting but, as a rule, as the purpose of assessment varies so do the ways in which it is carried out.

What are these purposes of assessment? Assessment can be used to select (or reject) students. This can be a crude screening device to eliminate the number of candidates to a manageable number, or it may be based on a genuine assessment of their ability to cope with the next stage of the education process. This can be a particular issue with workplace-based learning, if the processes of acquiring and demonstrating knowledge are very different from what the student might expect in the future if they wish to continue with their studies.

Assessment should/can be used to 'maintain standards'. Employers, professional bodies, academics and students themselves need reassurance that certification has some meaning that is independent of time and place. (There may be statutory or other requirements to assess students against a set of professional standards.) This may be particularly critical with workplace-based learning, where questions are often raised about the transferability of knowledge and skills acquired in one situation to another.

Assessment can be used as an extrinsic motivator of students. It is known that students neglect work that is not assessed in favour of work that is. The situation is more complex for workplace-based learners because, in one sense, they are continually being assessed on their day-to-day duties. Where academic requirements are for something additional or very different, the learner may find that there is a conflict between what is required in his or her role as an employee and that which is required as a 'student'. Evidence suggests that when the learner is in permanent paid employment, it is the student role that suffers.

It is important to distinguish between the motivating effect of knowing you are going to be assessed and that of knowing how you performed in that assessment. Providing feedback to learners is very important at the beginning of any stage in their educational development. As they become more confident and autonomous as learners, they will become more capable of self-assessment.

In workplace-based learning, formative assessment may well be the role of the workplace-based coach or mentor. Such people may themselves lack confidence in giving advice and guidance on 'academic' performance, particularly where they themselves may not be 'academically' qualified. The learners' own supervisors, particularly when they have not been trained in coaching and assessment, may indeed be unsuitable if their motivation is poor. It goes without saying that if they are unaware of the educational objectives of workplace-based learning, they can hardly be expected to serve as effective assessors for academic purposes. However, if they have the appropriate technical knowledge in the subject field, although they may lack expertise in academic grading, they may be better than a university-based tutor in evaluation of competence.

While university tutors may have experience as assessors, they may not be sufficiently familiar with the student and his or her work to undertake diagnostic assessment. Even where they are familiar with the learner, perhaps through part-time study, they may consider that the student's area of work lies outside their discipline or area of specialism. Some tutors may object to the principle of awarding credit for learning that takes place outside the classroom if they see it as a threat to their livelihood. Further, if it is not recognized as a legitimate part of their workload, they may see it as an additional burden, and motivation to undertake such assessments may be so low that it affects their efficiency and the effectiveness of the process.

Regardless of whether assessment is formative or summative, it is unlikely that one single person is going to have all the characteristics we are likely to be looking for in an assessor. We require that person to be both objective and familiar with a particular case, to be an expert in both assessment and the subject matter he or she is assessing, and, finally, to be motivated actually to undertake assessment. This suggests that more than one person should be involved in the assessment process, which will probably comprise multiple assessments. The outcome of such a process is unlikely to be effectively summarized by a percentage mark or a grade. However, it is precisely this that is required if a unit is to count towards degree classification.

In all the case histories that have been described in this chapter, at least some of the assessment required students to make a presentation (usually in writing) and not merely perform their usual working role. It is clearly a reasonable expectation of students seeking higher-level credit that they should demonstrate underpinning knowledge and an ability to handle intellectual material at a level that we demand from students at that stage in their academic career. However, this requirement has a more significant purpose in professional education than merely providing a hoop through which students must jump. Learning continues after the formal education process ceases: if professionals are to continue to learn and to create knowledge, they must have the appropriate tools.

CONCLUSION

This chapter began by saying that one of the purposes of higher education was to prepare people for work. Perhaps a better definition would be that its purpose is to give people the tools with which to reflect and learn from experience. In the case of the typical 18-year-old student fresh from school, much of that experience lies in the future; with mature and part-time students, experience of work may be past or current. HE should be sensitive to the differing needs of both groups and be prepared to acknowledge, support and give credit for appropriate learning wherever it occurs.

BIBLIOGRAPHY

Bines, H. (1992) Issues in course design. In Bines, H. and Watson, D. (eds) *Developing Professional Education*. Buckingham: SHRE and OUP.
Eraut, M. (1988) Learning about management: the role of the management course. In Day, C. and Poster, C. (eds) *Partnership in Education Management*. London: Routledge.
Kolb, D. (1984) *Experiential Learning*. New York: Prentice Hall.
Otter, S. (1992) *Learning Outcomes in Higher Education*. London: UDACE.

Name Index

Subject Index

2

CONTENTS

LOST AT SEA

Wind gusts shook the aircraft. Giant waves and sea spray made it hard to see anything. But the National Oceanic and Atmospheric Administration (NOAA) Hurricane Hunters aeroplane kept flying. The plane dipped closer to the ocean's surface than normal. It was 2 October 2015, and Hurricane Joaquin was pounding the Bahamas. And the SS *El Faro*, a United States cargo ship, was missing in the storm.

Hurricane Joaquin brought huge amounts of rainfall and caused extensive damage along the US east coast.